Learning Axure RP Interactive Prototypes

A practical, step-by-step guide to creating engaging prototypes with Axure

John Henry Krahenbuhl

[PACKT]
PUBLISHING

BIRMINGHAM - MUMBAI

Learning Axure RP Interactive Prototypes

First published: January 2015

Production reference: 1270115

Published by Packt Publishing Ltd.
Livery Place
35 Livery Street
Birmingham B3 2PB, UK.

ISBN 978-1-78355-205-4

www.packtpub.com

Credits

Author
John Henry Krahenbuhl

Reviewers
Ildikó Balla

Sam Spicer

Commissioning Editor
Usha Iyer

Acquisition Editor
Rebecca Youé

Content Development Editor
Vaibhav Pawar

Technical Editors
Pankaj Kadam

Bharat Patil

Copy Editors
Shambhavi Pai

Alfida Paiva

Laxmi Subramanian

Project Coordinator
Kranti Berde

Proofreaders
Mankee Cheng

Ameesha Green

Chris Smith

Indexer
Tejal Soni

Production Coordinator
Shantanu N. Zagade

Cover Work
Shantanu N. Zagade

About the Author

John Henry Krahenbuhl has over 20 years of experience in architecting practical, cost-effective, and innovative solutions. Being a creative thinker and having an entrepreneurial spirit has enabled him to be the lead or co-inventor on numerous utility patent applications. He is a multifaceted, collaborative management professional who is highly skilled at managing products through the entire life cycle, from design to obsolescence, including specification and use case definitions, schematic and PCB layouts, production software implementation, and hardware implementation. He's a passionate, resourceful leader who demands and delivers excellence in design and user experience.

> I would like to thank my family for their endless love and support: my children, Matt, Jason, Lauryn, and Henry, and especially my wife, my friend, my life coach, and the most amazing person I have ever had the privilege to love and admire—Melissa Krahenbuhl.

About the Reviewers

Ildikó Balla is a user experience designer living in Sydney, Australia, and working at www.reinteractive.net — Australia's largest Ruby on Rails-focused development company.

Her experience in the user experience field includes working on mobile, web, and desktop applications ranging from simple sites to complex back office solutions and e-commerce platforms. Specializing in interaction design and medium-fidelity prototyping, Axure has been Ildikó's tool of choice for the past 6 years.

Ildikó has also been a technical reviewer for *Axure RP Prototyping Cookbook* by John Henry Krahenbuhl and has contributed to a chapter in Ezra Schwartz and Elizabeth Srail's latest book, *Prototyping Essentials with Axure, Packt Publishing*.

Sam Spicer is a digital design professional with 14 years of experience. Beginning with frontend development, Sam progressed through his MS in human-computer interaction into the realm of information architecture in the early 2000s. Since then he has contributed to, and led, redesigns and replatforms for international brands ranging from e-commerce and financial services to retail and the food industry. When he's not geeking out on some obscure experience or technical thing, you can find him enjoying time with his family, brewing beer, baking, or otherwise getting into some sort of trouble. He has also reviewed *Prototyping Essentials with Axure, Packt Publishing*.

Thank you to my wife Nikki for her support and partnership without which I'd never be able to get anything accomplished!

www.PacktPub.com

Support files, eBooks, discount offers, and more

For support files and downloads related to your book, please visit www.PacktPub.com.

Did you know that Packt offers eBook versions of every book published, with PDF and ePub files available? You can upgrade to the eBook version at www.PacktPub.com and as a print book customer, you are entitled to a discount on the eBook copy. Get in touch with us at service@packtpub.com for more details.

At www.PacktPub.com, you can also read a collection of free technical articles, sign up for a range of free newsletters and receive exclusive discounts and offers on Packt books and eBooks.

https://www2.packtpub.com/books/subscription/packtlib

Do you need instant solutions to your IT questions? PacktLib is Packt's online digital book library. Here, you can search, access, and read Packt's entire library of books.

Why subscribe?

- Fully searchable across every book published by Packt
- Copy and paste, print, and bookmark content
- On demand and accessible via a web browser

Free access for Packt account holders

If you have an account with Packt at www.PacktPub.com, you can use this to access PacktLib today and view 9 entirely free books. Simply use your login credentials for immediate access.

Table of Contents

Preface

Axure has rapidly become one of the leading tools for rapid prototyping in use today. There are many reasons for Axure's popularity. You can easily create wireframes as well as generate a specification documentation.

Axure also provides the ability to quickly develop prototypes that can be leveraged in web browsers or as native Android, iPhone, or iPad applications. It is no wonder that Axure has become the tool of choice for a large percentage of the Fortune 100 corporations as well as User Experience Professionals worldwide.

Learning Axure RP Interactive Prototypes provides a rapid introduction to interactive prototyping. Starting with the fundamentals, you will create progressively complex experiences while learning basic, intermediate, and advanced interactions in Axure. You will apply what you learn to create an increasingly interactive prototype.

This book will show you how to create interactive prototypes with Axure RP 7 Pro. First, you will gain practical knowledge of Axure's pages, panes, and the design area. Then you will learn how to construct page and widget interactions.

Next, we will generate common interactions for a typical home page that will include a global header and footer as well as an interactive carousel. We will continue our journey by incorporating social media feeds from Facebook and Twitter. Your confidence with Axure will grow as you enhance your functional prototype with user account creation and login validation experiences.

Finally, you will fashion a dynamic shopping cart with a progress indicator and checkout interactions. By using Adaptive Views throughout your prototypes, you will transpose your designs and interactions for the desktop to tablet and mobile devices.

There are plentiful resources available to assist you no matter what your skill level. With a passionate community and exceptional technical support, any question you may have regarding Axure will quickly be answered. Visit http://www.axure.com/ community for access to Widget Libraries, the Axure Forum, and more resources. Welcome to the Axure community and enjoy the journey!

What this book covers

Chapter 1, Pages, the Design Area, and Panes, introduces fundamental interfaces and concepts. Master Axure's pages, panes, and the design area in addition to building a Sitemap for an e-commerce prototype.

Chapter 2, Home Page Structure and Interactions, presents interactions for a header, an interactive carousel, and includes a right column with live feeds from social media channels such as Facebook and Twitter.

Chapter 3, Registration and Sign In, creates an Inline Field Validation master, Registration, and Sign In pages and tracks a user's signed-in state.

Chapter 4, Dynamic Content Management, shows you how to leverage the Repeater widget to create a content management master.

Chapter 5, Product Pages and Interactions, provides examples for Catalog, Category, and Production Detail pages with immersive interactions.

Chapter 6, Search and Search Results, simulates Search interactions and populates a Search Results page by filtering the Repeater items shown on the content management master.

Chapter 7, The Shopping Bag Functionality and Interactions, builds a shopping bag that updates dynamically based on user interaction.

Chapter 8, Check Out Flow and Interactions, constructs a Check Out flow using forms and pages that include a dynamic progress indicator.

Appendix, Answers to Self-test Questions, reinforces concepts by reviewing chapter questions and answers.

What you need for this book

You will need Axure RP 7, an Internet connection, and a desire to learn interactive prototyping. If you do not currently have Axure, please visit http://www.axure.com to download a free trial version.

A few recipes will also require Axure RP 7 Pro, a graphics editing program (for example, Adobe Photoshop) and a word processing program that can open Microsoft Word's formatted documents (for example, MS Word).

Who this book is for

If you are a User Experience Professional, Designer, Information Architect, or Business Analyst who wants to gain interactive prototyping skills with Axure, this book is for you. This is also for users who have some experience creating wireframes as well as an interest in interaction design and want to take interactive prototypes to the next level.

Conventions

In this book, you will find a number of styles of text that distinguish between different kinds of information. Here are some examples of these styles, and an explanation of their meaning.

Code words in text, database table names, folder names, filenames, file extensions, pathnames, dummy URLs, user input, and Twitter handles are shown as follows: "Click on the green plus sign and type `ShoppingCartQty`."

New terms and **important words** are shown in bold. Words that you see on the screen, in menus or dialog boxes for example, appear in the text like this: "The **Sitemap** pane provides a top-down view of pages for a website."

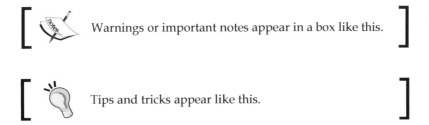

[Warnings or important notes appear in a box like this.]

[Tips and tricks appear like this.]

Reader feedback

Feedback from our readers is always welcome. Let us know what you think about this book—what you liked or may have disliked. Reader feedback is important for us to develop titles that you really get the most out of.

To send us general feedback, simply send an e-mail to feedback@packtpub.com, and mention the book title via the subject of your message.

If there is a topic that you have expertise in and you are interested in either writing or contributing to a book, see our author guide on www.packtpub.com/authors.

Customer support

Now that you are the proud owner of a Packt book, we have a number of things to help you to get the most from your purchase.

Downloading the example code

You can download the example code files for all Packt books you have purchased from your account at http://www.packtpub.com. If you purchased this book elsewhere, you can visit http://www.packtpub.com/support and register to have the files e-mailed directly to you.

Errata

Although we have taken every care to ensure the accuracy of our content, mistakes do happen. If you find a mistake in one of our books—maybe a mistake in the text or the code—we would be grateful if you would report this to us. By doing so, you can save other readers from frustration and help us improve subsequent versions of this book. If you find any errata, please report them by visiting http://www.packtpub.com/submit-errata, selecting your book, clicking on the **errata submission form** link, and entering the details of your errata. Once your errata are verified, your submission will be accepted and the errata will be uploaded to our website or added to any list of existing errata under the **Errata** section of that title.

To view the previously submitted errata, go to https://www.packtpub.com/books/content/support and enter the name of the book in the search field. The required information will appear under the **Errata** section.

Piracy

Piracy of copyright material on the Internet is an ongoing problem across all media. At Packt, we take the protection of our copyright and licenses very seriously. If you come across any illegal copies of our works, in any form, on the Internet, please provide us with the location address or website name immediately so that we can pursue a remedy.

Please contact us at copyright@packtpub.com with a link to the suspected pirated material.

We appreciate your help in protecting our authors, and our ability to bring you valuable content.

Questions

You can contact us at questions@packtpub.com if you are having a problem with any aspect of the book, and we will do our best to address it.

1
Pages, the Design Area, and Panes

A key to creating compelling interactions in **Axure RP** (**Rapid Prototyping**) is to quickly develop proficiency with Axure's environment and interface. Once you are familiar with specific aspects of the environment, you will be able to rapidly create interactive prototypes. The interface comprises a main menu, a toolbar, a sitemap, the design area, and several panes.

In this chapter, you will learn about exploring the environment and interface. This includes the following subtopics:

- Inspecting pages
  - The Sitemap pane
  - Creating a child page

- Investigating our design area
  - Opening pages
  - Showing the grid
  - Adding page guides

- Discovering panes
  - The Widgets pane and libraries
  - The Masters pane
  - The Page Properties pane
  - The Widget Interactions and Notes pane
  - The Widget Properties and Style pane
  - The Widget Manager pane

Exploring the environment and interface

Axure's environment has a similar feel to other desktop applications. When we open a RP document, the interface looks like this:

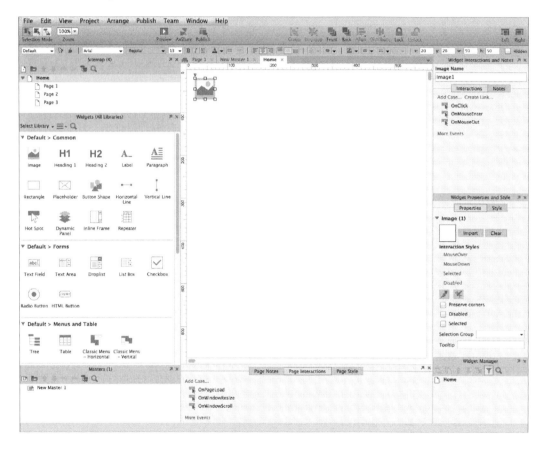

The interface is organized into the following sections: a main menu, a toolbar, the design area, and the surrounding panes. First, we will explore the interface as follows:

- At the top is the main menu that contains the following items:
    - **File**: This menu will have options to create new RP files, open and save as, import, open and save Team Project, print, export, and options for backup and recovery.
    - **Edit**: This menu has options such as **Cut**, **Copy**, **Paste**, **Find**, **Replace**, and an option to insert special characters.

- ° **View**: This menu has options such as **Panes**, **Toolbars**, **Reset View**, **Masks**, and several show options.

- ° **Project**: This menu has options for widgets and pages (for example, Style Editors and Notes Fields). It also has options such as **Adaptive Views...**, **Global Variables...**, and **Project Settings...**.

- ° **Arrange**: This menu will have **Group/Ungroup**, **Bring to Front/Send to Back**, **Align** (for example, Left, Right, Center, and so on) options, and options for **Grids and Guides**.

- ° **Publish**: This menu will have the new **Preview** option that enables quick viewing of our prototype, and also the **Generate HTML Files**, **Generate Word Documentation**, as well as **More Generators and Configurations...** options.

- ° **Team**: Team Projects allow us to share and work on single Projects in a Team environment. Items in this menu are **Create Team Project from Current File...**, **Get and Open Team Project**, as well as **Browse Team Project History...**.

- ° **Window**: This menu has the **Minimize** and **Zoom** options.

- ° **Help**: This menu has options to search, access Axure forums, manage the license key, and check for updates.

- Near the top of the Axure RP 7 interface is a toolbar. The toolbar comprises two sections stacked vertically, which are explained as follows:

  - ° The top toolbar section contains the following options:

    - ° **Selection Mode**: Intersected mode, Contained mode, and Connector mode.

    - ° **Zoom**: This is a drop-down list to set the default zoom level.

    - ° **Publishing**: Preview our prototype, AxShare (for example, publish our prototype to Axure's cloud-based sharing service), and **Publish** menu options.

    - ° **Arrangement of widgets**: The **Group**, **Ungroup**, **Front**, **Back**, **Align**, **Distribute**, **Lock**, and **Unlock** options.

    - ° **Interface layout**: This includes **Left** and **Right** options. Click to toggle (for example, show or hide) the left and right panes. When panes are shown, the **Left** or **Right** icon will change state, with visible panes on the icon shown in blue.

- ° The bottom toolbar section contains the following options:

   - ° Selected widget style drop-down list
   - ° Widget style editor
   - ° Format painter
   - ° Font formatting options (for example, font family, typeface, size, bold, italics, underline, color, bulleted list, and insert text link)
   - ° Text alignment (for example, left, center, right, top, middle, and bottom)
   - ° Fill color
   - ° Outer shadow
   - ° Line options (for example, color, width, pattern, and arrow style)
   - ° Widget location and visibility (for example, **x** coordinate and **y** coordinate, **w** for width, **h** for height, and **Hidden**)

In the center of the interface is the design area. The design area is where we open pages and drag and drop widgets to build our interface. The design area is surrounded on the left, right, and bottom by panes. The panes are organized as follows:

- The left-side column contains the following panes:
   - ° **Sitemap**: This pane provides a hierarchical overview of the pages in our design.
   - ° **Widgets**: This pane contains libraries of widgets that enable us to rapidly create wireframes and flow diagrams. Libraries of widgets can be downloaded, created, and shared.
   - ° **Masters**: This pane organizes templates that can be reused throughout our design. Common uses for masters are page elements, such as headers, footers, and so on.

- Under the design area, the bottom-center column contains the **Page Properties** pane. It has the following three tabs:
   - ° **Page Notes**
   - ° **Page Interactions**
   - ° **Page Style**

- The right-side column contains the following panes:
  - ○ **Widget Interactions and Notes**: It has the following two tabs:
    - ○ **Interactions**
    - ○ **Notes**
  - ○ **Widget Properties and Style**: It has the following two tabs:
    - ○ **Properties**
    - ○ **Style**
  - ○ **Widget Manager**: This pane enumerates widget states (for example, dynamic panel states).

Inspecting pages

Traditionally, the **Sitemap** pane provides a top-down view of pages for a website. In Axure, the **Sitemap** comprises pages and folders organized in a hierarchical fashion. Just under the toolbar, we will find the **Sitemap** pane.

The Sitemap pane

When we open a blank RP document, we will see four pages in the **Sitemap** pane. The pages are labeled Home, Page 1, Page 2, and Page 3, which are organized as follows:

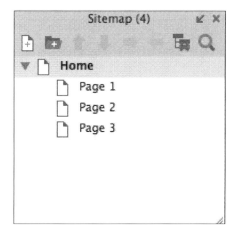

In the **Sitemap** pane, you will notice **(4)** next to **Sitemap**. This number indicates the total number of pages currently in the **Sitemap** pane.

At the top of the **Sitemap** pane, we see a row of eight icons as follows:

- Add Page
- Add Folder
- Move Up
- Move Down
- Indent
- Outdent
- Delete
- Search

Creating a child page

Icons of pages higher in the hierarchy are left justified. When a page becomes a parent page by having a child page association, a gray arrow is shown to the left of the page icon. The gray arrow enables us to collapse or view pages in that branch of the hierarchy.

There are several ways to create a child page. We can create a child page by clicking on the page in the **Sitemap** pane, clicking on the indent icon, and then clicking on the Move Up or Move Down icons to move the page.

Another method is to click and drag the page to the right and drag up or down if you want to move the page. You will see a blue box appear around the page that will become the parent page.

We can also create child pages by right-clicking on the parent page, moving the mouse over **Add**, and clicking on **Child Page**, as shown here:

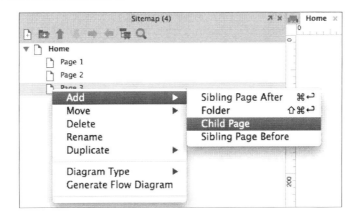

Investigating our design area

The design area is to the right of the **Sitemap** pane in the center of the interface, as shown here:

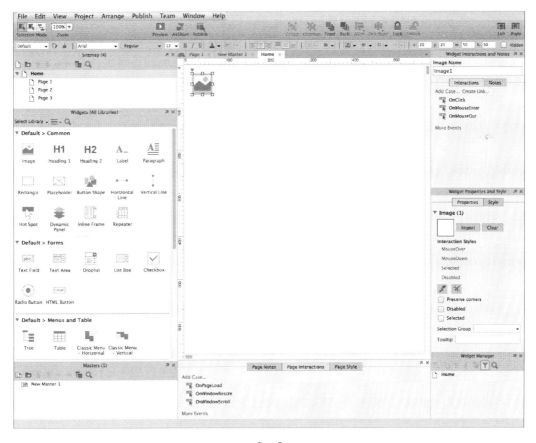

Opening pages

Pages can be opened in the design area by double-clicking on the page name or icon. Masters are also opened in the design area by double-clicking on the master name or icon. When a page or master is opened in the design area, a tab will be added to the design area with the name of the page or master. For example, double-clicking on the **Home** page in the **Sitemap** pane will display the page in the design area in a tab named **Home**.

When we open more than one page or master, the tabs will remain available in the design area until we choose to close the tab. Inactive tabs will be colored gray and the active tab will be white, as shown here:

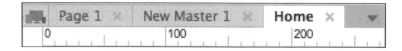

 To close a given tab, click on the cross next to the tab name. You can also manage tabs by clicking on the down arrow to the left of the tab names.

Showing the grid

When placing widgets in the design area, you may prefer having a grid to use as a visual reference. To show the grid, right-click on the design area, mouse over **Grid and Guides**, and click on **Show Grid**, as shown here:

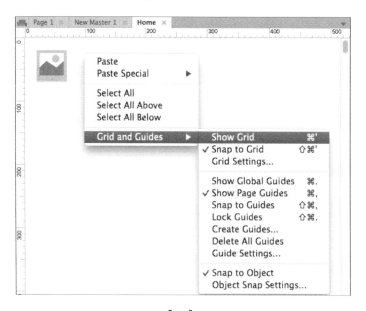

The default spacing for the grid is 20 pixels. To change the default spacing, right-click on the design area, mouse over **Grid and Guides**, and click on **Grid Settings...**.

Adding page guides

We can also add page guides to pages in our design. We can select from preset guides or add single page guides. To add page guides, right-click on the design area, mouse over **Grid and Guides**, and click on **Create Guides...**. In the **Create Guides** dialog window, click on the **Presets** drop-down list to select from the following:

- **960 Grid: 12 Column**
- **960 Grid: 16 Column**
- **1200 Grid: 12 Column**
- **1200 Grid: 15 Column**

We can also create custom guides by changing the default values offered in the **Create Guides** dialog window. The options presented are as follows:

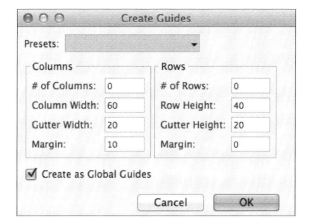

By default, guides are created as global guides. To create a guide just for the current page, uncheck the **Create as Global Guides** checkbox.

We can also create single guides for a page. To create a single guide, click on the left or top ruler and drag the guide onto the wireframe. To reposition a guide, click and drag the guide to the new position.

By default, single guides are blue and only appear on the current page. To make a global single guide that will be shown on all pages, hold down the *Command* key on a Mac (or the *Ctrl* key on Windows) while clicking and dragging the guide onto the wireframe. By default, global single guides are pink.

Discovering panes

As already mentioned briefly, the design area is surrounded on the left, right, and bottom by panes. You will now explore these panes in further detail.

The Widgets pane and libraries

In the left-side column under the **Sitemap** pane, we will find the **Widgets** pane, as shown here:

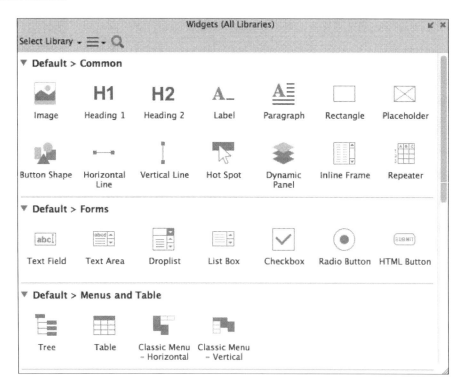

The **Widgets** pane allows us to view and leverage common interface objects, also known as widgets (for example, **Image**, **Button Shape**, **Rectangle**, and so on) in our design. Widgets are organized into custom libraries that can be shared and loaded into the **Widgets** pane.

The Masters panes

In the left-side column at the bottom under the **Widgets** pane is the **Masters** pane, as shown here:

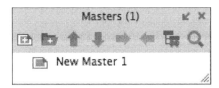

 In the **Masters** pane, you will notice **(1)** next to **Masters**. This number indicates the total number of masters currently in the sitemap.

The **Masters** pane contains of all the masters available in an RP file. Masters can range from a single widget to a collection of widgets used in our design. In most cases, masters enable you to make changes or updates in a single place. When we update a master, each page that contains the master will be updated as well.

Masters have three types of drop behavior. The drop behavior determines the location where the Master will be placed on the wireframe in the Design Area. The possible drop behavior options are as shown here:

 When placed on a page, **Break Away** masters can be edited just like widgets and do not change if the original master is updated.

The Page Properties pane

The **Page Properties** pane has three tabs: **Page Notes** (available with Axure RP Pro only), **Page Interactions**, and **Page Style**. The **Page Interactions** tab offers the following interactions:

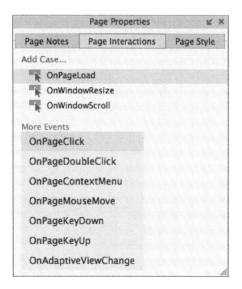

 There are three default events: **OnPageLoad**, **OnWindowResize**, and **OnWindowScroll**. Click on **More Events** to display the additional events, as shown in the previous screenshot.

The **Page Style** tab is used to change the style of individual pages, as well as page defaults. The **Page Style** tab offers the following options:

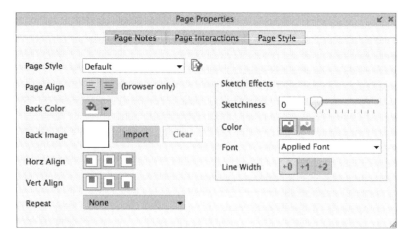

The Widget Interaction and Notes pane

The **Widget Interaction and Notes** pane has two tabs: **Interactions** and **Notes**.
The **Interactions** tab presents interaction options based on the widget selected.
An example from an Image widget is shown as follows:

 There are three default events: **OnClick**, **OnMouseEnter**, and
OnMouseOut. Click on **More Events** to display the additional
events, as shown in the previous screenshot.

The Widget Properties and Style pane

The **Widget Properties and Style** pane has two tabs: **Properties** and **Style**. The **Properties** tab presents interaction options based on the widget selected. An example from an Image widget is shown as follows:

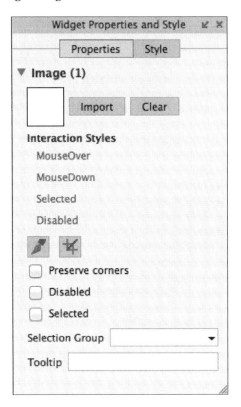

The **Style** tab is used to change the style of the widget selected. The **Style** tab has options organized into the following categories:

- **Location + Size**
- **Base Style**
- **Font**
- **Fills, Lines, + Borders**
- **Alignment + Padding**

The **Style** tab is shown as follows:

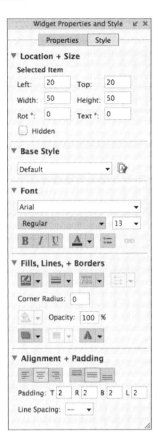

The Widget Manager pane

The **Widget Manager** pane is used to change the visibility of dynamic panels, as well as to manage panel states. The following is an example **Widget Manager** pane with two dynamic panels, labeled **Panel 1** and **Panel 2**, respectively:

Next to the dynamic panel labeled **Panel 1**, there is a blue rectangle. This indicates that the default for Panel 1 is Show in view. In contrast, next to the dynamic panel labeled Panel 2, there is a gray rectangle. This indicates that the default for **Panel 2** is Hide from view. Clicking on the icon will toggle the state.

At the top of the **Widget Manager** pane, we can see a row of seven icons as follows:

- Add State
- Duplicate State
- Move Up
- Move Down
- Delete
- Widget Filter
- Search

Summary

In this chapter, you learned about the various aspects of Axure's environment and interface. You explored the main menu, toolbar, sitemap, design area, and panes. You also became familiar with pages, widgets, and masters.

In the next chapter, we will create common interactions for several widely used web design elements. After organizing these elements into reusable masters, you will design a header, carousel, and global footer.

Self-test questions

- What sections does the Axure interface consist of?

- Can you show or hide individual widgets placed in the design area?

- When would we use a dynamic panel?

- What does it mean when you see a blue rectangle next to a dynamic panel in the **Widget Manager** pane?

- What does it mean when you see a gray rectangle next to a dynamic panel in the **Widget Manager** pane?

- How many tabs are there in the **Widget Interactions and Notes** pane and what are the names of the tabs?

- In the **Page Interactions** tab of the **Page Properties** pane, how many events are shown by default and what are the names of the events?

- In the **Page Interactions** tab of the **Page Properties** pane, how would you display additional events?

2
Home Page Structure and Interactions

By now, you have some familiarity with Axure's environment and interface. Using Axure's default common widget library and basic interactions, we can create compelling interactive prototypes. Throughout this book, we will utilize various common widgets and interactions to complete an e-commerce prototype.

We will first create our sitemap. Then, we will start our e-commerce prototype with the home page. Once completed, our home page will look like this:

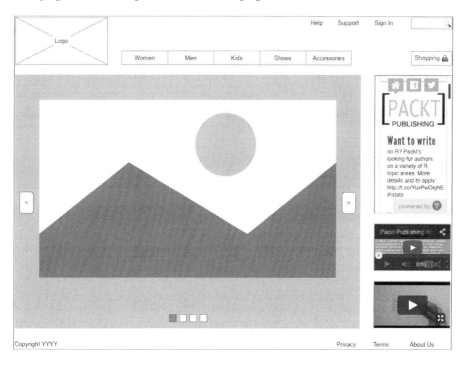

Downloading the example code

You can download the example code files for all Packt books you have purchased from your account at `http://www.packtpub.com`. If you purchased this book elsewhere, you can visit `http://www.packtpub.com/support` and register to have the files e-mailed directly to you.

A home page should be intuitive; it should capture one's attention and encourage further engagement with the site. For the home page, we will make use of the easily recognizable elements found on popular e-commerce sites.

In this chapter, you will learn about:

- Sitemap
- Header
    - Logo and links
    - Global navigation
    - Shopping cart
    - Search
- Carousel
    - Carousel dynamic panel
    - Autorotation
    - Previous and next
- Right column
    - Social media feed
    - Embedded video (YouTube and Vimeo)
- Global footer

Sitemap

We will first complete the initial phase of our sitemap for our e-commerce site.

To set up the **sitemap**, we perform the following steps:

1. Start Axure and, in the main menu, click on **File** and then **New** to create a new Axure RP document. In the **Sitemap** pane, click on the add page icon 10 times to add a total of 13 child pages under the **Home** page.

2. Rename each of the child pages using the following screenshot as a reference:

With our sitemap organized, we are now ready to focus on building the home page.

Header

When completed, the header for our e-commerce site will look like this:

Our header will include the following elements:

- Logo
- Global navigation
- Shopping cart
- Search

First, we will set up grid and page guides to assist with the placement of widgets. Next, we will drag and drop widgets from the **Widgets** pane onto the **Home** page, add interactions, and convert widgets in the header to a header master.

When you open a blank RP document, the interface looks like this:

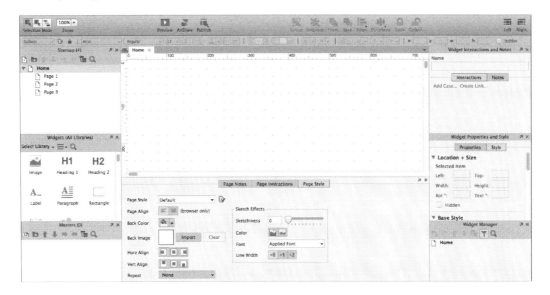

 When a blank RP document opens, the **Home** page is opened in the design area by default. When a page is currently displayed in the design area, you will see the page label highlighted in blue in the **Sitemap** pane.

To set up the grid and page guides, perform the following steps:

1. In the main menu, click on **Arrange**, then on **Grids and Guides**, and, finally, on **Create Guides...** to open the **Create Guides** dialog box. The **Create Guides** dialog box looks like this:

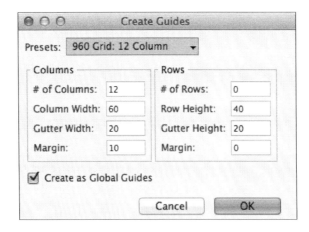

2. Select **960 Grid: 12 Column** from the **Presets** drop-down menu.

3. Make sure that the **Create as Global Guides** checkbox is selected.

4. In the main menu, click on **Arrange**, then on **Grids and Guides**, and, finally, click on **Grid Settings…** to open the **Grid Dialog** box. The **Grid Dialog** box looks like this:

5. In the **Grid Dialog** box, make sure that the **Show Grid** and **Snap to Grid** checkboxes are selected. Also, make sure that **Spacing** is set to 20 px.

 When **Snap to Grid** is enabled by moving a widget on to the design area, the widget will align to the closest point on the grid.

6. In the **Grid Dialog** box, click on the **Guides** tab. The **Grid Dialog** box will display the **Guides** tab as follows:

7. With the **Guides** tab selected in the **Grid Dialog** box, make sure that the checkboxes are selected for the following options:

    ° **Show Global Guides**

    ° **Show Page Guides**

    ° **Snap To Guides**

Guides are an aid to help ensure consistency across pages in our design. Global guides are shown in the design area on all pages, masters, and dynamic panel states. Page guides are only shown on the current page opened in the design area.

To create a page guide, drag from the ruler and drop a guide onto the design area. To create a global guide, hold the *Command* (Mac) or *Ctrl* (Windows) key, drag from the ruler, and drop onto the design area. With grids and page guides configured, we will now design our header. To start, we will place the logo and create an **OnClick** interaction.

Logo and links

To create our logo element, we will drag the **Placeholder** widget onto the **Home** page in the design area. We will then enable an **OnClick** interaction that will cause the **Home** page to open in the current window when the **Placeholder** widget is clicked.

To create the logo element, perform the following steps:

1. With the **Home** page opened in the design area, in the **Widgets** pane, click on the **Placeholder** widget. While holding down the mouse button, drag the **Placeholder** widget and place it at coordinates (10,20).

2. With the **Placeholder** widget selected, type Logo. We will see **Logo** in the center of the **Placeholder** widget, like so:

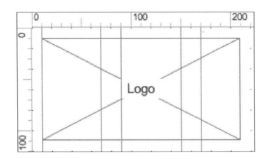

3. Next, we will name the **Placeholder** widget and add the **OnClick** interaction. With the **Placeholder** widget selected, perform the following steps:

   ○ In the **Widget Interactions and Notes** pane, click in the **Shape Name** field and type CompanyLogo.

   ○ In the **Widget Interactions and Notes** pane, click on the **Interactions** tab and then on **Create Link...**. In the **Sitemap** modal window, click on the **Home** page. You will see **Case 1** added to the **OnClick** interaction, as follows:

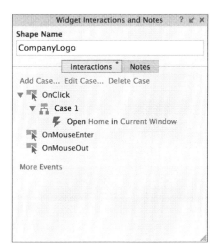

 Axure has numerous point updates, and as a result, in the Widgets Interactions and Notes pane, your version may show Shape Name (or a similar label for the name field) instead of Shape Footnote and Name.

4. We will now create three new links in our header using a **Dynamic Panel** and the **Label** widget. In the **Widgets** pane, click on the **Dynamic Panel** widget. While holding down the mouse button, drag the **Dynamic Panel** widget and place it at coordinates (570,10). With the **Dynamic Panel** widget selected, perform the following steps:

   ○ In the **Widget Interactions and Notes** pane, click in the **Dynamic Panel Name** field and type HeaderLinksDP.

   ○ In the toolbar, change the width **w:** to 300 and the height **h:** to 25.

5. In the **Widget Manager** pane, we will see the following:

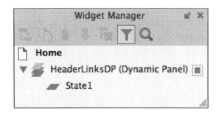

6. In the **Widget Manager** pane, double-click on **State1** to open it in the design area.

7. With **State1** selected, in the **Widgets** pane, click on the **Label** widget. While holding down the mouse button, drag the **Label** widget and place it at coordinates (80,4). With the **Label** widget selected, perform the following steps:

   1. Type `Help`. We will see **Help** displayed as text on the **Label** widget.

   2. In the **Widget Interactions and Notes** pane, click in the **Shape Name** field and type `HelpLink`.

   3. In the **Widget Interactions and Notes** pane, click on the **Interactions** tab and then click on **Create Link…**. In the **Sitemap** modal window, click on the **Help** page.

8. Repeat step 7 twice to create two additional links using the following table for coordinates, text displayed, shape name of the label widgets, and create link:

Coordinates	Text displayed	Shape name	Create link...
(140,4)	Support	SupportLink	Support
(220,4)	Sign In	SignInLink	Sign In

9. Slow double-click on **State1** and rename it to **Links**.

 When renaming a dynamic panel state, if the state is currently selected (that is, highlighted in blue), you only need to slow click on the state name to rename the state. If the state is not currently selected, you will need to slow double-click on the state name to rename the state.

We have now created the logo with three additional links. Our header should look like this:

Next, we will add global navigation using the **Classic Menu - Horizontal** widget.

Global navigation

We will now add global navigation using the **Classic Menu – Horizontal** widget. Once we have added the **Classic Menu – Horizontal** widget, our header should look like this:

Open the **Home** page in the design area. To create the global navigation element, perform the following steps:

1. In the **Widgets** pane, click on the **Classic Menu - Horizontal** widget. While holding down the left mouse button, drag the **Classic Menu - Horizontal** widget and place it at coordinates (240,80).

2. Right-click the first menu item labeled **File**, and in the flyout menu, click on **Add Menu Item After**. Your menu should look like this:

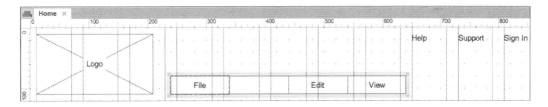

3. Repeat step 2, adding one more menu item. You should now have a total of five menu items.

4. Click on the first menu item to select it and type Women.

5. With the menu item selected, perform the following steps:
   - In the **Widget Interactions and Notes** pane, click in the **Menu Item Name** field and type HzMenuWomen.
   - In the **Widget Interactions and Notes** pane, click on the **Interactions** tab and then click on **Create Link...**. In the **Sitemap** modal window, click on the **Women** page.

6. Repeat step 5 to change the menu item displayed and menu item name for menu items 2–5 using the following table:

Menu item displayed	Menu item name	Create link...
Men	HzMenuMen	Men
Kids	HzMenuKids	Kids
Shoes	HzMenuShoes	Shoes
Accessories	HzMenuAccessories	Accessories

We have now created the global navigation with five menu items. Our header should now look like this:

   ° Next, we will add a shopping cart element using a **Rectangle** widget with a **Text Field** widget.

Shopping cart

We will now add a shopping cart element using a **Rectangle** widget and a special character for a shopping bag icon. Our shopping cart element will look like this:

To create the **Shopping Cart** element, perform the following steps:

1. From the **Widgets** pane, drag the **Rectangle** widget and place at coordinates (870,80). With the **Rectangle** widget selected, perform the following steps:

   1. Right-click on the **Rectangle** widget and click **Edit Text**.
      Type `Shopping`.

   2. In the toolbar, change the width **w** to `90` and the height **h** to `30`.

3. In the **Widget Interactions and Notes** pane, click in the **Shape Name** field and type `ShoppingButton`.

4. In the **Widget Properties and Style** pane, with the **Style** tab selected, scroll to **Alignment + Padding** and change padding by changing the value of **R** to `15`.

2. From the **Widgets** pane, drag the **Image** widget and place at coordinates (937,85). With the **Image** widget selected, perform the following steps:

   1. In the toolbar, change the width **w** to `20` and the height **h** to `20`.

   2. In the **Widget Interactions and Notes** pane, click in the **Image Name** field and type `ShoppingBagIcon`.

   3. Double-click the image and select the image you would like to use (that is, a shopping bag or shopping cart image).

 For our shopping bag icon, an image of a handbag emoji 👜 sized to 20 x 20 pixels was used. The handbag emoji as well as other useful emojis can be found at `http://emojipedia.org`.

Next, we will add an expandable search text field element using a dynamic panel widget with two states.

Search

One popular design pattern is to use an expandable search text field. To accomplish this, we will use a **Dynamic Panel** widget labeled SearchDP with two states: Collapsed and Expanded. The Collapsed state is the default state and will contain a **Text Field** widget. The **Text Field** widget will respond to the **OnMouseEnter** interaction and will perform the following actions:

- Move the **HeaderLinksDP (Dynamic Panel)** in *x*: `-80` pixels.

- Transitioning the Dynamic Panel to the Expanded state, using the slide left animation.

- Set focus on the Text Field widget labeled **SearchTextFieldExpanded**.

To create the Search text field, **Dynamic Panel**, and **States**, perform the following steps:

In the **Widgets** pane, click on the **Dynamic Panel** widget. While holding down the mouse button, drag the **Dynamic Panel** widget and place it at coordinates (790,10). With the **Dynamic Panel** widget selected, perform the following steps:

- Right-click on the **Dynamic Panel** widget and click on **Order**, then click on **Send to Back.**

- In the **Widget Interactions and Notes** pane, click in the **Dynamic Panel Name** field and type ExpandingSearchDP.

- In the toolbar, change the width **w:** to 170 and the height **h:** to 25.

In the **Widget Manager** pane, double-click on **State1** to open it in the design area. With **State1** selected, perform the following steps:

1. In the **Widgets** pane, click on the **Rectangle** widget. While holding down the mouse button, drag the **Rectangle** widget and place at coordinates (80,0). With the **Rectangle** widget selected, In the toolbar change the values of **w** to 90 and **h** to 24. In the **Widget Interactions and Notes** pane, click in the **Text Field Name** field and type SearchRectangleCollapsed.

2. From the **Widgets** pane, drag the **Image** widget and place at coordinates (149,2). In the toolbar, change the width **w** to 20 and the height **h** to 20. In the **Widget Interactions and Notes** pane, click in the **Image Name** field and type SearchIcon. Double-click the image and select the image you would like to use (that is, a left-pointing, magnifying glass image).

 For our search icon, an image of a left-pointing, magnifying glass emoji 🔍 sized to 20 x 20 pixels was used. This emoji as well as other useful emojis can be found at http://emojipedia.org.

In the **Widgets** pane, click on the **Text Field** widget. While holding down the left mouse button, drag the **Text Field** widget and place at coordinates (80,0). With the text field widget selected, perform the following steps:

1. In the **Widget Interactions and Notes** pane, click in the **Text Field Name** field and type SearchTextFieldCollapsed.

2. In the toolbar, change the value of **w** to 65 and **h** to 24.

3. Right-click on the **Text Field** widget and click on **Hide Border**.

4. In the **Widget Properties and Style** pane, with the **Style** tab selected, scroll to **Borders, Lines, + Fills**. Click on the down arrow next to the paint bucket icon. In the drop-down menu, click on the box with the red diagonal line to indicate no fill. The fill drop-down menu with no fill selected looks like this:

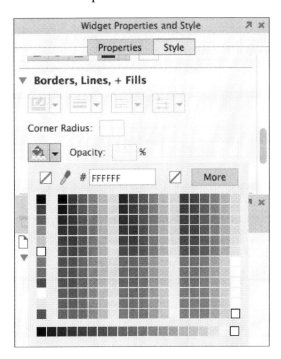

1. Right-click on **State1** and click **Duplicate State**.

2. Slow click on **State1** and rename it to **Collapsed**.

3. Slow double-click on **State2** and rename it to **Expanded**.

In the **Widget Manager** pane, double-click on **Expanded** to open it in the design area. With **Expanded** selected, perform the following steps:

• Click on the rectangle widget labeled **SearchRectangleCollapsed** to select it and perform the following steps:

 The **SearchRectangleCollapsed** widget is at coordinates (80,0) and is directly beneath the **SearchTextFieldCollapsed** widget at coordinates (80,0). Slow-double-click on the design area near coordinates (90,10) to select the **SearchRectangleCollapsed** widget. Once selected in the **Widget Interactions and Notes** pane, in the **Shape Name** field, you will see the name **SearchRectangleCollapsed**.

1. In the **Widget Interactions and Notes** pane, click in the **Shape Name** field and rename the widget `SearchRectangleExpanded`.

2. In the toolbar, change **x** to `0` and **w** to `170`.

- Click on the text field widget labeled **SearchTextFieldCollapsed** at coordinates (80,0) to select it and perform the following steps:

  1. In the **Widget Interactions and Notes** pane, click in the **Text Field Name** field and rename the widget `SearchTextFieldExpanded`.

  2. In the toolbar, change **x** to `0` and **w** to `145`.

With the search text field dynamic panel created, we are now ready to define the interactions that will cause the search text field element to expand and collapse. To create this effect, perform the steps given in the following sections:

1. In the **Widget Manager** pane, double-click on the **Collapsed** state to open it in the design area. In the design area, click on the text field widget named **SearchTextFieldCollapsed** at coordinates (80,0). With the text field widget selected in the **Widget Interactions and Notes** pane, click on the **Interactions** tab, then on **More Events**, and, finally, click on **OnMouseEnter**. A **Case Editor** dialog box will open. In the **Case Editor** dialog box, perform the steps given in the following section.

   Create the first action:

   1. Under **Click to add actions**, scroll to the **Dynamic Panels** drop-down menu and click on **Set Panel State**.

   2. Under **Configure actions**, click on the checkbox next to **Set ExpandingSearchDP state**.

   3. Change **Select the State** to **Expanded**.

   4. Change **Animate In** to **slide left t:** 250 ms.

Create the second action:

1. Under **Click to add actions**, scroll to the **Widgets** drop-down menu and click on **Move**.

2. Under **Configure actions**, click on the checkbox next to **HeaderLinksDP**.

3. Change **Move by x** to -80.

Create the third action:

1. Under **Click to add actions**, scroll to the **Miscellaneous** drop-down menu and click on **Wait**.

2. Under **Configure actions**, change **Wait time:** to 350 ms.

Create the fourth action:

1. Under **Click to add actions**, scroll to the **Widgets** drop-down menu and click on **Bring to Front/Back**.

2. Under **Configure actions**, click on the checkbox next to **SearchTextFieldExpanded**.

3. Next to **Order**, click on the radio button next to **Bring to Front**.

Create the fifth action:

1. Under **Click to add actions**, scroll to the **Widgets** drop-down menu and click on **Focus**.

2. Under **Configure actions**, click on the checkbox next to **SearchTextFieldExpanded**.

3. Click on **OK**.

In the **Widget Interactions and Notes** pane, click on the **Interactions** tab and then click on **Case 1**. In the main menu, click on **Edit** and then click on **Copy**.

In the design area, click on the rectangle widget named **SearchRectangleCollapsed** at coordinates (80,0) to select it. Recall that we must slow-double-click near coordinates (90,10) to select the **SearchRectangleCollapsed** since it is beneath the **SearchTextFieldCollapsed** widget. With the rectangle widget selected in the **Widget Interactions and Notes** pane, click on the **Interactions** tab, then click on **More Events**, and next to **OnMouseEnter,** click on the **Paste** button. The **OnMouseEnter** event with **Case 1** will be shown as follows:

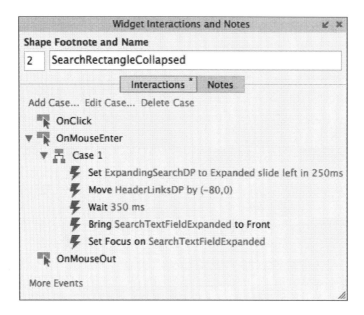

2. In the **Widget Manager** pane, double-click on the **Expanded** state to open it in the design area. Click on the text field widget named **SearchTextFieldExpanded** near coordinates (0,0) to select it. With the text field widget selected in the **Widget Interactions and Notes** pane, click on the **Interactions** tab, then on **More Events**, and, finally, click on **OnLostFocus**. A **Case Editor** dialog box will open. In the **Case Editor** dialog box, perform the following steps:

Create the condition. Click the **Add Condition** button. In the **Condition Builder** dialog box, in the outlined condition box perform the following steps:

1. In the first dropdown, select **cursor**.

2. In the second dropdown, select **is not over**.

3. In the third dropdown, select **area of widget**.

4. In the fourth text box dropdown, select **SearchRectangle**.

5. Click **OK**.

Create the first action:

1. Under **Click to add actions**, scroll to the **Dynamic Panels** drop-down menu and click on **Set Panel State**.

2. Under **Configure actions**, click on the checkbox next to **Set ExpandingSearchDP state**.

3. Change **Select the State** to **Collapsed**.

4. Change **Animate In** to **slide right t:** 200 ms.

Create the second action:

1. Under **Click to add actions**, scroll to the **Miscellaneous** drop-down menu and click on **Wait**.

2. Under **Configure actions**, change **Wait time:** to 150 ms.

Create the third action:

1. Under **Click to add actions**, scroll to the **Widgets** drop-down menu and click on **Move**.

2. Under **Configure actions**, click on the checkbox next to **HeaderLinksDP**.

3. Change **Move by x:** to 80.

Create the fourth action:

1. Under **Click to add actions**, scroll to the **Widgets** drop-down menu and click on **Set Text**.

2. Under **Configure actions**, click on the checkbox next to **SearchTextFieldExpanded**.

3. Under **Set text to**, click on the first dropdown and select **text on widget**. Click on the second dropdown and select **SearchTextFieldExpanded**. Your case editor will look like this:

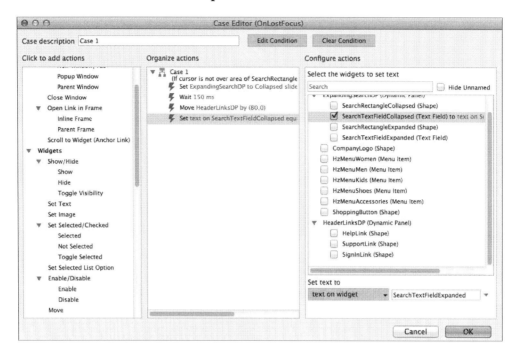

Create the fifth action:

1. Under **Click to add actions**, scroll to the **Widgets** drop-down menu and click on **Bring to Front/Back**.

2. Under **Configure actions**, click on the checkbox next to **HeaderLinksDP**.

3. Next to **Order**, click on the radio button next to **Bring to Front**.

4. Click on **OK**.

In the design area, click on the text field widget named **SearchTextFieldExpanded** to select it. Perform the following steps:

1. Right-click on the **SearchTextFieldExpanded** widget and click on **Assign Submit Button**.

2. In the **Assign Submit Button** dialog box, click on the checkbox next to **SearchRectangleExpanded**.

3. Click on **OK**.

4. In the design area, select the rectangle widget named **SearchRectangleExpanded** by slow-double-clicking near coordinates (10,10). With the **Rectangle** widget selected, go to the **Widget Interactions and Notes** pane, click on the **Interactions** tab, and click on **Create Link…**. In the **Sitemap** modal window, click on the **Search** page.

We have now created an expandable search text field widget that retains the text typed into the widget when the dynamic panel changes states. With the design completed for our header, we need to convert these widgets into a header master that can be leveraged on each page of our design.

To create a header master, open the **Home** page in the design area then navigate to **Edit | Select All** in the main menu. Right-click on any widget in the design area and click on **Convert to Master**. In the **Convert to Master** dialog box, type `Header`. For **Drop Behavior**, click on the radio button next to **Lock to Master Location**. Click on the **Continue** button. You will now see the header master appear in the **Masters** pane. With our header Master completed, next we will design an interactive carousel.

Carousel

Showcasing our e-commerce website's offers and products will be an autorotating carousel. When the user clicks on the main image on the carousel or the previous or next buttons, the autorotation will stop. Once we have added the carousel, our page should look like this:

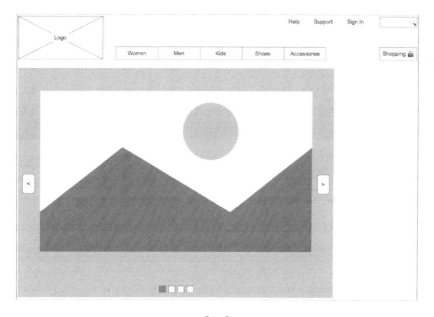

Carousel dynamic panel

To create the carousel dynamic panel and states, with the **Home** page opened in the design area, perform the following steps:

1. In the **Widgets** pane, click on the **Dynamic Panel** widget. While holding down the mouse button, drag the **Dynamic Panel** widget and place it at coordinates (10,130). With the **Dynamic Panel** widget selected, perform the following steps:

    1. Right-click on the **Dynamic Panel** widget and click on **Order,** then click on **Send to Back.**

    2. In the **Widget Interactions and Notes** pane, click in the **Dynamic Panel Name** field and type CarouselDP.

    3. In the toolbar, change the width **w** to 750 and the height **h** to 530.

2. In the **Widget Manager** pane, double-click on **State1** to open it in the design area. With **State1** selected, in the **Widgets** pane, click on the **Image** widget. While holding down the mouse button, drag the **Image** widget and place it at coordinates (0,0). With the rectangle widget selected, perform the following steps:

    1. In the **Widget Interactions and Notes** pane, click in the **Image Name** field and type Image1.

    2. In the toolbar, change the width **w** to 750 and the height **h** to 530.

3. With **State1** still open in the design area, click on the **Rectangle** widget in the **Widgets** pane. While holding down the mouse button, drag the **Rectangle** widget and place it at coordinates (335,500). With the **Rectangle** widget selected, perform the following steps:

    1. In the **Widget Interactions and Notes** pane, click in the **Shape Name** field and type Indicator1.

    2. In the toolbar, change the width **w:** to 16 and the height **h:** to 16.

4. Repeat step 3 three times to create three additional rectangles using the following table for the coordinates and shape names:

Coordinates	Shape name
(357,500)	Indicator2
(379,500)	Indicator3
(401,500)	Indicator4

5. In the **Widget Manager** pane, under the **CarouselDP (Dynamic Panel)**, right-click on **State1** and click on **Duplicate State**.

6. Repeat step 5 two times to create a total of four states.

7. We will now set the fill color for each indicator on **State1** through **State4**. In the **Widget Manager** pane, double-click on **State1** to open it in the design area and perform the following steps:

    1. Click on the **Rectangle** widget labeled **Indicator1** to select it.

    2. In the **Widget Properties and Style** pane, with the **Style** tab selected, scroll to **Borders, Lines, + Fills**. Click on the down arrow next to the paint bucket icon. In the drop-down menu, enter 999999 in the **#** text field.

8. Repeat step 7 three times to set the fill color for each indicator on **State2** through **State4**, using the following table for states and shape names:

State	Shape name
State2	Indicator2
State3	Indicator3
State4	Indicator4

We now have a carousel with four states and indicators. Next, we will enable the autorotation interaction.

Autorotation

To start our autorotating carousel, we will leverage the **OnPageLoad** page interaction. Next, for each state of the **CarouselDP (Dynamic Panel)**, we will use OnPanelStateChange, wait for 2000 ms, and then verify whether the user has clicked on the carousel image before changing the state of the **CarouselDP (Dynamic Panel)**.

To verify whether the user has clicked on the carousel image, we will create a global variable named CarouselClicked. To create the global variable, perform the following steps:

1. In the main menu, click on **Project** and then on **Global Variables...**.

2. In the **Global Variables...** dialog box, click on the **+** sign and type CarouselClicked.

3. Click on **OK**.

Next, we will create a **CheckForClick Hot Spot** widget. The **CheckForClick** widget will be used to stop the autorotation of the carousel if the carousel image or previous or next buttons have been clicked. To create the **CheckForClick Hot Spot** widget with interactions, perform the following steps:

In the **Widgets** pane, click on the **Hot Spot** widget. While holding down the mouse button, drag the **Hot Spot** widget and place it at coordinates (240,520). With the **Hot Spot** widget selected, perform the following steps:

1. In the **Widget Interactions and Notes** pane, click in the **Hot Spot Name** field and type CheckForClick.

2. Right-click on the **Hot Spot** widget and click on **Set Hidden**. This will hide the **Hot Spot** widget from view.

In the **Widget Interactions and Notes** pane, click on the **Interactions** tab, then on **More Events**, and, finally, click on **OnFocus**. A **Case Editor** dialog box will open. In the **Case Editor** dialog box, perform the following steps:

Create the condition.

- Click on the **Add Condition** button. In the **Condition Builder** dialog box, perform the following steps in the outlined condition box:
    1. In the first dropdown, select **value of variable**.
    2. In the second dropdown, select **CarouselClicked**.
    3. In the third dropdown, select **equals**.
    4. In the fourth dropdown, select **value**.
    5. In the text field, enter 0. Your **Condition Builder** will look like this:

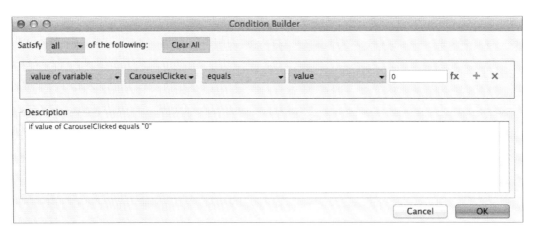

    6. Click on **OK**.

Create the action:

1. Under **Click to add actions**, scroll to the **Dynamic Panels** drop-down menu and click on **Set Panel State**.

2. Under **Configure actions**, click on the checkbox next to **Set CarouselDP state**.

3. Change **Select the state** to **Next**.

4. Click on the checkbox next to **Wrap from last to first**.

5. Change **Animate In** to **slide left t:** 500 ms.

6. Change **Animate Out** to **slide left t:** 500 ms.

7. Click on **OK**.

With the **CarouselClicked global variable** and the **CheckForClick** widget defined, we are now ready to use the **OnPageLoad** interaction. Perform the following steps:

1. In the **Sitemap** pane, double-click on the **Home** page to open it in the design area.

2. Under the design area in the **Page** pane, click on the **Page Interactions** tab.

3. Click on **Add Case...** to open the **Case Editor** dialog box. In the **Case Editor** dialog box, perform the following steps:

Create the first action:

1. Under **Variables**, click on **Set Variable Value**.

2. Under **Configure actions**, click on the checkbox next to **CarouselClicked** in the **Select the variables to set** section.

3. Under **Configure actions**, in the first drop-down menu, select **value** and enter 0 in the text field in the **Set variable to** section.

Create the second action:

1. Under **Click to add actions**, scroll to the **Miscellaneous** drop-down menu and click on **Wait**.

2. Under **Configure actions**, change **Wait time:** to 2000 ms.

Create the third action:

1. Under **Click to add actions**, scroll to the **Widgets** drop-down menu and click on **Focus**.

2. Under **Configure actions**, click on the checkbox next to **CheckForClick** in the **Select widget to focus** section.

3. Click on **OK**.

With the **OnPageLoad** interaction defined, we are now ready to complete the autorotation interaction. To complete the autorotation interaction, click on the **CarouselDP (Dynamic Panel)** to select it and perform the following steps:

1. In the **Widget Interactions and Notes** pane, click on the **Interactions** tab and double-click on **OnClick**. A **Case Editor** dialog box will open. In the **Case Editor** dialog box, perform the following steps:

    1. Under **Click to add actions**, scroll to the **Variables** drop-down menu and click on **Set Variable Value**.

    2. Under **Configure actions**, click on the checkbox next to **CarouselClicked** in the **Select the variables to set** section.

    3. Under **Configure actions**, in the first drop-down menu, select **value** and enter 1 in the text field in the **Set variable to** section.

    4. Click on **OK**.

2. In the **Widget Interactions and Notes** pane, click on the **Interactions** tab and double-click on **OnPanelStateChange**. A **Case Editor** dialog box will open. In the **Case Editor** dialog box, perform the following steps:

    Create the conditions.

    Click on the **Add Condition** button. In the **Condition Builder** dialog box, in the outlined condition box, perform the following steps:

    1. In the first dropdown, select **state of panel**.

    2. In the second dropdown, select **CarouselDP**.

    3. In the third dropdown, select **equals**.

    4. In the fourth dropdown, select **state**.

    5. In the fifth dropdown, select **State1**.

    6. Click on the green plus sign to add a second condition.

In the **Condition Builder** dialog box, perform the following steps in the outlined condition box for the second condition:

1. In the first dropdown, select **value of variable**.

2. In the second dropdown, select **CarouselClicked**.

3. In the third dropdown, select **equals**.

4. In the fourth dropdown, select **value**.

5. In the text field, enter 0.

6. Click on **OK**.

Create the first action:

1. Under **Click to add actions**, scroll to the **Miscellaneous** drop-down menu and click on **Wait**.

2. Under **Configure actions**, change **Wait time:** to 2000 ms.

Create the second action:

1. Under **Click to add actions**, scroll to the **Widgets** drop-down menu and click on **Focus**.

2. Under **Configure actions**, click on the checkbox next to **CheckForClick** in the **Select widget to focus** section.

3. Click on **OK**.

3. Repeat step 2 three times to create the additional interactions for the remaining states of the CarouselDP Dynamic Panel. Use the following table for the case descriptions to create with the modified conditions (that is, changing the first condition, in the fifth drop-down menu):

Case description	Condition
Case 2	State2
Case 3	State3
Case 4	State4

We have now created an autorotating carousel that will stop when a user clicks on the image shown. Next, we will create Previous and Next buttons using Rectangle widgets and **OnClick** interactions.

Previous and next

We will now create previous and next buttons to control our autorotating carousel. To create the previous and next buttons with interactions, perform the following steps:

To create the previous button with interactions, click on the **Rectangle** widget in the **Widgets** pane. Drag the **Rectangle** widget and place it at coordinates (20,375). With the rectangle widget selected, perform the following steps:

- In the toolbar, change the width **w** to 30 and the height **h** to 45.
- In the **Widget Interactions and Notes** pane, click in the **Shape Name** field and type PreviousButton.
- In the **Widget Interactions and Notes** pane, with the **Interactions** tab selected, click on **Add Case...** to open the **Case Editor** dialog box. In the **Case Editor** dialog box, perform the following steps:

Create the first action:

1. Under **Variables**, click on **Set Variable Value**.
2. Under **Configure actions**, click on the checkbox next to **CarouselClicked** in the **Select the variables to set** section.
3. Under **Configure actions**, in the first drop-down menu, select **value** and enter 1 in the text field in the **Set variable to** section.

Create the second action:

1. Under **Click to add actions**, scroll to the **Dynamic Panels** drop-down menu and click on **Set Panel State**.
2. Under **Configure actions**, click on the checkbox next to **Set CarouselDP state**.
3. Change **Select the state** to **Previous**.
4. Click on the checkbox next to **Wrap from last to first**.
5. Change **Animate In** to **slide right t:** 500 ms.
6. Change **Animate Out** to **slide right t:** 500 **ms**.
7. Click on **OK**.
8. Right-click on the **rectangle** widget and click on **Edit Text**. Type <.

To create the next button with interactions, click on the **Rectangle** widget in the **Widgets** pane. Drag the **Rectangle** widget and place it at coordinates (720,375). With the rectangle widget selected, perform the following steps:

- In the toolbar, change the width **w:** to 30 and the height **h:** to 45.

- In the **Widget Interactions and Notes** pane, click in the **Shape Name** field and type NextButton.

- In the **Widget Interactions and Notes** pane, with the **Interactions** tab selected, click on **Add Case...** to open the **Case Editor** dialog box. In the **Case Editor** dialog box, perform the following steps:

Create the first action:

1. Under **Variables**, click on **Set Variable Value**.

2. Under **Configure actions**, click on the checkbox next to **CarouselClicked** in the **Select the variables to set** section.

3. Under **Configure actions**, in the first drop-down menu, select value and enter 1 in the text field in the **Set variable to** section.

Create the second action:

1. Under **Click to add actions**, scroll to the **Dynamic Panels** drop-down menu and click on **Set Panel State**.

2. Under **Configure actions**, click on the checkbox next to **Set CarouselDP state**.

3. Change **Select the state** to **Next**.

4. Click on the checkbox next to **Wrap from last to first**.

5. Change **Animate In** to **slide left t** 500 ms.

6. Change **Animate Out** to **slide left t** 500 ms.

7. Click on **OK**.

8. Right-click on the **Rectangle** widget and click on **Edit Text**. Type >.

Our **Home** page with the carousel including previous and next buttons looks like this:

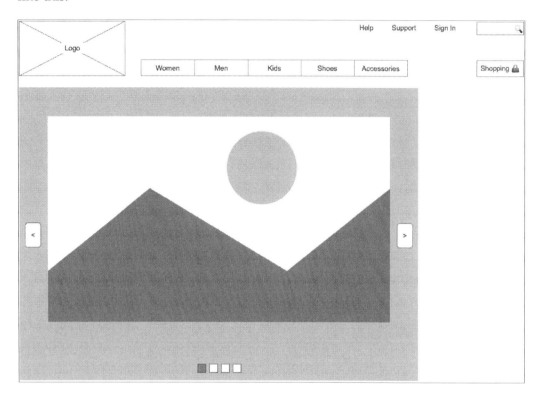

With our carousel completed, we are now ready to design the right column.

Right column

We will now add a social media feed, a YouTube video, and a Vimeo video in the right column of our e-commerce **Home** page. Once added, our **Home** page will look like this:

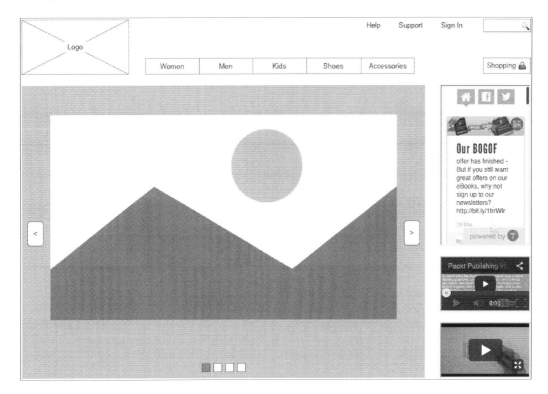

Social media feed

We will now leverage an inline frame widget to create a social media feed. There are various social aggregator services available. For this prototype, we will use Tint (`http://www.tintup.com`).

Tint offers a basic service that allows you to connect to two social media networks for free. After creating an account and adding a Tint (that is, a social media feed), you will be given a URL to your new feed. To add the social media feed to your prototype, click on the **Inline Frame** widget in the **Widgets** pane. Drag the **Inline Frame** widget and place it at coordinates (790,1300). With the **Inline Frame** widget selected, perform the following steps:

1. In the **Widget Interactions and Notes** pane, click in the **Inline Frame Name** field and type SocialMediaFeed.

2. In the toolbar, change the value of **w** to `170` and **h** to `290`.

3. Right-click on the **SocialMediaFeed Inline Frame** widget, click on **Scrollbars**, and click on **Never Show Scrollbars**.

4. Right-click on the **SocialMediaFeed Inline Frame** widget and click on **Frame Target.** In the **Link Properties** dialog box, click on the radio button next to **Link to an external url or file**. In the **Hyperlink** field, paste the embed link to your Tint (for example, `http://www.tintup.com/axuredemo`).

By using an inline frame widget and a social media aggregator, we were able to add a social media feed to our prototype. Next, we will embed videos in our prototype.

Embedded video (YouTube and Vimeo)

The key to embedding videos from YouTube and Vimeo is using the **Inline Frame** widget and setting the frame target to the correct embed code.

To get the embed code for a YouTube video, perform the following steps:

1. On the YouTube page for our selected video, click on the **Share** menu item under the video.

2. Click on the **Embed** menu item.

3. Copy the embed URL (for example, `http://www.youtube.com/embed/NrOzIRHLvCU`).

To get the embed code for a Vimeo video, perform the following steps:

1. On the Vimeo page for our selected video, click on the **Share** menu item to the right of the video.

2. An overlay titled **Share** will appear. Copy the **Embed** URL (for example, `http://player.vimeo.com/video/50288794`).

To embed YouTube and Vimeo video, perform the following steps:

1. In the **Widgets** pane, click on the **Inline Frame** widget. Drag the **Inline Frame** widget and place it at coordinates (790,440). With the **Inline Frame** widget selected, perform the following steps:

    1. In the **Widget Interactions and Notes** pane, click in the **Inline Frame Name** field and type `YouTubeVideo`.

    2. In the toolbar, change the value of **w** to `170` and **h** to `100`.

3. Right-click on the **YouTubeVideo Inline Frame** widget, click on **Scrollbars** and then on **Never Show Scrollbars**.

4. Right-click on the **YouTubeVideo Inline Frame** widget and click on **Frame Target**. In the **Link Properties** dialog box, click on the radio button next to **Link to an external url or file**. In the **Hyperlink** field, paste the embed link to your YouTube video.

2. In the **Widgets** pane, click on the **Inline Frame** widget. Drag the **Inline Frame** widget and place it at coordinates (790,560). With the **Inline Frame** widget selected, perform the following steps:

   ° In the **Widget Interactions and Notes** pane, click in the **Inline Frame Name** field and type `VimeoVideo`.

   ° In the toolbar, change the value of **w** to `170` and **h** to `100`.

   ° Right-click on the **VimeoVideo Inline Frame** widget, click on **Scrollbars**, and then on **Never Show Scrollbars**.

   ° Right-click on the **VimeoVideo Inline Frame** widget and click on **Frame Target**. In the **Link Properties** dialog box, click on the radio button next to **Link to an external url or file**. In the **Hyperlink** field, paste the embed link to the Vimeo video.

By using two inline frame widgets, we were able to embed a YouTube as well as a Vimeo video. Next, we will construct a global footer.

Global footer

We will now create a global footer master. Perform the following steps:

1. In the **Masters** pane, click on the **Add Master** icon. Slow click the master labeled **New Master 1** to select it, type `Footer`, and press *Enter*.

2. In the **Widgets** pane, click on the **Label** widget. While holding down the mouse button, drag the **Label** widget and place it at coordinates (10,685). With the **Label** widget selected, perform the following steps:

   1. Type `Copyright YYYY`. You will see **Copyright YYYY** displayed as text on the **Label** widget.

   2. In the **Widget Interactions and Notes** pane, click in the **Shape Name** field and type `CopyrightLink`.

3. In the **Widgets** pane, click on the **Label** widget. While holding down the mouse button, drag the **Label** widget and place it at coordinates (10,685). With the **Label** widget selected, perform the following steps:

    1. Type `Privacy`. You will see **Privacy** displayed as text on the **Label** widget.

    2. In the **Widget Interactions and Notes** pane, click in the **Shape Name** field and type `PrivacyLink`.

    3. In the **Widget Interactions and Notes** pane, click on the **Interactions** tab, and then click on **Create Link…**. In the **Sitemap** modal window, click on the **Privacy** page.

4. Repeat step 3 twice to create two additional links using the following table for coordinates, text displayed, shape name of the label widgets, and create link:

Coordinates	Text displayed	Shape name	Create link…
(790,685)	Terms	TermsLink	Terms
(870,685)	About Us	AboutUsLink	About Us

To place the **Global Footer** on the **Home** page, open the **Home** page in the design area. From the **Masters** pane, drag-and-drop the **Footer** master onto the design area. Our completed, home page now looks like this:

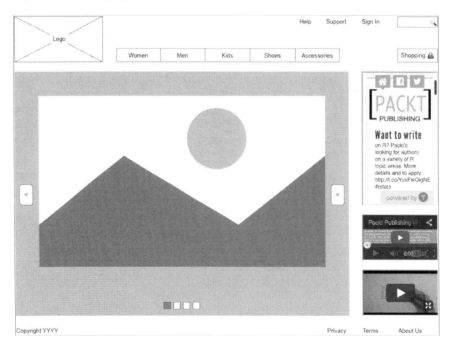

Summary

In this chapter, we first created a sitemap for our e-commerce prototype. Next, we focused on creating the home page. After building a header master with an expanding search bar, we built an autorotating carousel and a right column that contained a social media feed, in addition to YouTube and Vimeo videos. Finally, we created a global footer master.

In the next chapter, we will build an account sign up page, as well as product and detail pages.

Self-test questions

- What was the first activity we performed in this chapter before we started the home page design?

- Why did we convert the widgets that make up the header into a master?

- What drop behavior did we select for our header master and why?

- On the SearchDP dynamic panel, what interaction(s) on which widget(s) enable the search bar to expand?

- How did we start the autorotation of the carousel?

- What widget stops the autorotation of the carousel and on what conditions?

- What widget did we use to embed YouTube and Vimeo videos into our prototype?

3
Registration and Sign In

Inline Field Validation provides users real-time feedback. The feedback is localized to the field of interaction and causes minimal disruption to the task flow. **Inline Field Validation** enables users to quickly recover from errors, and it occurs prior to the user submitting a form. If the user submits the form before resolving the error, a global error message will be displayed in addition to the individual field error messages.

By creating an **Inline Field Validation** master, we have a single place to update validation rules. We will also be able to use the Validation master on both our **Registration** and our **SignIn** pages. We will now create Registration variables, an **Inline Field Validation** master, a **Registration** page, and a **SignIn** page.

In this chapter, we will learn about:

- Defining Registration Variables and Inline Field Validation
  - ○ Creating Registration Variables
  - ○ Creating an Inline Field Validation master

- Creating our Registration page
  - ○ Validation and Feedback for our Registration page
  - ○ Designing the Confirmation page

- Making our Sign In page
  - ○ Validation and Feedback for our Sign In page

Defining Registration variables and Inline Field Validation

We will start by reviewing our **Sitemap** to ensure that we have created all the pages needed for Registration and SignIn. You will notice that we need to create pages for Registration and Confirmation.

To create a child page labeled **Account SignUp** with a **Confirmation** page, perform the following steps:

1. In the **Sitemap** pane, right-click on the **Home** page.
2. Click **Add** and click on **Child Page**.
3. Type Registration.
4. In the **Sitemap** pane, right-click on the **Registration** page.
5. Click on **Add** and then click on **Child Page**.
6. Type Confirmation.

With the **Registration** page created, we are now ready to create variables enabling us to track the user-entered e-mail ID and password.

Creating Registration variables

We now will create Axure variables that will allow us to store the user-entered e-mail ID and password. We will also create variables to assist in tracking the validity of the e-mail ID and password once the user has signed in.

To create Registration variables, click on **Project** in the main menu and then click on **Global Variables**. In the **Global Variables** dialog, perform the following steps:

1. Click the green **+** sign and type DefaultAccountEmail. Click on the **Default Value** field and type Axure@test.com.
2. Repeat the first step five more times to create additional variables using the following table for the variable name and default value fields:

Variable name	Default value
DefaultAccountPassword	Axure1
UserAccount1Email	
UserAccount1Password	
AccountVerified	0
PasswordVerified	0

3. Once completed, your **Global Variables** dialog will look like the following screenshot:

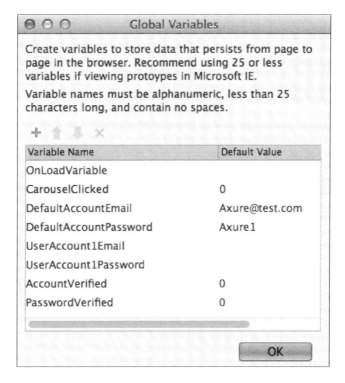

4. Click on **OK**.

With your **Sitemap** updated and variables created, you are now ready to design the **Inline Field Validation** master.

Designing an Inline Field Validation master

We will now create an **Inline Field Validation** master. The **Inline Field Validation** master will be used on both the **SignIn** and the **SignUp** pages. Raised events allow us to create tailored events. This enables us to create customizable interactions for each instance of a master. We will leverage raised events on the master to differentiate the events on each page.

When completed, your **Inline Field Validation** master will look like the following screenshot:

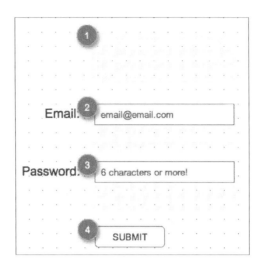

As shown in the preceding screenshot, the **Inline Field Validation** master has four key areas stacked vertically:

1. The Global Error message area
2. The Email text field and Error message area
3. The Password text field and Error message area
4. The **Submit** button

 The yellow highlighted areas shown on the design area indicate that the associated widget's default visibility is hidden.

The **Inline Field Validation** master will have all error message areas hidden by default. When the user's mouse enters the Email or Password text fields, an **OnFocus** event will trigger to set focus on the text field and clear the placeholder text. When focus is lost from the Email or Password text fields, the text on the text field widget is verified. If no text was entered, placeholder text is then set on the text field. If text was entered, the text on the widget is verified. If the text entered is not valid, an error message will be shown. If the user does not correct an error shown and clicks the **Submit** button, the **Submit** button will shake and a Global Error message will be made visible in addition to the Inline Error messages.

Creating the Inline Field Validation master

We will first create a master labeled **Inline Field Validation**. To create the **Inline Field Validation** master, perform the following steps:

1. In the **Masters** pane, click on the **Add Master** icon. Slow click the master labeled **New Master 1** to select, type `Inline Field Validation`, and press *Enter*.

2. In the **Masters** pane, right-click on the icon next to the **Inline Field Validation** master, move the mouse over **Drop Behavior**, and click on **Lock to Master Location**.

3. In the **Masters** pane, double-click on the icon next to the **Inline Field Validation** master to open it in the design area.

We are now ready to add raised events for the **Inline Field Validation** master.

Perform the following steps to do so:

1. In the main menu, click **Arrange** and click **Manage raised events (Masters Only)....**

2. In the **Raised Events** dialog box, click the green **+** sign and type `OnValidSignInEmail`.

3. Repeat the second step five times to create additional **Raised Events** using the following table for each raised event name:

Raised event name
OnValidSignUpEmail
OnValidSignInPassword
OnValidSignUpPassword
OnSignInSubmitClick
OnSignUpSubmitClick

4. Click on **OK**. We are now ready to place widgets and define common interactions for the **Inline Field Validation** master.

 The **Inline Field Validation** master should still be opened in the design area. If not, in the **Masters** pane, double-click on the icon next to the **Inline Field Validation** master to open it in the design area.

Placing widgets for the Global Error message

To place widgets for the Global Error message, in the **Widgets** pane, drag the **Rectangle** widget and place at coordinates (429,200). With the **Rectangle** widget selected, in the toolbar, change the value of **w** to 212 and **h** to 74. Click on the checkbox next to **Hidden**.

In the **Widget Interactions and Notes** pane, click in the **Shape Name** field and type GlobalErrorMsgRectangle.

In the **Widget Properties and Style** pane, with the **Style** tab selected, scroll to **Borders, Lines, + Fills** and perform the following steps:

1. Click the down arrow next to the pencil (line color) icon . In the drop-down menu, enter FF0000 in the **#** text field.

2. Click the down arrow next to the paint bucket (fill color) icon . In the drop-down menu, enter FF0000 in the **#** text field.

3. From the **Widgets** pane, drag the **Label** widget and place at coordinates (432,219). With the **Label** widget selected, perform the following:

   1. Type There was a problem. Please correct and try again. You will see the error message displayed as text on the **Label** widget.

   2. In the toolbar change the value of **w** to 205 and **h** to 40. Click the checkbox next to **Hidden**.

   3. In the **Widget Interactions and Notes** pane, click in the **Shape Name** field and type GlobalErrorMsgLabel.

   4. In the **Widget Properties and Style** pane, with the **Style** tab selected, scroll to **Font** and change the font size to 16. Click the down arrow next to the A (text color) icon . In the drop-down menu, in the **#** text field enter FFFFFF.

   5. In the **Widget Properties and Style** pane, with the **Style** tab selected, scroll to **Borders, Lines, + Fills**. Click on the down arrow next to the pencil (line color) icon. In the drop-down menu, click on the box with the red diagonal line to indicate no outline. Click the down arrow next to the paint bucket (fill color) icon. In the drop-down menu, click the box with the red diagonal line to indicate no fill.

Placing widgets for the Email text field and the Error message

To place widgets for the Email text field and Error message, perform the steps given in the following section.

From the **Widgets** pane, drag the **Label** widget and place at coordinates (364,304). With the **Label** widget selected, perform the following:

1. Type Email:. You will see **Email:** displayed as text on the **Label** widget.
2. In the toolbar, change the value of **w** to 51 and **h** to 21.
3. In the **Widget Interactions and Notes** pane, click in the **Shape Name** field and type EmailLabel.
4. In the **Widget Properties and Style** pane, with the **Style** tab selected, scroll to **Font** and change the font size to 18.

From the **Widgets** pane, drag the **Rectangle** widget and place at coordinates (429,296). With the **Rectangle** widget selected, perform the following:

1. In the toolbar, change the value of **w** to 212 and **h** to 74. Click the checkbox next to **Hidden**.
2. In the **Widget Interactions and Notes** pane, click in the **Shape Name** field and type EmailMsgRectangle.
3. In the **Widget Properties and Style** pane, with the **Style** tab selected, scroll to **Borders, Lines, + Fills** and perform the following:
   1. Click the down arrow next to the pencil (line color) icon. In the drop-down menu, enter FF0000 in the **#** text field.
   2. Click the down arrow next to the paint bucket (fill color) icon. In the drop-down menu, enter FF0000 in the **#** text field.

From the **Widgets** pane, drag the **Rectangle** widget and place at coordinates (435,300). With the **Rectangle** widget selected, perform the following:

1. In the toolbar, change the value of **w** to 200 and **h** to 30.
2. In the **Widget Interactions and Notes** pane, click in the **Shape Name** field and type EmailRectangle.
3. In the **Widget Properties and Style** pane, with the **Style** tab selected, scroll to **Font** and change the font size to 18.

From the **Widgets** pane, drag the **Label** widget and place at coordinates (441,300). With the **Label** widget selected, perform the following:

1. Type `email@email.com`. You will see **email@email.com** displayed as text on the **Label** widget.

2. In the toolbar, change the value of **w** to `151` and **h** to `30`.

3. In the **Widget Interactions and Notes** pane, click in the **Shape Name** field and type `EmailTextField`.

4. In the **Widget Properties and Style** pane, with the **Style** tab selected, scroll to **Font** and click the down arrow next to the A (text color) icon. In the drop-down menu, enter `666666` in the **#** text field.

In the **Widget Properties and Style** pane, with the **Style** tab selected, scroll to **Borders, Lines, + Fills** and perform the following steps:

1. Click the down arrow next to the paint bucket (fill color) icon. In the drop-down menu, click the box with the red diagonal line to indicate no fill.

2. From the **Widgets** pane, drag the **Label** widget and place at coordinates (436,333). With the **Label** widget selected, perform the following:

    1. Type `Doesn't seem to be a valid email`. You will see the error message displayed as text on the **Label** widget.

    2. In the toolbar, change the value of **w** to `199` and **h** to `34`. Click the checkbox next to **Hidden**.

    3. In the **Widget Interactions and Notes** pane, click in the **Shape Name** field and type `EmailMsgLabel`.

    4. In the **Widget Properties and Style** pane, with the **Style** tab selected, scroll to **Font** and click the down arrow next to the A (text color) icon. In the drop-down menu, enter `FFFFFF` in the **#** text field.

    5. In the **Widget Properties and Style** pane, with the **Style** tab selected, scroll to **Borders, Lines, + Fills** and perform the following:

        1. Click the down arrow next to the pencil (line color) icon. In the drop-down menu, click the box with the red diagonal line to indicate no outline.

        2. Click the down arrow next to the paint bucket (fill color) icon. In the drop-down menu, click the box with the red diagonal line to indicate no fill.

Placing widgets for the Password text field and Error message

To place widgets for the Password text field and Error message, perform the following steps:

From the **Widgets** pane, drag the **Label** widget and place at coordinates (330,384). With the **Label** widget selected, perform the following:

1. Type `Password:`. You will see **Password:** displayed as text on the **Label** widget.
2. In the toolbar, change the value of **w** to `85` and **h** to `21`.
3. In the **Widget Interactions and Notes** pane, click in the **Shape Name** field and type `PasswordLabel`.
4. In the **Widget Properties and Style** pane, with the **Style** tab selected, scroll to **Font** and change the font size to `18`.

In the **Widgets** pane, click on the **Rectangle** widget. While holding down the mouse button, drag the **Rectangle** widget and place at coordinates (429,376). With the **Rectangle** widget selected, perform the following:

1. In the toolbar, change the value of **w** to `212` and **h** to `74`. Click the checkbox next to **Hidden**.
2. In the **Widget Interactions and Notes** pane, click in the **Shape Name** field and type `PasswordMsgRectangle`.
3. In the **Widget Properties and Style** pane, with the **Style** tab selected, scroll to **Borders, Lines, + Fills** and perform the following:
    1. Click the down arrow next to the pencil (line color) icon. In the drop-down menu, enter `FF0000` in the **#** text field.
    2. Click the down arrow next to the paint bucket (fill color) icon. In the drop-down menu, enter `FF0000` in the **#** text field.

From the **Widgets** pane, drag the **Rectangle** widget and place at coordinates (435,380). With the **Rectangle** widget selected, perform the following:

1. In the toolbar, change the value of **w** to `200` and **h** to `30`.
2. In the **Widget Interactions and Notes** pane, click in the **Shape Name** field and type `PasswordRectangle`.
3. In the **Widget Properties and Style** pane, with the **Style** tab selected, scroll to **Font** and change the font size to `18`.

From the **Widgets** pane, drag the **Label** widget and place at coordinates (441,380). With the **Label** widget selected, perform the following:

1. Type 6 characters or more! You will see **6 characters or more!** displayed as text on the **Label** widget.
2. In the toolbar, change the value of **w** to 151 and **h** to 30.
3. In the **Widget Interactions and Notes** pane, click in the **Shape Name** field and type PasswordTextField.
4. In the **Widget Properties and Style** pane, with the **Style** tab selected, scroll to **Font** and perform the following:
5. Click the down arrow next to the A (Text Color) icon. In the drop-down menu, enter 666666 in the **#** text field.
6. In the **Widget Properties and Style** pane, with the **Style** tab selected, scroll to **Borders, Lines, + Fills** and perform the following:
7. Click the down arrow next to the paint bucket (fill color) icon. In the drop-down menu, click the box with the red diagonal line to indicate no fill.

From the **Widgets** pane, drag the **Label** widget and place at coordinates (436,413). With the **Label** widget selected, perform the following:

1. Type Password must be at least 6 characters.. You will see the error message displayed as text on the **Label** widget.
2. In the toolbar, change the value of **w** to 199 and **h** to 34. Click the checkbox next to **Hidden**.
3. In the **Widget Interactions and Notes** pane, click in the **Shape Name** field and type PasswordMsgLabel.
4. In the **Widget Properties and Style** pane, with the **Style** tab selected, scroll to **Font** and perform the following:
5. Click the down arrow next to the A (text color) icon. In the drop-down menu, enter FFFFFF in the # text field.
6. In the **Widget Properties and Style** pane, with the **Style** tab selected, scroll to **Borders, Lines, + Fills** and perform the following:
   1. Click the down arrow next to the pencil (line color) icon. In the drop-down menu, click the box with the red diagonal line to indicate no outline.
   2. Click the down arrow next to the paint bucket (fill color) icon. In the drop-down menu, click the box with the red diagonal line to indicate no fill.

Placing the Submit button

To place the **Submit** button from the **Widgets** pane, drag the **Button Shape** widget and place at coordinates (435,470). With the **Button Shape** widget selected, perform the following:

1. Type SUBMIT. You will see **SUBMIT** displayed as text on the **Label** widget.
2. In the toolbar, change the value of **w** to 100 and **h** to 30.
3. In the **Widget Interactions and Notes** pane, click in the **Shape Name** field and type SubmitButton.

With all of the widgets in place, we are now ready to define the common interactions for the **Inline Field Validation** master. We will now define interactions for the EmailTextField, PasswordTextField, and SubmitButton.

Enabling Interactions for the Email text field

For the **EmailTextField**, we will create new cases the OnMouseEnter, OnFocus, and OnLostFocus events. Once complete, the **Widgets Interactions and Notes** pane for the **EmailTextField** will look like this:

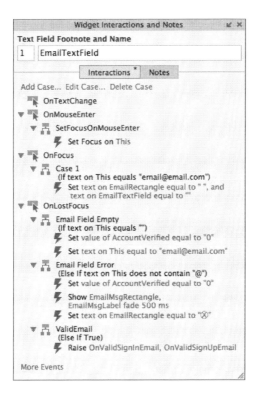

Creating the SetFocusOnMouseEnter case for the OnMouseEnter event

To create a case for the OnMouseEnter event, with the **EmailTextField** widget at coordinates (441,300) selected in the **Widget Interactions and Notes** pane, click the **Interactions** tab, click **More Events**, and then click **OnMouseEnter**. A **Case Editor** dialog box will open. In the **Case Editor** dialog, perform the steps given in the following section.

Creating the action

Perform the following steps to create the action:

1. In the **Case Description** field, enter SetFocusOnMouseEnter.
2. Under **Click to add actions**, scroll to the **Widget** drop-down menu and click on **Focus**.
3. Under **Configure actions**, click the checkbox next to **This Widget**.
4. Click **OK**.

Creating the case for the OnFocus event

With the **EmailTextField** widget selected, in the **Widget Interactions and Notes** pane, click the **Interactions** tab and double-click on the **OnFocus** event. In the **Case Description** field on the **Case Editor** dialog, type CheckItemCount0 and perform the steps given in the following sections.

Creating the condition

Perform the following steps to create the condition:

1. Click the **Add Condition** button.
2. In the **Condition Builder** dialog box, in the outlined condition box perform the following:
    1. In the first drop-down, select **text on widget**.
    2. In the second drop-down, select **This**.
    3. In the third drop-down, select **equals**.
    4. In the fourth drop-down, select **value**.
    5. In the text field enter email@email.com.
    6. Click **OK**.

Adding and configuring the actions

Perform the following steps to create the actions:

1. Under **Click to add actions**, scroll to the **Widgets** drop-down menu and click on **set text**.

2. Under **Configure actions**, select the checkboxes next to **EmailRectangle** and **EmailTextField**.

3. To set the text on the **EmailRectangle** and **EmailTextField** widgets to "", under **Set text to**, the first drop-down defaults to **value** and the **Set text** field defaults to "". So by default, the text will be set to "".

4. Click **OK**.

Creating the cases for the OnLostFocus event

For the **OnLostFocus** event, there will be three cases, namely, Email Field Empty, Email Field Error, and ValidEmail. To create the cases for the **OnLostFocus** event, perform the steps given in the following sections.

Defining the Email Field Empty case

With the **EmailTextField** widget selected, in the **Widget Interactions and Notes** pane, click on the **Interactions** tab and double-click on the **OnLostFocus** event. A **Case Editor** dialog box will open. In the **Case Editor** dialog, perform the steps given in the following sections.

Creating the condition

1. In the **Case Description** field, type Email Field Empty.

2. Click on the **Add Condition** button.

3. In the **Condition Builder** dialog box, perform the following steps in the outlined condition box:

    1. In the first drop-down, select **text on widget**.

    2. In the second drop-down, select **This**.

    3. In the third drop-down, select **equals**.

    4. In the fourth drop-down, select **value**.

    5. Leave the final text field blank.

    6. Click on **OK.**

Creating the actions

To set **AccountVerified** as equal to 0, perform the following steps:

1. Under **Click to add actions**, scroll to the **Variables** drop-down menu and click on **Set Variable Value**.

2. Under **Configure actions**, click the checkbox next to **AccountVerified**.

3. Under **Set variable to**, the first drop-down defaults to **value**. Enter 0 in the **Set variable** field.

To set the text in the **EmailTextField**, perform the following steps:

1. Under **Click to add actions**, scroll to the **Widgets** drop-down menu and click on **set text**.

2. Under **Configure actions**, click the checkbox next to **EmailTextField**.

3. Under **Set text to**, click on the first drop-down and select **value**. Click on the second field and enter `email@email.com`.

4. Click on **OK**.

Defining the Email Field Error case

With the **EmailTextField** widget selected, in the **Widget Interactions and Notes** pane, click the **Interactions** tab and double-click on the **OnLostFocus** event. A **Case Editor** dialog box will open. In the **Case Editor** dialog, perform the steps given in the following sections.

Creating the condition

1. In the **Case Description** field, enter `Email Field Error`.

2. Click on the **Add Condition** button.

3. In the **Condition Builder** dialog box, perform the following steps in the outlined condition box:

    1. In the first drop-down, select **text on widget**.

    2. In the second drop-down, select **This**.

    3. In the third drop-down, select **does not contain**.

    4. In the fourth drop-down, select **value**.

    5. In the text field, enter @.

    6. Click **OK**.

Creating the actions

To set **AccountVerified** as equal to 0, perform the following steps:

1. Under **Click to add actions**, scroll to the **Variables** drop-down menu and click on **Set Variable Value**.

2. Under **Configure actions**, click the checkboxes next to **AccountVerified**.

3. Under **Set variable to**, the first drop-down defaults to **value**. Enter 0 in the **Set variable** field.

To show **EmailMsgRectangle** and **EmailMsgLabel**, perform the following steps:

1. Under **Click to add actions**, scroll to the **Widgets** drop-down menu, click the **Show/Hide** drop-down, and click on **Show**.

2. Under **Configure actions**, click on the checkboxes next to **EmailMsgRectangle** and **EmailMsgLabel**.

3. Next to **Animate**, click on the drop-down and then click on **fade**. Leave **t:** set to **500** ms.

To set the text on the **EmailRectangle**, perform the following steps:

1. Under **Click to add actions**, scroll to the **Widgets** drop-down menu and click on **Set Text**.

2. Under **Configure actions**, click on the checkbox next to **EmailRectangle**.

3. Under **Set text to** click on the first drop-down and select **value**. Click on the second field and enter x.

> We can enter any character into the set text field by copying and pasting the character. For example, ⊗.

4. Click on **OK**.

Defining the ValidEmail case

With the **EmailTextField** widget selected, in the **Widget Interactions and Notes** pane, click the **Interactions** tab and double-click on the **OnLostFocus** event. A **Case Editor** dialog box will open.

In the **Case Editor**, to raise events, perform the following steps:

1. Under **Click to add actions**, scroll to the **Miscellaneous** drop-down menu and click on **Raise Event**.

2. Under **Configure actions**, click on the checkboxes next to **OnValidSignInEmail** and **OnValidSignUpEmail**.

3. Click on **OK**.

Enabling interactions for the PasswordTextField

For the **PasswordTextField**, we will create new cases for the **OnMouseEnter**, **OnFocus**, and **OnLostFocus** events. Once complete, the **Widgets Interactions and Notes** pane for the **PasswordTextField** will look like this:

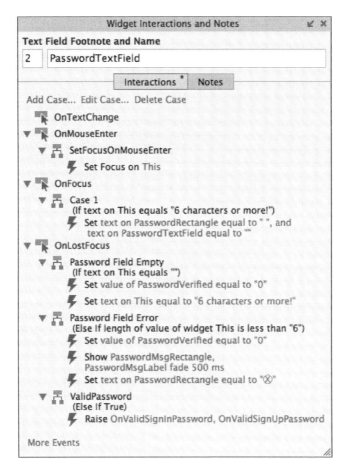

Creating a case for the OnMouseEnter event

With the **PasswordTextField** widget at coordinates (441,380) selected, in the **Widget Interactions and Notes** pane, click on the **Interactions** tab, click **More Events**, and then click on **OnMouseEnter**. A **Case Editor** dialog box will open. In the **Case Editor** dialog, perform the following steps to create an action:

1. In the **Case Description** field, type `SetFocusOnMouseEnter`.
2. Under **Click to add actions**, scroll to the **Widget** drop-down menu and click on **Focus**.
3. Under **Configure actions**, click the checkbox next to **This Widget**.
4. Click on **OK**.

Creating the case for the OnFocus event

With the **PasswordTextField** widget selected, in the **Widget Interactions and Notes** pane, click the **Interactions** tab and double-click **OnFocus**. A **Case Editor** dialog box will open. In the **Case Editor** dialog, perform the steps given in the following sections.

Creating the condition

1. Click on the **Add Condition** button.
2. In the **Condition Builder** dialog box, perform the following steps in the outlined condition box:
   1. In the first drop-down, select **text on widget**.
   2. In the second drop-down, select **This**.
   3. In the third drop-down, select **equals**.
   4. In the fourth drop-down, select **value**.
   5. In the text field, enter `6 characters or more!`

Creating the action

1. Under **Click to add actions**, scroll to the **Widgets** drop-down menu and click on **set text**.
2. Under **Configure actions**, click on the checkboxes next to **PasswordRectangle** and **PasswordTextField**.
3. To set the text on the **PasswordRectangle** and **PasswordTextField** widgets to "", under **Set text to**, the first drop-down defaults to **value** and the **Set text** field defaults to "". So by default, the text will be set to "".
4. Click on **OK**.

Creating the cases for the OnLostFocus event

For the **OnLostFocus** event, there will be three cases, namely, Password Field Empty, Password Field Error, and ValidPassword. To create the cases for the **OnLostFocus** event, perform the following steps.

Defining the Password Field Empty case

With the **PasswordTextField** widget selected, in the **Widget Interactions and Notes** pane, click the **Interactions** tab and double-click **OnLostFocus**. A **Case Editor** dialog box will open. In the **Case Editor** dialog, perform the steps given in the following sections.

Creating the condition

1. In the **Case Description** field, enter Password Field Empty.
2. Click on the **Add Condition** button.
3. In the **Condition Builder** dialog box, in the outlined condition box, perform the following steps:

    1. In the first drop-down, select **text on widget**.
    2. In the second drop-down, select **This**.
    3. In the third drop-down, select **equals**.
    4. In the fourth drop-down, select **value**.
    5. In the text field, enter " ".
    6. Click on **OK**.

Creating the actions

To set **PasswordVerified** as equal to 0, perform the following steps:

1. Under **Click to add actions**, scroll to the **Variables** drop-down menu and click on **Set Variable Value**.
2. Under **Configure actions**, click on the checkbox next to **PasswordVerified**.
3. Under **Set variable to**, the first drop-down defaults to **value**. Enter 0 in the **Set variable** field.

To set the text on the **PasswordTextField**, perform the following steps:

1. Under **Click to add actions**, scroll to the **Widgets** drop-down menu and click on **set text**.

2. Under **Configure actions**, click on the checkbox next to **PasswordTextField**.

3. Under **Set text to**, click on the first drop-down and select **value**. Click on the second field and enter `6 characters or more!`

4. Click on **OK**.

Defining the Password Field Error case

With the **PasswordTextField** widget selected, in the **Widget Interactions and Notes** pane, click on the **Interactions** tab and double-click **OnLostFocus**. A **Case Editor** dialog box will open. In the **Case Editor** dialog, perform the steps given in the following sections.

Creating the condition

1. In the **Case Description** field, enter `Password Field Error`.

2. Click on the **Add Condition** button.

3. In the **Condition Builder** dialog box, perform the following steps in the outlined condition box:

    1. In the first drop-down, select **length of widget value**.

    2. In the second drop-down, select **This**.

    3. In the third drop-down, select **is less than**.

    4. In the fourth drop-down, select **value**.

    5. In the text field, enter `6`.

    6. Click on **OK**.

Creating the actions:

To set **PasswordVerified** as equal to 0, perform the following steps:

1. Under **Click to add actions**, scroll to the **Variables** drop-down menu and click on **Set Variable Value**.

2. Under **Configure actions**, click on the checkboxes next to **PasswordVerified**.

3. Under **Set variable to**, the first drop-down defaults to **value**. Enter `0` in the **Set variable** field.

To show PasswordMsgRectangle and PasswordMsgLabel, perform the following steps:

1. Under **Click to add actions**, scroll to the **Widgets** drop-down menu, click the **Show/Hide** drop-down, and click on **Show**.

2. Under **Configure actions**, click on the checkboxes next to **PaswordMsgRectangle** and **PasswordMsgLabel**.

3. Next to **Animate**, click the drop-down and click **fade**. Leave **t:** set to **500** ms.

To set the text on the **PasswordRectangle**, perform the following steps:

1. Under **Click to add actions**, scroll to the **Widgets** drop-down menu and click on **set text**.

2. Under **Configure actions**, click on the checkbox next to **PasswordRectangle**.

3. Under **Set text to**, click on the first drop-down and select **value**. Click on the second field and enter x.

 Note: We can enter any character into the **Set text** field by copying and pasting the character. For example, ⊗.

4. Click on **OK**.

Defining the ValidPassword case

With the **PasswordTextField** widget selected, in the **Widget Interactions and Notes** pane, click the **Interactions** tab and double-click on the **OnLostFocus** event. A **Case Editor** dialog box will open. In the **Case Editor** dialog perform the steps given in the following section.

Creating the action:

To raise events, perform the following steps:

1. Under **Click to add actions**, scroll to the **Miscellaneous** drop-down menu and click on **Raise Event**.

2. Under **Configure actions**, click on the checkboxes next to **OnValidSignInPassword** and **OnValidSignUpPassword**.

3. Click on **OK**.

Enabling interactions for the Submit button

For the **SubmitButton**, we will create new cases for the **OnClick** and **OnMouseEnter** events. Once complete, the **Widgets Interactions and Notes** pane for the **SubmitButton** will look like this:

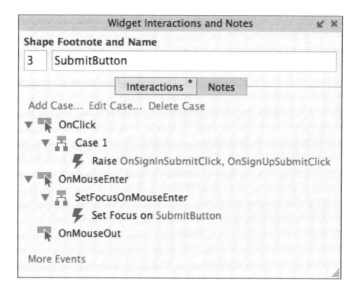

Creating the case for the OnClick event

With the **SubmitButton** widget at coordinates (435,470) selected, in the **Widget Interactions and Notes** pane, click on the **Interactions** tab and double-click the **OnClick** event. A **Case Editor** dialog box will open. In the **Case Editor** dialog, perform the following steps:

Create the action:

To raise events, perform the following steps:

1. Under **Click to add actions**, scroll to the **Miscellaneous** drop-down menu and click on **Raise Event**.

2. Under **Configure actions**, click the checkboxes next to **OnSignInSubmitClick** and **OnSignUpSubmitClick**.

3. Click on **OK**.

Creating the case for the OnMouseEnter event

With the **SubmitButton** widget selected, in the **Widget Interactions and Notes** pane, click the **Interactions** tab, click **More Events**, and then click **OnMouseEnter**. A **Case Editor** dialog box will open. In the **Case Editor** dialog, perform the following steps:

Create the action:

1. In the **Case Description** field, enter `SetFocusOnMouseEnter`.
2. Under **Click to add actions**, scroll to the **Widget** drop-down menu and click on **Focus**.
3. Under **Configure actions**, click the checkbox next to **SubmitButton**.
4. Click on **OK**.

With our **Sitemap** updated, Global Variables created, and the **Inline Field Validation** master complete, we are now ready to design the Registration page.

Creating our Registration page

To create our **Registration** page, we will use a **Heading 1** widget as well as the Header, Footer, and **Inline Field Validation** masters. When completed, our **Registration** page will look as follows:

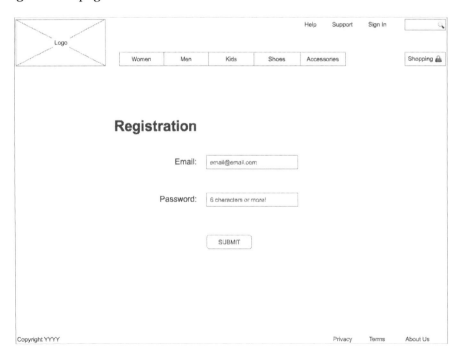

To create the **Registration** page, perform the following steps:

1. In the **Sitemap** pane, double-click on the **Registration** page to open it in the design area.

2. From the **Masters** pane, drag the **Header** master and drop at any location on the wireframe.

 As the **Header** master has **Drop Behavior** set to **Lock to Master Location**, we can drop the master anywhere in the design area. With this drop behavior specified, a master and the master's associated widgets will be placed at the same coordinates as specified in the master.

3. From the **Masters** pane, drag the **Footer** master and place at coordinates (10,685).

4. From the **Widgets** pane, drag the **Heading 1** widget and place at coordinates (228,220).

5. With the **Heading 1** widget selected, type `Registration`.

6. In the **Widget Interactions and Notes** pane, click in the **Shape Name** field and type `RegistrationHeading1`.

7. From the **Masters** pane, drag the **Inline Field Validation** master and drop at any location on the wireframe. In the **Widget Interactions and Notes** pane, click in the **Inline Field Validation Name** field and type `AccountSignUp`. With the **Registration** page layout completed, we are now ready to define the Validation and Feedback interactions.

Validation and Feedback for our Registration page

To perform validation and provide user feedback on the **Registration** page, we will leverage the following three **Inline Field Validation** master's raised events:

* OnValidSignUpEmail
* OnValidSignUpPassword
* OnSignUpSubmitClick

We will name the instance of the **Inline Field Validation** master on the **Registration** page **AccountSignUp**. For **AccountSignUp**, we will create new cases for the three raised events. Once complete, the **Widgets Interactions and Notes** pane for **AccountSignUp** will look like this:

Creating the case for the OnValidSignUpEmail event

With the Registration page opened in the design area, click near coordinates (450,200) to select the **AccountSignUp InLine Field Validation** (master). In the **Widget Interactions and Notes** pane, click the **Interactions** tab and double-click on **OnValidSignUpEmail**. A **Case Editor** dialog box will open. In the **Case Editor** dialog, perform the steps given in the following section.

Creating the action

To set the value of the **UserAccount1Email** variable, perform the following steps:

1. Under **Click to add actions**, scroll to the **Variables** drop-down menu and click on **Set Variable Value**.

2. Under **Configure actions**, click on the checkbox next to **UserAccount1Email**.

3. Under **Set variable to**, click on the first drop-down and click on **text on widget**.

4. Click on the second drop-down next to the **Set variable** field, click on the down arrow next to **AccountSignUp**, and click on **EmailTextField**.

To set **AccountVerified** as equal to 1, perform the following steps:

1. Under **Click to add actions**, scroll to the **Variables** drop-down menu and click on **Set Variable Value**.

2. Under **Configure actions**, click the checkbox next to **AccountVerified**.

3. Under **Set variable to**, the first drop-down defaults to **value**. Enter 1 in the **Set variable** field.

To hide **AccountSignUp/EmailMsgRectangle** and **AccountSignUp/EmailMsgLabel**, perform the following steps:

1. Under **Click to add actions**, scroll to the **Widgets** drop-down menu, click the **Show/Hide** drop-down, and then click on **Hide**.

2. Under **Configure actions**, scroll to the **AccountSignUp** drop-down, click to expand, and click the checkbox next to **EmailMsgRectangle**.

3. Next to **Animate**, click the drop-down and click **fade**. Leave **t:** set to **500** ms.

4. Under **Configure actions**, scroll to the **SignIn** drop-down, click to expand, and click the checkbox next to **EmailMsgLabel**.

5. Next to **Animate**, click the drop-down and click **none**.

To set the text on the **AccountSignUp/EmailRectangle**, perform the following steps:

1. Under **Click to add actions**, scroll to the **Widgets** drop-down menu and click on **Set Text**.

2. Under **Configure actions**, scroll to the **AccountSignUp** drop-down, click to expand, and click the checkbox next to **EmailRectangle**.

3. Under **Set text to,** click the first drop-down and select **value**. Click the second field and enter &#10003.

 The value **&#10003** is the checkmark symbol in hexadecimal.

4. Click on **OK**.

Creating the case for the OnValidSignUpPassword event

To create the case for the OnValidSignUpPassword event, with **AccountSignUp** selected, in the **Widget Interactions and Notes** pane, click the **Interactions** tab and double-click **OnValidSignUpPassword**. A **Case Editor** dialog box will open. In the **Case Editor** dialog, perform the steps given in the following section.

Creating the action:

To set the value of the **UserAccount1Password** variable, perform the following steps:

1. Under **Click to add actions**, scroll to the **Variables** drop-down menu and click on **Set Variable Value**.
2. Under **Configure actions**, click the checkbox next to **UserAccount1Password**.
3. Under **Set variable to,** click the first drop-down and click **text on widget**.
4. Click the second drop-down next to the **Set variable** field, click the down arrow next to **AccountSignUp**, and click **PasswordTextField**.

To set **PasswordVerified** as equal to 1, perform the following steps:

1. Under **Click to add actions**, scroll to the **Variables** drop-down menu and click on **Set Variable Value**.
2. Under **Configure actions**, click the checkbox next to **PasswordVerified**.
3. Under **Set variable to,** the first drop-down defaults to **value**. Enter 1 in the **Set variable** field.

To hide **AccountSignUp/PasswordMsgRectangle** and **AccountSignUp/ PasswordMsgLabel**, perform the following steps:

1. Under **Click to add actions**, scroll to the **Widgets** drop-down menu, click the **Show/Hide** drop-down, and then click on **Hide**.

2. Under **Configure actions**, scroll to the **AccountSignUp** drop-down, click to expand, and then click the checkboxes next to **PasswordMsgRectangle** and **PasswordMsgLabel**.

3. Next to **Animate**, click the drop-down and click **fade**. Leave **t:** set to **500** ms.

To set the text on the **AccountSignUp/PasswordRectangle**, perform the following steps:

1. Under **Click to add actions**, scroll to the **Widgets** drop-down menu and click on **Set Text**.

2. Under **Configure actions**, scroll to the **AccountSignUp** drop-down, click to expand, and click the checkbox next to **PasswordRectangle**.

3. Under **Set text to**, click the first drop-down and select **value**. Click the second field and enter `&#10003`.

4. Click **OK**.

Creating cases for the OnSignUpSubmitClick event

For the **OnSignUpSubmitClick** event, there will be two cases, namely, Successful Login and GlobalError. To create the cases for the **OnSignUpSubmitClick** event, perform the following steps.

Defining the Successful Login case

With **AccountSignUp** selected, in the **Widget Interactions and Notes** pane, click the **Interactions** tab and double-click **OnSignUpSubmitClick**. A **Case Editor** dialog box will open. In the **Case Editor** dialog, perform the steps given in the following sections.

Creating the conditions

Add the first condition:

1. In the **Case Description** field, enter Successful Login.

2. Click the **Add Condition** button.

3. In the **Condition Builder** dialog box, perform the following steps in the outlined condition box:

    1. In the first drop-down, select **value of variable**.

    2. In the second drop-down, select **AccountVerified**.

    3. In the third drop-down, select **equals**.

    4. In the fourth drop-down, select **value**.

    5. In the text field, enter 1.

Add the second condition:

1. Click the green **+** sign to add a second condition.

2. In the **Condition Builder** dialog box, perform the following steps in the outlined condition box:

    1. In the first drop-down, select **value of variable**.

    2. In the second drop-down, select **PasswordVerified**.

    3. In the third drop-down, select **equals**.

    4. In the fourth drop-down, select **value**.

    5. In the text field, enter 1.

    6. Click on **OK**.

Creating the actions

To set the value of the **AccountVerified** variable, perform the following steps:

1. Under **Click to add actions**, scroll to the **Variables** drop-down menu and click on **Set Variable Value**.

2. Under **Configure actions**, click on the checkbox next to **AccountVerified**.

3. Under **Set variable to**, click the first drop-down and click **text on widget**.

4. Click on the second drop-down next to the **Set variable** field, click the down arrow next to **AccountSignUp**, and click **EmailTextField**.

To open the Confirmation page in the Current Window, perform the following steps:

1. Under **Click to add actions**, click the **Links** drop-down menu, click the **Open Link** drop-down menu, and click on **Current Window**.

2. Under **Configure actions**, with the **Link to a page in this design** radio button selected, click the **Confirmation** page in the **Sitemap**.

3. Click on **OK**.

Defining the GlobalError case

With **AccountSignUp** selected, in the **Widget Interactions and Notes** pane, click the **Interactions** tab and double-click **OnSignUpSubmitClick**. A **Case Editor** dialog box will open. In the **Case Editor** dialog, perform the steps given in the following sections.

Name the Case

1. In the **Case Description** field, enter GlobalError.

Creating the actions

To show **AccountSignUp/GlobalErrorMsgRectangle** and **AccountSignUp/ GlobalErrorMsgLabel**, perform the following steps:

1. Under **Click to add actions**, scroll to the **Widgets** drop-down menu, click the **Show/Hide** drop-down, and click on **Show**.

2. Under **Configure actions**, scroll to the **AccountSignUp** drop-down, click to expand, and click the checkboxes next to **GlobalErrorMsgRectangle** and **GlobalErrorMsgLabel**.

To create the horizontal shaking effect on the **SubmitButton**, we will move the **AccountSignUp/SubmitButton** three times. Perform the following steps:

1. To define the first **Move** interaction:

    1. Under **Click to add actions**, scroll to the **Widgets** drop-down menu and click on **Move**.

    2. Under **Configure actions**, scroll to the **AccountSignUp** drop-down, click to expand, and click the checkbox next to **SubmitButton**.

    3. In the **Move** drop-down, click on **to**. In the **x:** field, enter 430 and in the **y:** field, enter 470.

    4. In the **Animate** drop-down, click **bounce**. In the **t** field, enter 150.

2. To define the second **Move** interaction:

    1. Under **Click to add actions**, scroll to the **Widgets** drop-down menu and click on **Move**.

    2. Under **Configure actions**, scroll to the **AccountSignUp** drop-down, click to expand, and click the checkbox next to **SubmitButton**.

    3. In the **Move** drop-down, click on **to**. In the **x:** field, enter 440 and in the **y:** field, enter 470.

    4. In the **Animate** drop-down, click **bounce**. In the **t:** field, enter 150.

3. To define the third **Move** interaction:

    1. Under **Click to add actions**, scroll to the **Widgets** drop-down menu and click on **Move**.

    2. Under **Configure actions**, scroll to the **AccountSignUp** drop-down, click to expand and click the checkbox next to **SubmitButton**.

    3. In the **Move** drop-down, click on **to**. In the **x:** field, enter 435. In the **y:** field, enter 470.

    4. In the **Animate** drop-down, click **linear**. In the **t:** field, enter 100.

    5. Click **OK**.

With the **Registration** page and interactions completed, we are now ready to design the **Confirmation** page.

Designing the Confirmation page

When a user logs in or creates a new account, the user lands on a **Confirmation** page. Our completed **Confirmation** page will look like this:

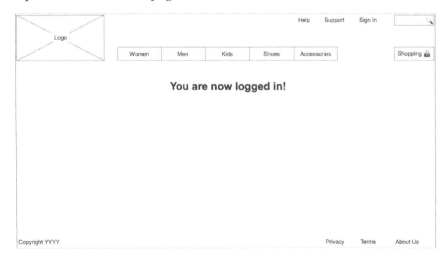

To create the basic **Confirmation** page, perform the following steps:

1. In the **Sitemap** pane, double-click on the **Confirmation** page to open it in the design area.

2. From the **Masters** pane, drag the **Header** master and drop at any location on the wireframe.

3. From the **Masters** pane, drag the **Footer** master and place at coordinates (10,725).

4. From the Widgets pane, drag the **Heading 2** widget and place at coordinates (360,152). In the toolbar, click on the checkbox next to **Hidden**.

5. With the **Heading 2** widget selected, type `You are now logged in!`.

6. In the **Widget Interactions and Notes** pane, click in the **Shape Name** field and type `ConfirmationMessage`.

When the **Confirmation** page opens, we use the **OnPageLoad** Event to set text on the **WelcomeMessage** in the Header, set the panel state of the **HeaderLinksDP** to **LinksSignOut** and show the **ConfirmationMessage**.

To enable the **OnPageLoad** interactions for the **Confirmation** page, perform the following steps:

1. Under the design area in the **Page** pane, click on the **Page Interactions** tab.

2. Click on **Add Case...** to open the **Case Editor** dialog box. In the **Case Editor** dialog box, perform the following steps:

   Creating the condition.

   Perform the following steps to create the condition:

   1. Click the **Add Condition** button.

   2. In the **Condition Builder** dialog box, in the outlined condition box perform the following: In the first dropdown, select **value of variable**.

   3. In the second dropdown, select **AccountVerified**.

   4. In the third dropdown, select **contains**.

   5. In the fourth dropdown, select **value**.

   6. In the text field enter @.

   7. Click **OK**.

Creating the actions

To set the text on the **Header/WelcomeMessage**, perform the following steps:

1. Under **Click to add actions**, scroll to the **Widgets** drop-down menu and click on **set text**.

2. Under **Configure actions**, scroll to the **Header** dropdown, click to expand, and click the checkbox next to **WelcomeMessage**.

3. Under **Set text to**, click on the first dropdown and select **value**. Click on the second field and enter `Welcome, [[AccountVerified]]!`.

To show the **Header/WelcomeMessage**, perform the following steps:

1. Under **Click to add actions**, scroll to the **Widgets** drop-down menu, click the **Show/Hide** dropdown, and click on **Show**.

2. Under **Configure actions**, scroll to the **Header** dropdown, click to expand, and click the checkbox next to **WelcomeMessage**.

To set the panel state of the **Header/HeaderLinksDP**, perform the following steps:

1. Under **Click to add actions**, scroll to the **Dynamic Panels** drop-down menu and click on **Set Panel State**.

2. Under **Configure actions**, scroll to the **Header** dropdown, click to expand, and click the checkbox next to **HeaderLinksDP**.

3. Change **Select the State** to **LinksSignOut**.

To show the **ConfirmationMessage**, perform the following steps:

1. Under **Click to add actions**, scroll to the **Widgets** drop-down menu, click the **Show/Hide** drop-down, and click on **Show**.

2. Under **Configure actions**, click the checkbox next to **ConfirmationMessage**.

3. Click **OK**.

With the **Registration** and **Confirmation** pages completed, we are now ready to design the **Sign In** page.

Making our Sign In page

To create our **Sign In** page, you will use a **Heading 1** widget as well as the Header, Footer, and **Inline Field Validation** masters. When completed, our **Sign In** page will look as follows:

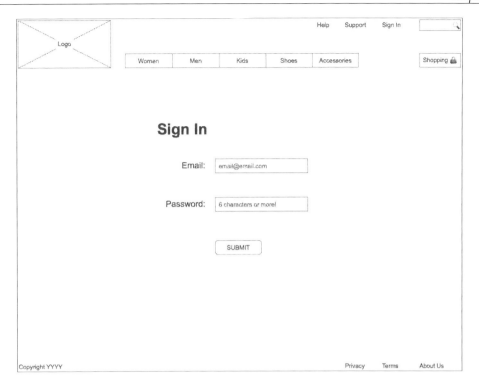

To create the **Sign In** page, perform the following steps:

1. In the **Sitemap** pane, double-click on the **Sign In** page to open it in the design area.

2. From the **Masters** pane, drag the **Header** master and drop it at any location on the wireframe.

3. From the **Masters** pane, drag the **Footer** master and place at coordinates (10,725).

4. From the **Widgets** pane, drag the **Heading 1** widget and place at coordinates (308,220).

5. With the **Heading 1** widget selected, type Sign In.

6. In the **Widget Interactions and Notes** pane, click in the **Shape Name** field and type SignInHeading1.

7. From the **Masters** pane, drag the **Inline Field Validation** master and drop at any location on the wireframe. In the **Widgets and Interactions and Notes** pane, click in the **Inline Field Validation Name** field and type SignIn. With the **Sign In** page layout completed, we are now ready to define the validation and feedback interactions.

Validation and Feedback for our Sign In page

To perform validation and provide user feedback on the **Sign In** page, we will leverage the following two raised events of the **Inline Field Validation** master:

- OnValidSignInEmail
- OnSignInSubmitClick

We will name the instance of the **Inline Field Validation** master on the **Registration** page **SignIn**. For **SignIn**, we will create new cases for the two raised events. Once complete, the **Widgets Interactions and Notes** pane for **SignIn** will look as follows:

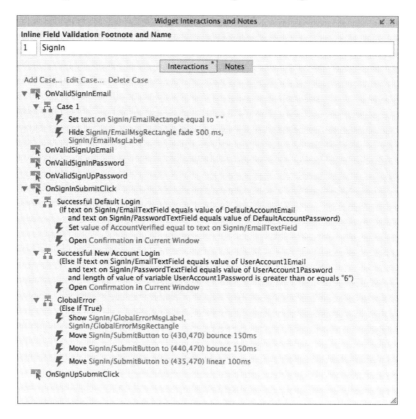

Creating the case for the OnValidSignInEmail event

With **AccountSignUp** selected, in the **Widget Interactions and Notes** pane, click the **Interactions** tab and double-click **OnValidSignUpEmail**. A **Case Editor** dialog box will open. In the **Case Editor** dialog, perform the steps given in the following sections.

Creating the action

To set the text on the **EmailRectangle** widget, perform the following steps:

1. Under **Click to add actions**, scroll to the **Variables** drop-down menu and click on **Set Text**.

2. Under **Configure actions**, scroll to the **SignIn** drop-down, click to expand, and click the checkbox next to **EmailRectangle**.

3. Under **Set text to**, click the first drop-down and click **value**.

To hide **SignIn/EmailMsgRectangle** and **SignIn/EmailMsgLabel**, perform the following steps:

1. Under **Click to add actions**, scroll to the **Widgets** drop-down menu, click the **Show/Hide** drop-down and click on **Hide**.

2. Under **Configure actions**, scroll to the **SignIn** drop-down, click to expand, and click the checkbox next to **EmailMsgRectangle**.

3. Next to **Animate**, click the drop-down and click **fade**. Leave **t:** set to **500** ms.

4. Under **Configure actions**, scroll to the **SignIn** drop-down, click to expand, and click the checkbox next to **EmailMsgLabel**.

5. Next to **Animate**, click the drop-down and click **none**.

6. Click **OK**.

Creating cases for the OnSignInSubmitClick event

For the **OnSignInSubmitClick** event, there will be three cases, namely, Successful Default Login, Successful New Account Login, and GlobalError. To create the cases for the **OnSignInSubmitClick** event, perform the following steps:

Defining the Successful Default Login case

With **SignIn** selected, in the **Widget Interactions and Notes** pane, click the **Interactions** tab and double-click **OnSignInSubmitClick**. A **Case Editor** dialog box will open. In the **Case Editor** dialog, perform the following steps:

Creating the conditions

Add the first condition:

1. In the **Case Description** field, enter `Successful Default Login`.

2. Click the **Add Condition** button.

3. In the **Condition Builder** dialog box, in the outlined condition box, perform the following steps:

    1. In the first drop-down, select **text on widget**.
    2. In the second drop-down, click the **SignIn** drop-down and click **EmailTextField**.
    3. In the third drop-down, select **equals**.
    4. In the fourth drop-down, select **value of variable**.
    5. In the fifth drop-down, select **DefaultAccountEmail**.

Add the second condition:

1. Click the green **+** sign to add a second condition.
2. In the **Condition Builder** dialog box, in the outlined condition box, perform the following steps:

    1. In the first drop-down, select **text on widget**.
    2. In the second drop-down, click the **SignIn** drop-down and click **PasswordTextField**.
    3. In the third drop-down, select **equals**.
    4. In the fourth drop-down, select **value of variable**.
    5. In the fifth drop-down, select **DefaultAccountPassword**.
    6. Click **OK**.

Creating the actions

To set the value of the **AccountVerified** variable, perform the following steps:

1. Under **Click to add actions**, scroll to the **Variables** drop-down menu and click on **Set Variable Value**.
2. Under **Configure actions**, click the checkbox next to **AccountVerified**.
3. Under **Set variable to**, click the first drop-down and click **text on widget**.
4. Click the second drop-down next to the **Set variable** field, click the down arrow next to **SignIn**, and click **EmailTextField**.

To open the Confirmation page in the Current Window, perform the following steps:

1. Under **Click to add actions**, click the **Links** drop-down menu, click the **Open Link** drop-down menu, and then click on **Current Window**.

2. Under **Configure actions**, with the **Link to a page in this design** radio button selected, click the **Confirmation** page in the **Sitemap**.

3. Click **OK**.

Defining the Successful new Account Login case

With **SignIn** selected, in the **Widget Interactions and Notes** pane, click the **Interactions** tab, double-click **OnSignInSubmitClick**. A **Case Editor** dialog box will open. In the **Case Editor** dialog, perform the steps given in the following sections.

Creating the conditions

Add the first condition:

1. In the **Case Description** field, enter Successful new Account Login.

2. Click the **Add Condition** button.

3. In the **Condition Builder** dialog box, perform the following steps in the outlined condition box:

   1. In the first drop-down, select **text on widget**.

   2. In the second drop-down, click the **SignIn** drop-down and click **EmailTextField**.

   3. In the third drop-down, select **equals**.

   4. In the fourth drop-down, select **value of variable**.

   5. In the fifth drop-down, select **UserAccount1Email**.

Add the second condition:

1. Click the green **+** sign to add a second condition.

2. In the **Condition Builder** dialog box, perform the following steps in the outlined condition box:

   1. In the first drop-down, select **text on widget**.

   2. In the second drop-down, click the **SignIn** drop-down and click **PasswordTextField**.

   3. In the third drop-down, select **equals**.

   4. In the fourth drop-down, select **value of variable**.

   5. In the fifth drop-down, select **UserAccount1Password**.

Add the third condition:

1. Click the green **+** sign to add a third condition.

2. In the **Condition Builder** dialog box, perform the following steps in the outlined condition box:

    1. In the first drop-down, select **length of variable value**.
    2. In the second drop-down, click **UserAccount1Password**.
    3. In the third drop-down, select **is greater than or equals**.
    4. In the fourth drop-down, select **value**.
    5. In the text field, enter 6.
    6. Click **OK**.

Creating the action

To open the Confirmation page in the Current Window, perform the following steps:

1. Under **Click to add actions**, click the **Links** drop-down menu, click the **Open Link** drop-down menu, and then click on **Current Window**.

2. Under **Configure actions**, with the **Link to a page in this design** Radio Button selected, click the **Confirmation** page in the **Sitemap**.

3. Click **OK**.

Defining the GlobalError case

With **SignIn** selected, in the **Widget Interactions and Notes** pane, click the **Interactions** tab and double-click **OnSignInSubmitClick**. A **Case Editor** dialog box will open. In the **Case Editor** dialog, perform the steps given in the following sections.

Name the Case

1. In the **Case Description** field, enter GlobalError.

Create the actions

To show **SignIn/GlobalErrorMsgRectangle** and **SignIn/GlobalErrorMsgLabel**, perform the following steps:

1. Under **Click to add actions**, scroll to the **Widgets** drop-down menu, click the **Show/Hide** drop-down, and click on **Show**.

2. Under **Configure actions**, scroll to the **AccountSignUp** drop-down, click to expand, and click the checkboxes next to **GlobalErrorMsgRectangle** and **GlobalErrorMsgLabel**.

To create the horizontal shaking effect on the **SubmitButton**, you will **Move** the **SignIn/SubmitButton** three times. Perform the following steps:

1. To define the first **Move** interaction:

   1. Under **Click to add actions**, scroll to the **Widgets** drop-down menu and click on **Move**.

   2. Under **Configure actions**, scroll to the **SignIn** drop-down, click to expand, and click the checkbox next to **SubmitButton**.

   3. In the **Move** drop-down, click **to**. In the **x:** field, enter 430 and in the **y:** field, enter 470.

   4. In the **Animate** drop-down, click **bounce**. In the **t:** field, enter 150.

2. To define the second **Move** interaction:

   1. Under **Click to add actions**, scroll to the **Widgets** drop-down menu, and click on **Move**.

   2. Under **Configure actions**, scroll to the **SignIn** drop-down, click to expand, and then click the checkbox next to **SubmitButton**.

   3. In the **Move** drop-down, click **to**. In the **x:** field, enter 440 and in the **y:** field, enter 470.

   4. In the **Animate** drop-down, click **bounce**. In the **t:** field, enter 150.

3. To define the third **Move** interaction:

   1. Under **Click to add actions**, scroll to the **Widgets** drop-down menu and click on **Move**.

   2. Under **Configure actions**, scroll to the **SignIn** drop-down, click to expand, and click the checkbox next to **SubmitButton**.

   3. In the **Move** drop-down, click **to**. In the **x:** field, enter 435. In the **y:** field, enter 470.

   4. In the **Animate** drop-down, click **linear**. In the **t:** field, enter 100.

   5. Click **OK**.

Congratulations, we have completed the design of the **Registration**, **SignIn**, and **Confirmation** pages!

Summary

In this chapter, we created Registration Variables, an **Inline Field Validation** master, a Registration page, and a Sign In page. We first defined Registration Variables to store login and password information.

We created an **Inline Field Validation** master that leveraged raised events. We then created a **Registration** page using a Header, a Footer, and **Inline Field Validation** masters. Using unique **raised events**, we defined specific interactions for the **Inline Field Validation** master on the **Registration** page. Next, we created a simple Confirmation page.

Finally, we created a **SignIn** page using a Header, a Footer, and **Inline Field Validation** masters. Once again, using unique raised events, we defined specific interactions for the **Inline Field Validation** master on the **SignIn** page.

In the next chapter, we will leverage a Repeater widget as a Content Management System (CMS), enabling us to dynamically switch content for the Catalog, Category, and Product Detail pages.

Self-test questions

- What was the first thing we reviewed prior to creating our Inline Field Validation master?
- What was the purpose of creating Global Registration Variables?
- What do the yellow highlighted areas in the design area indicate?
- Why did we create an Inline Field Validation master?
- Why did we use raised events for the Inline Field Validation master?
- How many error message areas are defined on the Inline Field Validation master?
- What are the names of the error message widgets for the Inline Field Validation master?
- What type and how many actions did we use to create the horizontal shaking effect for the Submit button?

4
Dynamic Content Management

Several exciting new features were introduced in Axure RP 7. One such feature is known as the **Repeater** widget. The **Repeater** widget enables us to create a **Repeater Dataset** that repeats and dynamically updates an associated Repeater item. In addition, events and interactions can be defined that filter, sort, and paginate data displayed on the Repeater item.

In our project, we will leverage the **Repeater** widget to simulate a **Content Management System (CMS)**. This single **Repeater** will then be used to dynamically update the Catalog, Category, and Product Detail pages.

In this chapter, you will learn about:

- Designing our Catalog Repeater
  - Simulating a Content Management System (CMS)

- Creating our Category Repeater
  - Defining and Creating Category Repeater interactions

- Facetted Filtering, Sorting, and Pagination widgets
- interactions for Facetted Filtering, Sorting, and Pagination

  - Defining Facetted Filtering interactions
  - Creating Sorting interactions
  - Enabling Pagination

Designing our Catalog Repeater

The first step is to perform a Content Inventory and decide which content we will need for the Catalog, Category, and Product Detail designs. We will then populate a Repeater Dataset with data. There are two primary parts to a **Repeater**: the **Repeater Dataset** and the **Repeater item**. In its simplest use, a repeater iterates through the **Repeater Dataset** dynamically updating the Repeater item widgets as specified by the **OnitemLoad** event. Using a single **Repeater** to simulate a Content Management System is a more advanced implementation.

Simulating a Content Management System

Since we want to use a single **Repeater** for Catalog, Category, and Product Detail designs, we will create a Content Management System repeater named **CMS Repeater** master. The **Category** page will be built from Repeater item master. Catalog and Product Detail designs will be created using two separate Dynamic Panels.

Once completed, the **Repeater Dataset** tab for our **CMS Repeater** master will look like this:

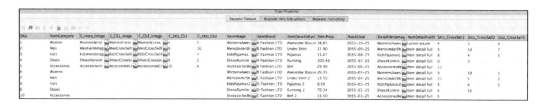

 Repeater Datasets are analogous to SQL database schemas, where data is organized by columns (that is attributes) and rows (that is tuples).

The following table associates repeater column names to repeater item or dynamic panel and widget names:

Column number	Repeater column name	Repeater item or dynamic panel	Widget name
1	SKU	All	Used for tracking individual items during interactions and events
2	ItemCategory	All	
3	C_Hero_Image	CatalogDynamicPanel	CatalogHeroImage
4	C_CS1_Image	CatalogDynamicPanel	CrossSell1_Image
5	C_CS2_Image	CatalogDynamicPanel	CrossSell2_Image

Column number	Repeater column name	Repeater item or dynamic panel	Widget name
6	C_SKU_CS1	CatalogDynamicPanel	Used for tracking catalog cross sell items during interactions and events
7	C_SKU_CS2	CatalogDynamicPanel	
8	ItemImage	Repeater item, DetailDynamicPanel	ItemImageRepeater
9	ItemBrand	Repeater item, DetailDynamicPanel	ItemBrandRepeater
10	ItemDescription	Repeater item, DetailDynamicPanel	ItemDescriptionRepeater
11	ItemPrice	Repeater item, DetailDynamicPanel	ItemPriceRepeater
12	StockDate	Repeater item	Used for sorting by date
13	DetailHeroImage	DetailDynamicPanel	HeroImageDetail
14	ItemDetailFullDescription	DetailDynamicPanel	ItemDescriptionDetail
15	SKU_CrossSell1	DetailDynamicPanel	ItemImageCrossSell1, ItemBrandCrossSell1, ItemDescriptionCrossSell1, and ItemPriceCrossSell1
16	SKU_CrossSell2	DetailDynamicPanel	ItemImageCrossSell2, ItemBrandCrossSell2, ItemDescriptionCrossSell2, and ItemPriceCrossSell2
17	SKU_CrossSell3	DetailDynamicPanel	ItemImageCrossSell3, ItemBrandCrossSell3, ItemDescriptionCrossSell3, and ItemPriceCrossSell3

Defining the CMS Repeater master

By leveraging the **CMS Repeater** master in our design, we will have a centralized widget in which we can quickly add and update content for our prototype. To create the **CMS Repeater** master, perform the following steps:

1. In the **Masters** pane, click on the **Add Master** icon. Slow click the master labeled **New Master 1**, type CMS Repeater and press *Enter*.

2. In the **Masters** pane, right-click on the icon next to **CMS Repeater** master, mouse over **Drop Behavior** and click on **Lock to Master Location**.

3. In the **Masters** pane, double-click on the icon next to the **CMS Repeater** master to open in the design area.

We are now ready to place the **Repeater** widget and place widgets on the Repeater item.

Placing the Repeater widget

To place the **Repeater** widget and format the **Repeater** widget from the **Widgets** pane, drag the **Repeater** widget and place at coordinates (160,170). With the **Repeater** widget selected, perform the following steps:

- In the **Widget interactions and Notes** pane, click on the **Repeater Name** field and type `CategoryRepeater`.

- Double-click on the **Repeater** to open **CategoryRepeater** Repeater item in the design area

- Under the design area in the **Repeater** pane, click on the **Repeater Style** tab. To change the default **Repeater Style**, perform the following steps:

    ◦ Under the **Layout** dropdown, click on the radio button next to **Horizontal**.

    ◦ Under the **Layout** dropdown, click on the checkbox next to **Wrap (Grid)** and in the **Items per column** field enter `4`.

    ◦ Under the **Pagination** dropdown, click on the checkbox next to **Multiple pages**, in the **Items per page** field enter `8`, and in the **Starting page** field enter `1`.

Adjusting and placing widgets on the Repeater item

To adjust and place widgets on the Repeater item, perform the following steps:

1. In the design area, click on the Repeater item at coordinates (0,0). With the **Repeater** widget selected, perform the following steps:

    1. In the toolbar, change the value of **w** to `200` and **h** to `270`.

    2. In the **Widget interactions and Notes** pane, click on the **Shape Name** field and type `CategoryBackground`.

2. From the **Widgets** pane, drag the **Image** widget and place at coordinates (13,10). With the **Image** widget selected, perform the following steps:

    1. In the toolbar, change the value of **w** to `173` and **h** to `173`.

    2. In the **Widget interactions and Notes** pane, click in the **Shape Name** field and type `ItemImageRepeater`.

3. From the **Widgets** pane, drag the **Heading 2** widget and place at coordinates (13,190). With the **Heading 2** widget selected, perform the following steps:

    1. In the toolbar, change the value of **w** to 173 and **h** to 18.

    2. In the **Widget interactions and Notes** pane, click in the **Shape Name** field and type ItemBrandRepeater.

    3. In the **Widget Properties and Style** pane, with the **Style** tab selected scroll to **Font** and change the font size to 16.

4. From the **Widgets** pane, drag the **Label** widget and place at coordinates (13,210). With the **Label** widget selected, perform the following steps:

    1. Type Description that could take up to two lines.. You will see the error message displayed on the **Label** widget.

    2. In the toolbar, change the value of **w** to 173 and **h** to 30.

    3. In the **Widget interactions and Notes** pane, click in the **Shape Name** field and type ItemDescriptionRepeater.

5. From the **Widgets** pane, drag the **Label** widget and place at coordinates (13,245). With the **Label** widget selected, perform the following steps:

    1. Type $. You will see the text displayed as text on the **Label** widget.

    2. In the toolbar, change the value of **w** to 15 and **h** to 15.

    3. In the **Widget interactions and Notes** pane, click in the **Shape Name** field and type CurrencySymbolRepeater.

6. From the **Widgets** pane, drag the **Label** widget and place at coordinates (28,245). With the **Label** widget selected, perform the following steps:

    1. Type ###.##. You will see the text displayed on the **Label** widget.

    2. In the toolbar, change the value of **w** to 158 and **h** to 15.

    3. In the **Widget interactions and Notes** pane, click in the **Shape Name** field and type ItemPriceRepeater.

With Repeater item widgets placed, we are ready to define the Repeater Dataset. SKU is the first column of the Repeater Dataset and is a unique index to track individual items in our Catalog. columns 2–7 are used for the Catalog page. columns 8–12 are used to update the Repeater item displayed on the Category page. columns 13–17 are used for Product Detail pages.

Creating and populating the CMS Repeater Dataset

Next we will create and populate the **Repeater Dataset**. We will accomplish this by updating the columns by three sections: columns 1–7, columns 8–12, and columns 13–17.

Updating columns 1-7 of the CMS Repeater Dataset

To create and populate columns 1–7 of the **Repeater Dataset**:

1. With the Repeater item still open in the design area, perform the following steps:

    1. Under the design area in the **Repeater** pane, click on the **Repeater Dataset** tab. To change the default **Repeater** column heading, double-click on **Column0** and type SKU to rename.

    2. Double-click on **Add Column** six times renaming each column as follows:

Repeater column name
ItemCategory
C_Hero_Image
C_CS1_Image
C_CS2_Image
C_SKU_CS1
C_SKU_CS2

2. With Repeater item table column headings 1–7 defined, we are now ready to populate data items for each row 1–10.

> For column headings with image in the title, you will right-click in the corresponding cell and click on **Import Image...** in the drop-down menu.
>
> Sample images and code downloads are available at http://www.packtpub.com/learning-axure-rp-interactive-prototypes. To download, click on the support tab and then on the **Download now** button.

    ° Use the following table to update columns 1–5 and rows 1–10. Click on **Add Row** to add new rows 4–10. Populate each column and row with the following data:

SKU	ItemCategory	C_Hero_Image	C_CS1_Image	C_CS2_Image
1	Women	WomenHeroImage.png	WomenCrossSellImage1.png	WomenCrossSellImage2.png
2	Men	MenHeroImage.png	MenCrossSellImage1.png	MenCrossSellImage2.png
3	Kids	KidsHeroImage.png	KidsCrossSellImage1.png	KidsCrossSellImage2.png
4	Shoes	ShoesHeroImage.png	ShoesCrossSellImage1.png	ShoesCrossSellImage2.png
5	Accessories	AccessoriesHeroImage.png	AccessoriesCrossSellImage1.png	AccessoriesCrossSellImage2.png
6	Women			
7	Men			
8	Kids			
9	Shoes			
10	Accessories			

- ○ Use the following table to update columns 6–7 and rows 1–5. Populate each column and row with the following data:

SKU (Reference Only)	C_SKU_CS1	C_SKU_CS2
1	4	5
2	9	10
3	8	4
4	9	2
5	10	6

Updating columns 8-12 of the CMS Repeater Dataset

Perform the following steps to create and populate columns 8–12 of the **Repeater Dataset**:

1. With the Repeater item still open in the design area, perform the following steps:

    1. Under the design area in the **Repeater** pane, click on the **Repeater Dataset** tab. To change the default **Repeater** column heading, double-click on **Add Column** five times renaming each column as follows:

Repeater column name
ItemImage
ItemBrand
ItemDescription

Repeater column name
ItemPrice
StockDate

2. With Repeater item table column headings 8–12 defined, we are now ready to populate data items for each row from 1–10.

   ○ Use the following table to update columns 8–12 and rows 1–10. Populate each column and row with the f ollowing data:

SKU (Reference Only)	ItemImage	ItemBrand	ItemDescription	ItemPrice	StockDate
1	WomensAwesomeBlouse.png	A Fashion LTD	Awesome Blouse	34.85	2055-10-25
2	MensUnderShirt.png	B Fashion LTD	Under Shirt	11.00	2055-09-25
3	KidsPajamas.png	C Fashion LTD	Pajamas	15.67	2055-08-25
4	ShoesRunning.png	A Fashion LTD	Running	109.49	2055-07-25
5	AccessoriesBelt.png	B Fashion LTD	Belt	29.99	2055-06-25
6	WomensAwesome Blouse2(0).png	B Fashion LTD	Awesome Blouse 2	29.35	2055-05-25
7	MensUnderShirt2.png	C Fashion LTD	Under Shirt 2	13.50	2055-04-25
8	KidsPajamas2.png	D Fashion LTD	Pajamas 2	9.99	2055-03-25
9	ShoesRunning2.png	D Fashion LTD	Running 2	79.34	2055-02-25
10	AccessoriesBelt2.png	C Fashion LTD	Belt 2	15.50	2055-01-25

Updating columns 13–17 of the CMS Repeater Dataset

Perform the following steps to create and populate columns 13–17 of the **Repeater Dataset**:

1. With Repeater item still open in the design area, perform the following steps:

   1. Under the design area in the **Repeater** pane, click on the **Repeater Dataset** tab. To change the default **Repeater** column heading, double-click on **Add Column** five times renaming each column as follows:

Repeater column name
DetailHeroImage
ItemDetailFullDescription
SKU_CrossSell1
SKU_CrossSell2
SKU_CrossSell3

2. With Repeater item table column headings 13–17 defined, we are now ready to populate data items for each row 1–10.

   ○ Use the following table to update columns 13–17 and rows 1–10. Populate each column and row with the following data:

SKU (Reference Only)	DetailHeroImage	ItemDetailFullDescription	SKU_ CrossSell1	SKU_ CrossSell2	SKU_ CrossSell3
1	WomensAwesome Blouse(0).png	Lorem ipsum dolor sit amet, consectetur adipiscing elit. Aenean euismod bibendum laoreet. Proin gravida dolor sit amet lacus accumsan et viverra justo commodo. Proin sodales pulvinar tempor. Cum sociis natoque penatibus et magnis dis parturient montes, nascetur ridiculus mus. Nam fermentum, nulla luctus pharetra vulputate, felis tellus mollis orci, sed rhoncus sapien nunc eget odio.	4	5	6
2	MensUnderShirt(0).png	Item detail full description here.....	5	10	7
3	KidsPajamas(0).png	Item detail full description here.....	8	4	5
4	ShoesRunning(0).png	Item detail full description here.....	9	5	
5	AccessoriesBelt(0).png	Item detail full description here.....	10		
6	WomensAwesome Blouse2.png	Item detail full description here.....	9	10	1
7	MensUnderShirt2(0).png	Item detail full description here.....	10	5	2
8	KidsPajamas2(0).png	Item detail full description here.....	3	4	5
9	ShoesRunning2(0).png	Item detail full description here.....	4	10	
10	AccessoriesBelt2(0).png	Item detail full description here.....	5		

With Repeater item widgets placed and the **Repeater Dataset** defined, we are now ready to create CMS variables.

Creating CMS variables

Now we will create Axure variables that will allow us to store global variables for our CMS. To create CMS variables, in the main menu, click on **Project** and then on **Global Variables…**. In the **Global Variables** dialog, perform the following steps:

1. Click on the green plus sign and type ShowCatalog. Click in the **Default Value** field and type 0.

2. Repeat step 1 eight more times to create additional variables using the following table for variable name and default value fields:

Variable name	Default value
SKU_CrossSell1	0
SKU_CrossSell2	0
SKU_CrossSell3	0
ShowDetail	0
RepeaterCount	0
BrandFilter	None
PriceFilter	None
CategoryFilter	None
SetCategory	0

Once completed, our **Global Variables** dialog will look like this:

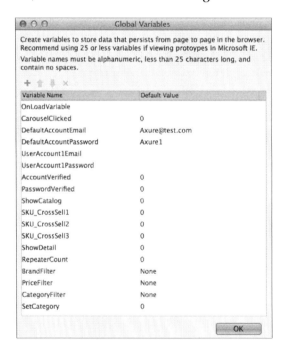

3. Click on **OK**.

With Repeater item widgets placed, the **Repeater Dataset** defined, and CMS Variables created, we are now ready to design the Category repeater using the **CMS Repeater** master with interactions.

Creating our Category Repeater

The Category Repeater is dynamically updated with content from the **Repeater Dataset** and built using the Repeater item. In addition, the **CMS Repeater** master also provides facetted filtering with sorting capabilities. Once created, the **Category** page will leverage a Repeater item with the following named widgets:

- CategoryBackground
- ItemImageRepeater
- ItemBrandRepeater
- ItemDescriptionRepeater
- CurrencySymbolRepeater
- ItemPriceRepeater

Once completed, our Category Repeater will look like this:

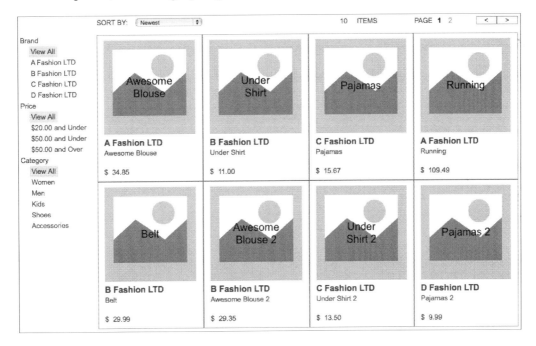

We will first define interactions for the CategoryRepeater and Repeater OnItemLoad events. Next we will add facetted filtering, sorting, and pagination controls to the **CMS Repeater** master.

Defining and Creating Category Repeater interactions

We will start by defining interactions for the CategoryRepeater OnItemLoad event. Once completed, the **OnItemLoad** event will have a total of 10 cases and the CategoryRepeater widget interactions pane will look like this:

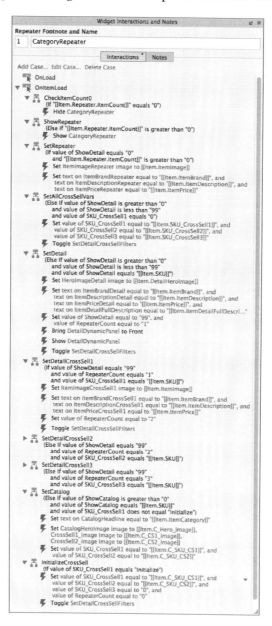

Updating our Category Repeater

To create the interactions, open the **CMS Repeater** master in the design area and perform the steps given in the upcoming section.

Defining the CheckItemCount0 case

To define the **CheckItemCount0** case, click on the **CategoryRepeater**. In the **Widget Interactions and Notes** pane with the **Interactions** tab selected, double-click on the **OnItemLoad** event. A **Case Editor** dialog box will open. In the **Case Description** field on the **Case Editor** dialog, type CheckItemCount0 and perform the steps given in the upcoming sections.

Creating conditions

Perform the following steps to create the condition:

1. In the first dropdown, select **value**
2. In the second field, enter [[Item.Repeater.itemCount]].
3. In the third dropdown, select **equals**.
4. In the fourth dropdown, select **value**.
5. In the text field, enter 0.
6. Click on **OK**.

Adding and configuring actions

To hide the **CategoryRepeater**, perform the following steps:

1. Under **Click to add actions**, scroll to the **Widgets** drop-down menu. Under the **Set Show/Hide** dropdown, click on **Hide**.
2. Under **Configure actions**, click on the checkbox next to **CategoryRepeater**.
3. Click on **OK**.

Defining the ShowRepeater case

To define the **ShowRepeater** case, do the following:

In the **Widget Interactions and Notes** pane with the **Interactions** tab selected, double-click on the **OnItemLoad** event. A **Case Editor** dialog box will open. In the **Case Description** text field in the **Case Editor** dialog, type ShowRepeater.

Creating conditions

Perform the following steps to create the condition:

1. In the first dropdown, select **value**.
2. In the second field, enter `[[Item.Repeater.itemCount]]`.
3. In the third dropdown, select **is greater than**.
4. In the fourth dropdown, select **value**.
5. In the text field, enter `0`.
6. Click on **OK**.

Adding and configuring actions

To show the **CategoryRepeater**, perform the following steps:

1. Under **Click to add actions**, scroll to the **Widgets** drop-down menu. Under the **Set Show/Hide** drop-down, click on **Show**.
2. Under **Configure actions**, click on the checkbox next to **CategoryRepeater**.
3. Click on **OK**.

Defining the SetRepeater case

To define the **SetRepeater** case, do the following:

In the **Widget Interactions and Notes** pane with the **Interactions** tab selected, double-click on the **OnItemLoad** event. A **Case Editor** dialog box will open. In the **Case Description** field, on the **Case Editor** dialog, type `SetRepeater`.

Creating conditions

We need to add two conditions in the **SetRepeater** case.

To add the first condition perform the following steps:

1. Click on the **Add Condition** button.
2. In the **Condition Builder** dialog box, in the outlined condition box, perform the following steps:

    1. In the first dropdown, select **value of variable**.
    2. In the second dropdown, select **ShowDetail**.
    3. In the third dropdown, select **equals**.
    4. In the fourth dropdown, select **value**.
    5. In the text field, enter `0`.

To add the second condition perform the following steps:

1. Click on the green plus sign to add a second condition.

2. In the **Condition Builder** dialog box, in the outlined condition box perform the following steps:

    1. In the first dropdown, select **value**.

    2. In the second field, enter `[[Item.Repeater.itemCount]]`.

    3. In the third dropdown, select **is greater than**.

    4. In the fourth dropdown, select **value**.

    5. In the text field, enter `0`.

3. Click on **OK**.

Adding and configuring actions

To set the image on the **ItemImageRepeater** widget, perform the following steps:

1. Under **Click to add actions**, scroll to the **Widgets** drop-down menu and click on **set image**.

2. Under **Configure actions** in the **Select the image widgets to set the image** section, click on the checkbox next to **ItemImageRepeater**.

3. Under **Configure actions** in the **Default** section, select **value** in the first drop-down menu and enter `[[Item.ItemImage]]` in the text field.

4. To set the text on the **ItemBrandRepeater** widget perform the following steps:

    ° Under **Click to add actions**, scroll to the **Widgets** drop-down menu and click on **set the text**.

    ° Under **Configure actions** in the **Select the widgets to set text** section, click on the checkbox next to **ItemBrandRepeater**.

    ° Under **Configure actions** in the **set the text to** section, select **value** in the first drop-down menu and enter `[[Item.ItemBrand]]` in the text field.

5. To set the text on the **ItemDescriptionRepeater** widget, perform the following steps:

    1. Under **Click to add actions**, scroll to the **Widgets** drop-down menu and click on **set the text**.

2. Under **Configure action**, in the **Select the widgets to set text** section, click on the checkbox next to **ItemDescriptionRepeater**.

3. Under **Configure actions** in the **set the text to** section, select **value** in the first drop-down menu and enter `[[Item.ItemDescription]]` in the text field.

6. To set the text on the **ItemPriceRepeater** widget, perform the following steps:

    1. Under **Click to add actions**, scroll to the **Widgets** drop-down menu and click on **set the text**.

    2. Under **Configure actions** in the **Select the widgets to set text** section, click on the checkbox next to **ItemPriceRepeater**.

    3. Under **Configure actions** in the **set the text to** section, select **value** in the first drop-down menu and enter `[[Item.ItemPrice]]` in the text field.

7. Click on **OK**.

8. Under the **OnItemLoad** event, right-click on the **SetRepeater** case and click on **Toggle IF/ELSE IF**.

Defining the SetAllCrossSellVars case

To define the **SetAllCrossSellVars** case, do the following:

In the **Widget Interactions and Notes** pane with the **Interactions** tab selected, double-click on the **OnItemLoad** event. A **Case Editor** dialog box will open. Within the **Case Editor** dialog in the **Case Description** field, type `SetAllCrossSellVars` and perform the actions mentioned in the upcoming sections.

Create the conditions

To add the first condition, perform the following steps:

- Click on the **Add Condition** button.

- In the **Condition Builder** dialog box, perform the following steps in the outlined condition box:

    1. In the first dropdown, select **value of variable**.

    2. In the second dropdown, select **ShowDetail**.

    3. In the third dropdown, select **is greater than**.

    4. In the fourth dropdown, select **value**.

    5. In the text field, enter `0`.

To add the second condition perform the following steps:

- Click on the green plus sign to add a second condition.
- In the **Condition Builder** dialog box, perform the following steps in the outlined condition box:
  1. In the first dropdown, select **value of variable**.
  2. In the second dropdown, select **ShowDetail**.
  3. In the third dropdown, select **is less than**.
  4. In the fourth dropdown, select **value**.
  5. In the text field, enter 99.

To add the third condition, perform the following steps:

- Click on the green plus sign to add a third condition.
- In the **Condition Builder** dialog box, perform the following steps in the outlined condition box:
  1. In the first dropdown, select **value of variable**.
  2. In the second dropdown, select **SKU_CrossSell1**.
  3. In the third dropdown, select **equals**.
  4. In the fourth dropdown, select **value**.
  5. In the text field, enter 0.
  6. Click on **OK**.

Create the actions

1. To set variable value for **SKU_CrossSell1**, **SKU_CrossSell2**, and **SKU_CrossSell3** perform the following steps:
   1. Under **Click to add actions**, scroll to the **Variables** drop-down menu and click on **set variable value**.
   2. Under **Configure actions** in the **Select the variables to set** section, click on the checkbox next to **SKU_CrossSell1**.
   3. Under **Configure actions** in the **Set variable to** section, select **value** in the first drop-down menu and enter `[[Item.SKU_CrossSell1]]` in the text field.
   4. Under **Configure actions** in the **Select the variables to set** section, click on the checkbox next to **SKU_CrossSell2**.

5. Under **Configure actions** in the **Set variable to** section, select **value** in the first drop-down menu and enter `[[Item.SKU_CrossSell2]]` in the text field.

6. Under **Configure actions** in the **Select the variables to set** section, click on the checkbox next to **SKU_CrossSell3**.

7. Under **Configure actions** in the **Set variable to** section, select **value** in the first drop-down menu and enter `[[Item.SKU_CrossSell3]]` in the text field.

2. To toggle the **SetDetailCrossSellFilters** and cause the Repeater to reload, perform the following steps:

   1. Under **Click to add actions**, scroll to the **Widgets** drop-down menu. Under the **Show/Hide** drop-down menu, click on **Toggle Visibility**.

   2. Under **Configure actions**, in the **Select the widgets to hide/show** section, click on the checkbox next to **SetDetailCrossSellFilters**.

3. Click on **OK**.

Defining the SetDetail case

To define the **SetDetail** case, do the following:

In the **Widget Interactions and Notes** pane with the **Interactions** tab selected, double-click on the **OnItemLoad** event. A **Case Editor** dialog box will open. Within the **Case Editor** dialog in the **Case Description** field, type `SetDetail` and perform the actions mentioned in the upcoming sections.

Create the conditions

To add the first condition, perform the following steps:

- Click on the **Add Condition** button.

- In the **Condition Builder** dialog box, perform the following steps in the outlined condition box:

  1. In the first dropdown, select **value of variable**.
  2. In the second dropdown, select **ShowDetail**.
  3. In the third dropdown, select **is greater than**.
  4. In the fourth dropdown, select **value**.
  5. In the text field, enter `0`.

To add the second condition, perform the following steps:

- Click on the green plus sign to add a second condition.
- In the **Condition Builder** dialog box, perform the following steps in the outlined condition box:

  1. In the first dropdown, select **value of variable**.
  2. In the second dropdown, select **ShowDetail**.
  3. In the third dropdown, select **is less than**.
  4. In the fourth dropdown, select **value**.
  5. In the text field, enter 99.

To add the third condition, perform the following steps:

- Click on the green plus sign to add a third condition.
- In the **Condition Builder** dialog box, perform the following steps in the outlined condition box:

  1. In the first dropdown, select **value of variable**.
  2. In the second dropdown, select **ShowDetail**.
  3. In the third dropdown, select **equals**.
  4. In the fourth dropdown, select **value**.
  5. In the text field, enter [[Item.SKU]].
  6. Click on **OK**.

Create the actions

1. To set the image on **HeroImageDetail**, perform the following steps:

   1. Under **Click to add actions**, scroll to the **Widgets** drop-down menu and click on **set image**.
   2. Under **Configure actions**, in the **Select the image widgets to set the image** section, click on the checkbox next to **HeroImageDetail**.
   3. Under **Configure actions** in the **Default** section, select **value** in the first drop-down menu and enter [[Item.DetailHeroImage]] in the text field.

2. To set the text on **ItemBrandDetail**, **ItemDescriptionDetail**, **ItemPriceDetail** and **ItemDetailFullDescription** perform the following steps:

    1. Under **Click to add actions**, scroll to the **Widgets** drop-down menu and click on **set the text**.

    2. Under **Configure actions** in the **Select the widgets to set text** section, click on the checkbox next to **ItemBrandDetail**.

    3. Under **Configure actions** in the **Set variable to** section, select **value** in the first drop-down menu and enter `[[Item.ItemBrand]]` in the text field.

    4. Under **Configure actions** in the **Select the widgets to set text** section, click on the checkbox next to **ItemDescriptionDetail**.

    5. Under **Configure actions** in the **Set variable to** section, select **value** in the first drop-down menu and enter `[[Item.ItemDescription]]` in the text field.

    6. Under **Configure actions** in the **Select the widgets to set text** section, click on the checkbox next to **ItemPriceDetail**.

    7. Under **Configure actions** in the **Set variable to** section, select **value** in the first drop-down menu and enter `[[Item.ItemPrice]]` in the text field.

    8. Under **Configure actions** in the **Select the widgets to set text** section, click on the checkbox next to **ItemDetailFullDescription**.

    9. Under **Configure actions** in the **Set variable to** section, select **value** in the first drop-down menu and enter `[[Item.ItemDetailFullDescription]]` in the text field.

3. To set variable value for **ShowDetail** and **RepeaterCount**, perform the following steps:

    1. Under **Click to add actions**, scroll to the **Variables** drop-down menu and click on **set variable value**.

    2. Under **Configure actions** in the **Select the variables to set** section, click on the checkbox next to **ShowDetail**.

    3. Under **Configure actions** in the **Set variable to** section, select **value** in the first drop-down menu and enter `99` in the text field.

    4. Under **Configure actions** in the **Select the variables to set** section, click on the checkbox next to **RepeaterCount**.

    5. Under **Configure actions** in the **Set variable to** section, select **value** in the first drop-down menu and enter `1` in the text field.

4. To bring to front the **DetailDynamicPanel**, perform the following steps:

    1. Under **Click to add actions**, scroll to the **Widgets** drop-down menu. Under the **Bring to Front/Back** dropdown, click on **Bring to Front**.

    2. Under **Configure actions**, click on the checkbox next to **DetailDynamicPanel**.

5. To show the **DetailDynamicPanel**, perform the following steps:

    1. Under **Click to add actions**, scroll to the **Widgets** drop-down menu. Under the **Set Show/Hide** dropdown, click on **Show**.

    2. Under **Configure actions**, click on the checkbox next to **DetailDynamicPanel**.

6. To toggle the **SetDetailCrossSellFilters** and cause the Repeater to reload, perform the following steps:

    1. Under **Click to add actions**, scroll to the **Widgets** drop-down menu. Under the Show/Hide drop-down menu, click on **Toggle Visibility**.

    2. Under **Configure actions** in the **Select the widgets to hide/show** section, click on the checkbox next to **SetDetailCrossSellFilters**.

7. Click on **OK**.

Defining the SetDetailCrossSell1 case

To define the **SetDetailCrossSell1** case:

In the **Widget Interactions and Notes** pane with the **Interactions** tab selected, double-click on the **OnItemLoad** event. A **Case Editor** dialog box will open. Within the **Case Editor** dialog in the **Case Description** field, type SetDetailCrossSell1 and perform the actions given in the upcoming sections.

Create the conditions

To add the first condition, perform the following steps:

- Click on the **Add Condition** button.

- In the **Condition Builder** dialog box, in the outlined condition box perform the following steps:

    1. In the first dropdown, select **value of variable**.
    2. In the second dropdown, select **ShowDetail**.
    3. In the third dropdown, select **equals**.
    4. In the fourth dropdown, select **value**.
    5. In the text field, enter 99.

To add the second condition, perform the following steps:

- Click on the green plus sign to add a second condition.
- In the **Condition Builder** dialog box, in the outlined condition box perform the following steps:
    1. In the first dropdown, select **value of variable**.
    2. In the second dropdown, select **RepeaterCount**.
    3. In the third dropdown, select **equals**.
    4. In the fourth dropdown, select **value**.
    5. In the text field, enter 1.

To add the third condition, perform the following steps:

- Click on the green plus sign to add a third condition.
- In the **Condition Builder** dialog box, in the outlined condition box perform the following steps:
    1. In the first dropdown, select **value of variable**.
    2. In the second dropdown, select **SKU_CrossSell1**.
    3. In the third dropdown, select **equals**.
    4. In the fourth dropdown, select **value**.
    5. In the text field, enter `[[Item.SKU]]`.
    6. Click on **OK**.

Create the actions

1. To set image on **ItemImageCrossSell1** perform the following steps:
    1. Under **Click to add actions**, scroll to the **Widgets** drop-down menu and click on **set image**.
    2. Under **Configure actions** in the **Select the image widgets to set the image** section, click on the checkbox next to **ItemImageCrossSell1**.
    3. Under **Configure actions** in the **Default** section, select **value** in the first drop-down menu and enter `[[Item.ItemImage]]` in the text field.

2. To set the text on **ItemBrandCrossSell1**, **ItemDescriptionCrossSell1**, and **ItemPriceCrossSell1**, perform the following steps:

    1. Under **Click to add actions**, scroll to the **Widgets** drop-down menu and click on **set the text**.

    2. Under **Configure actions** in the **Select the widgets to set text** section, click on the checkbox next to **ItemBrandCrossSell1**.

    3. Under **Configure actions** in the **Set variable to** section, select **value** in the first drop-down menu and enter `[[Item.ItemBrand]]` in the text field.

    4. Under **Configure actions** in the **Select the widgets to set text** section, click on the checkbox next to **ItemDescriptionCrossSell1**.

    5. Under **Configure actions** in the **Set variable to** section, select **value** in the first drop-down menu and enter `[[Item.ItemDescription]]` in the text field.

    6. Under **Configure actions** in the **Select the widgets to set text** section, click on the checkbox next to **ItemPriceCrossSell1**.

    7. Under **Configure actions** in the **Set variable to** section, select **value** in the first drop-down menu and enter `[[Item.ItemPrice]]` in the text field.

3. To set variable value for **RepeaterCount**, perform the following steps:

    1. Under **Click to add actions**, scroll to the **Variables** drop-down menu and click on **set variable value**.

    2. Under **Configure actions** in the **Select the variables to set** section, click on the checkbox next to **RepeaterCount**.

    3. Under **Configure actions** in the **Set variable to** section, select **value** in the first drop-down menu and enter 2 in the text field.

4. To toggle the **SetDetailCrossSellFilters** and cause the **Repeater** to reload, perform the following steps:

    1. Under **Click to add actions**, scroll to the **Widgets** drop-down menu. Under the **Show/Hide** drop-down menu, click on **Toggle Visibility**.

    2. Under **Configure actions** in the **Select the widgets to hide/show** section, click on the checkbox next to **SetDetailCrossSellFilters**.

5. Click on **OK**.

6. Under the **OnItemLoad** event, right-click on the **SetDetailCrossSell1** case and click on **Toggle IF/ELSE IF**.

Defining the SetDetailCrossSell2 case

To define the **SetDetailCrossSell2** case, do the following:

In the **Widget Interactions and Notes** pane with the **Interactions** tab selected, double-click on the **OnItemLoad** event. A **Case Editor** dialog box will open. Within the **Case Editor** dialog in the **Case Description** field, type `SetDetailCrossSell2` and perform the actions mentioned in the upcoming sections.

Create the conditions

To add the first condition, perform the following steps:

- Click on the **Add Condition** button.
- In the **Condition Builder** dialog box, perform the following steps in the outlined condition box:

  1. In the first dropdown, select **value of variable**.
  2. In the second dropdown, select **ShowDetail**.
  3. In the third dropdown, select **equals**.
  4. In the fourth dropdown, select **value**.
  5. In the text field, enter `99`.

To add the second condition, perform the following steps:

- Click on the green plus sign to add a second condition.
- In the **Condition Builder** dialog box, perform the following steps in the outlined condition box:

  1. In the first dropdown, select **value of variable**.
  2. In the second dropdown, select **RepeaterCount**.
  3. In the third dropdown, select **equals**.
  4. In the fourth dropdown, select **value**.
  5. In the text field, enter `2`.

To add the third condition, perform the following steps:

- Click on the green plus sign to add a third condition.
- In the **Condition Builder** dialog box, perform the following steps in the outlined condition box:

  1. In the first dropdown, select **value of variable**.
  2. In the second dropdown, select **SKU_CrossSell2**.

3. In the third dropdown, select **equals**.

4. In the fourth dropdown, select **value**.

5. In the text field, enter `[[Item.SKU]]`.

6. Click on **OK**.

Create the actions

1. To set image on **ItemImageCrossSell2**, perform the following steps:

   1. Under **Click to add actions**, scroll to the **Widgets** drop-down menu and click on **set image**.

   2. Under **Configure actions** in the **Select the image widgets to set the image** section, click on the checkbox next to **ItemImageCrossSell2**.

   3. Under **Configure actions**, in the **Default** section, select **value** in the first drop-down menu and enter `[[Item.ItemImage]]` in the text field.

2. To set the text on **ItemBrandCrossSell2**, **ItemDescriptionCrossSell2**, and **ItemPriceCrossSell2**, perform the following steps:

   1. Under **Click to add actions**, scroll to the **Widgets** drop-down menu and click on **set the text**.

   2. Under **Configure actions** in the **Select the widgets to set text** section, click on the checkbox next to **ItemBrandCrossSell2**.

   3. Under **Configure actions** in the **Set variable to** section, select **value** in the first drop-down menu and enter `[[Item.ItemBrand]]` in the text field.

   4. Under **Configure actions** in the **Select the widgets to set text** section, click on the checkbox next to **ItemDescriptionCrossSell2**.

   5. Under **Configure actions** in the **Set variable to** section, select **value** in the first drop-down menu and enter `[[Item.ItemDescription]]` in the text field.

   6. Under **Configure actions** in the **Select the widgets to set text** section, click on the checkbox next to **ItemPriceCrossSell2**.

   7. Under **Configure actions** in the **Set variable to** section, select **value** in the first drop-down menu and enter `[[Item.ItemPrice]]` in the text field.

3. To show the **CrossSell2** widgets, perform the following steps:

   1. Under **Click to add actions**, scroll to the **Widgets** drop-down menu. Under the **Set Show/Hide** dropdown, click on **Show**.

   2. Under **Configure actions**, click on the checkbox next to **ItemImageCrossSell2, ItemBrandCrossSell2, ItemDescriptionCrossSell2, ItemPriceCrossSell2,** and **CurrencySymbolCrossSell2**.

4. To set the variable value for **RepeaterCount**, perform the following steps:

   1. Under **Click to add actions**, scroll to the **Variables** drop-down menu and click on **set variable value**.

   2. Under **Configure actions** in the **Select the variables to set** section, click on the checkbox next to **RepeaterCount**.

   3. Under **Configure actions** in the **Set variable to** section, select **value** in the first drop-down menu and enter 3 in the text field.

5. To toggle the **SetDetailCrossSellFilters** and cause the **Repeater** to reload, perform the following steps:

   1. Under **Click to add actions**, scroll to the **Widgets** drop-down menu. Under the **Show/Hide** drop-down menu, click on **Toggle Visibility**.

   2. Under **Configure actions**, in the **Select the widgets to hide/show** section, click on the checkbox next to **SetDetailCrossSellFilters**.

6. Click on **OK**.

Defining the SetDetailCrossSell3 case

To define the **SetDetailCrossSell3** case, do the following:

In the **Widget Interactions and Notes** pane with the **Interactions** tab selected, double-click on the **OnItemLoad** event. A **Case Editor** dialog box will open. Within the **Case Editor** dialog in the **Case Description** field, type `SetDetailCrossSell3` and perform the steps mentioned in the upcoming section.

Create the conditions

To add the first condition, perform the following steps:

- Click on the **Add Condition** button.
- In the **Condition Builder** dialog box, perform the following steps in the outlined condition box:
    1. In the first dropdown, select **value of variable**.
    2. In the second dropdown, select **ShowDetail**.
    3. In the third dropdown, select **equals**.
    4. In the fourth dropdown, select **value**.
    5. In the text field, enter 99.

To add the second condition, perform the following steps:

- Click on the green plus sign to add a second condition.
- In the **Condition Builder** dialog box, perform the following steps in the outlined condition box:
    1. In the first dropdown, select **value of variable**.
    2. In the second dropdown, select **RepeaterCount**.
    3. In the third dropdown, select **equals**.
    4. In the fourth dropdown, select **value**.
    5. In the text field, enter 3.

To add the third condition, perform the following steps:

- Click on the green plus sign to add a third condition.
- In the **Condition Builder** dialog box, perform the following steps in the outlined condition box:
    1. In the first dropdown, select **value of variable**.
    2. In the second dropdown, select **SKU_CrossSell3**.
    3. In the third dropdown, select **equals**.
    4. In the fourth dropdown, select **value**.
    5. In the text field, enter [[Item.SKU]].
    6. Click on **OK**.

Create the actions

1. To set image on **ItemImageCrossSell3**, perform the following steps:

    1. Under **Click to add actions**, scroll to the **Widgets** drop-down menu and click on **set image**.

    2. Under **Configure actions**, in the **Select the image widgets to set the image** section, click on the checkbox next to **ItemImageCrossSell3**.

    3. Under **Configure actions**, in the **Default** section, select **value** in the first drop-down menu and enter `[[Item.ItemImage]]` in the text field.

2. To set the text on **ItemBrandCrossSell3**, **ItemDescriptionCrossSell3**, and **ItemPriceCrossSell3**, perform the following steps:

    1. Under **Click to add actions**, scroll to the **Widgets** drop-down menu and click on **set the text**.

    2. Under **Configure actions** in the **Select the widgets to set text** section, click on the checkbox next to **ItemBrandCrossSell3**.

    3. Under **Configure actions** in the **Set variable to** section, select **value** in the first drop-down menu and enter `[[Item.ItemBrand]]` in the text field.

    4. Under **Configure actions** in the **Select the widgets to set text** section, click on the checkbox next to **ItemDescriptionCrossSell3**.

    5. Under **Configure actions** in the **Set variable to** section, select **value** in the first drop-down menu and enter `[[Item.ItemDescription]]` in the text field.

    6. Under **Configure actions** in the **Select the widgets to set text** section, click on the checkbox next to **ItemPriceCrossSell3**.

    7. Under **Configure actions** in the **Set variable to** section, select **value** in the first drop-down menu and enter `[[Item.ItemPrice]]` in the text field.

3. To show the **CrossSell3** widgets, perform the following steps:

    1. Under **Click to add actions**, scroll to the **Widgets** drop-down menu. Under the **Set Show/Hide** dropdown, click on **Show**.

    2. Under **Configure actions**, click on the checkbox next to **ItemImageCrossSell3, ItemBrandCrossSell3, ItemDescriptionCrossSell3, ItemPriceCrossSell3,** and **CurrencySymbolCrossSell3**.

4. Click on **OK**.

Defining the SetCatalog case

In the **Widget Interactions and Notes** pane with the **Interactions** tab selected, double-click on the **OnItemLoad** event. A **Case Editor** dialog box will open. Within the **Case Editor** dialog in the **Case Description** field, type SetCatalog and perform the steps mentioned in upcoming sections.

Create the conditions

To add the first condition, perform the following steps:

- Click on the **Add Condition** button.
- In the **Condition Builder** dialog box, perform the following steps in the outlined condition box:

  1. In the first dropdown, select **value of variable**.
  2. In the second dropdown, select **ShowCatalog**.
  3. In the third dropdown, select **is greater than**.
  4. In the fourth dropdown, select **value**.
  5. In the text field, enter 0.

To add the second condition, perform the following steps:

- Click on the green plus sign to add a second condition.
- In the **Condition Builder** dialog box, perform the following steps in the outlined condition box:

  1. In the first dropdown, select **value of variable**.
  2. In the second dropdown, select **ShowCatalog**.
  3. In the third dropdown, select **equals**.
  4. In the fourth dropdown, select **value**.
  5. In the text field, enter [[Item.SKU]].

To add the third condition, perform the following steps:

- Click on the green plus sign to add a third condition.
- In the **Condition Builder** dialog box, perform the following steps in the outlined condition box:

  1. In the first dropdown, select **value of variable**.
  2. In the second dropdown, select **SKU_CrossSell1**.

3. In the third dropdown, select **does not equal**.

4. In the fourth dropdown, select **value**.

5. In the text field, enter `Initalize`.

6. Click on **OK**.

Create the actions

1. To set image for Catalog Hero and CrossSells, perform the following steps:

   1. Under **Click to add actions**, scroll to the **Widgets** drop-down menu and click on **set image**.

   2. Under **Configure actions** in the **Select the image widgets to set the image** section, click on the checkbox next to **CatalogHeroImage**.

   3. Under **Configure actions** in the **Default** section, select **value** in the first drop-down menu and enter `[[Item.C_Hero_Image]]` in the text field.

   4. Under **Configure actions** in the **Select the image widgets to set the image** section, click on the checkbox next to **CrossSell1_Image**.

   5. Under **Configure actions** in the **Default** section, select **value** in the first drop-down menu and enter `[[Item.C_CS1_Image]]` in the text field.

   6. Under **Configure actions** in the **Select the image widgets to set the image** section, click on the checkbox next to **CrossSell2_Image**.

   7. Under **Configure actions**, in the **Default** section, select **value** in the first drop-down menu and enter `[[Item.C_CS2_Image]]` in the text field.

2. To set the variable for **SKU_CrossSell1** and **SKU_CrossSell2**, perform the following steps:

   1. Under **Click to add actions**, scroll to the **Variables** drop-down menu and click on **set variable value**.

   2. Under **Configure actions** in the **Select the variables to set** section, click on the checkbox next to **SKU_CrossSell1**.

   3. Under **Configure actions** in the **Set variable to** section, select **value** in the first drop-down menu and enter `[[Item.C_SKU_CS1]]` in the text field.

4. Under **Configure actions** in the **Select the variables to set** section, click on the checkbox next to **SKU_CrossSell2**.

5. Under **Configure actions** in the **Set variable to** section, select **value** in the first drop-down menu and enter `[[Item.C_SKU_CS2]]` in the text field.

3. To set the text on **CatalogHeadline**, perform the following steps:

    1. Under **Click to add actions**, scroll to the **Widgets** drop-down menu and click on **set the text**.

    2. Under **Configure actions**, in the **Select the widgets to set text** section, click on the checkbox next to **CatalogHeadline**.

    3. Under **Configure actions** in the **set the text to** section, select value in the first drop-down menu and enter `[[Item.ItemCategory]]` in the text field.

4. Click on **OK**.

Defining the InitializeCrossSell case

In the **Widget Interactions and Notes** pane with the Interactions tab selected, double-click on the **OnItemLoad** event. A **Case Editor** dialog box will open. Within the **Case Editor** dialog in the **Case Description** field, type `InitializeCrossSell` and perform the steps mentioned in the upcoming sections.

Create the condition

1. Click on the **Add Condition** button.

2. In the **Condition Builder** dialog box, perform the following steps in the outlined condition box:

    1. In the first dropdown, select **value of variable**.

    2. In the second dropdown, select **SKU_CrossSell1**.

    3. In the third dropdown, select **equals**.

    4. In the fourth dropdown, select **value**.

    5. In the text field, enter `Initalize`.

3. Click on **OK**.

Create the actions

1. To set the variable for **SKU_CrossSell1**, **SKU_CrossSell2**, **SKU_CrossSell3**, and **RepeaterCount**, perform the following steps:

    1. Under **Click to add actions**, scroll to the **Variables** drop-down menu and click on **set variable value**.

    2. Under **Configure actions** in the **Select the variables to set** section, click on the checkbox next to **SKU_CrossSell1**.

    3. Under **Configure actions** in the **Set variable to** section, select **value** in the first drop-down menu and enter `[[Item.C_SKU_CS1]]` in the text field.

    4. Under **Configure actions** in the **Select the variables to set** section, click on the checkbox next to **SKU_CrossSell2**.

    5. Under **Configure actions** in the **Set variable to** section, select **value** in the first drop-down menu and enter `[[Item.C_SKU_CS2]]` in the text field.

    6. Under **Configure actions** in the **Select the variables to set** section, click on the checkbox next to **SKU_CrossSell3**.

    7. Under **Configure actions** in the **Set variable to** section, select **value** in the first drop-down menu and enter `0` in the text field.

    8. Under **Configure actions** in the **Select the variables to set** section, click on the checkbox next to **RepeaterCount**.

    9. Under **Configure actions** in the **Set variable to** section, select **value** in the first drop-down menu and enter `0` in the text field.

2. To toggle the **SetDetailCrossSellFilters** and cause the **Repeater** to reload, perform the following steps:

    1. Under **Click to add actions**, scroll to the **Widgets** drop-down menu. Under the **Show/Hide** drop-down menu, click on **Toggle Visibility**.

    2. Under **Configure actions** in the **Select the widgets to hide/show** section, click on the checkbox next to **SetDetailCrossSellFilters**.

3. Click on **OK**.

4. Under the **OnItemLoad** event, right-click on the **InitializeCrossSell** case, and click on **Toggle IF/ELSE IF**.

With the **CategoryRepeater OnItemLoad** cases completed, we are now ready to define the Repeater item interaction.

Creating our Repeater item interaction

The Repeater item supports an **OnClick** event on the **ItemImageRepeater** widget. With the interaction defined, the design area with the Repeater item and the Widget interactions pane will look like this:

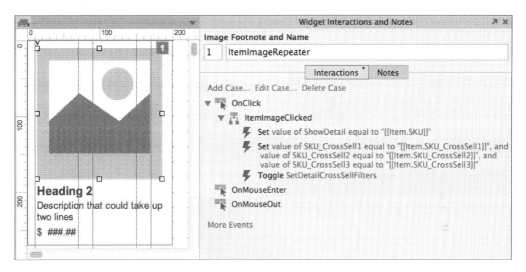

To create the interaction, open the **CMS Repeater** master in the design area and double-click on the **Repeater** to open the **CategoryRepeater** Repeater item in the design area. Click on the **ItemImageRepeater** at coordinates (13,10), in the **Widget Interactions and Notes** pane, double-click on the **OnClick** event. A **Case Editor** dialog box will open. In the **Case Description** field on the **Case Editor** dialog, type `ItemImageClicked`.

Creating and configuring actions

1. To set a variable value for **ShowDetail**, perform the following steps:

    1. Under **Click to add actions**, scroll to the **Variables** drop-down menu and click on **set variable value**.

    2. Under **Configure actions** in the **Select the variables to set** section, click on the checkbox next to **ShowDetail**.

    3. Under **Configure actions** in the **Set variable to** section, select **value** in the first drop-down menu and enter `[[Item.SKU]]` in the text field.

2. To set variable value for **SKU_CrossSell1**, **SKU_CrossSell2**, and **SKU_CrossSell3**, perform the following steps:

    1. Under **Click to add actions**, scroll to the **Variables** drop-down menu and click on **set variable value**.

    2. Under **Configure actions** in the **Select the variables to set** section, click on the checkbox next to **SKU_CrossSell1**.

    3. Under **Configure actions** in the **Set variable to** section, select **value** in the first drop-down menu and enter `[[Item.SKU_CrossSell1]]` in the text field.

    4. Under **Configure actions** in the **Select the variables to set** section, click on the checkbox next to **SKU_CrossSell2**.

    5. Under **Configure actions** in the **Set variable to** section, select **value** in the first drop-down menu and enter `[[Item.SKU_CrossSell2]]` in the text field.

    6. Under **Configure actions** in the **Select the variables to set** section, click on the checkbox next to **SKU_CrossSell3**.

    7. Under **Configure actions** in the **Set variable to** section, select **value** in the first drop-down menu and enter `[[Item.SKU_CrossSell3]]` in the text field.

3. To toggle the **SetDetailCrossSellFilters** and cause the **Repeater** to reload, perform the following steps:

    1. Under **Click to add actions**, scroll to the **Widgets** drop-down menu. Under the **Show/Hide** drop-down menu, click on **Toggle Visibility**.

    2. Under **Configure actions** in the **Select the widgets to hide/show** section, click on the checkbox next to **SetDetailCrossSellFilters**.

4. Click on **OK**.

With the **CategoryRepeater** and Repeater item interactions defined, we are now ready to create interactions for facetted filtering, sorting, and pagination.

Facetted Filtering, Sorting, and Pagination Widgets

We will start by placing widgets for facetted filtering, sorting, and pagination controls on the **CMS Repeater** master.

Designing the Facetted filters

To design the Facetted filters, in the **Masters** pane, double-click on the icon next to the **CMS Repeater** master to open in the design area. To add Brand Facetted filtering, from the **Widgets** pane, drag the **Tree** widget and place at coordinates (10,170).

With the **Tree** widget selected, perform the following steps:

- In the **Widget interactions and Notes** pane, click in the **Tree Name** field and type BrandFacettedFilterTree.

- Right-click on **Item 1** to open the **Tree Properties** pop up. Uncheck the checkbox next to **Show Expand/Collapse Icon**.

- Click on **Item 1** and type Brand. In the **Widget interactions and Notes** pane, click in the **Tree Node Name** field and type BrandFilter.

- Click on **Item 1.1** and type View All. In the **Widget interactions and Notes** pane, click in the **Tree Node Name** field and type BrandFilterViewAll.

- In the **Widget Properties and Style** pane, with the **Properties** tab selected scroll to the **Tree Node** dropdown and perform the following steps:

  1. Under **Interaction Styles**, click on **MouseOver**
  2. Click on the checkbox next to **Fill Color**.
  3. Click on the down arrow next to the paint bucket (Fill Color) icon.
  4. In the # field, enter C9C9C9.
  5. Under **Interaction Styles**, click on **Selected**.
  6. Click on the checkbox next to **Fill Color**.
  7. Click on the down arrow next to the paint bucket (Fill Color) icon.
  8. In the # field, enter E4E4E4.
  9. Click on **OK**.

- Click on **Item 1.2** and type A Fashion LTD. In the **Widget interactions and Notes** pane, click in the **Tree Node Name** field and type BrandFilterAFashionLTD.

- Click on **Item 1.3** and type B Fashion LTD. In the **Widget interactions and Notes** pane, click in the **Tree Node Name** field and type BrandFilterBFashionLTD.

- Right-click on **B Fashion LTD**, mouse over **Add**, and click on **Add Sibling After**.

- Click on **enter text...** and type C Fashion LTD. In the **Widget interactions and Notes** pane, click in the **Tree Node Name** field and type BrandFilterCFashionLTD.

- Right-click on **C Fashion LTD**, mouse over **Add**, and click on **Add Sibling After**.

- Click on **enter text...** and type D Fashion LTD. In the **Widget interactions and Notes** pane, click in the **Tree Node Name** field and type BrandFilterDFashionLTD.

Adding Price Facetted filtering

To add Price Facetted filtering, from the **Widgets** pane, drag the **Tree** widget and place at coordinates (10,290). With the **Tree** widget selected, perform the following steps:

1. In the **Widget interactions and Notes** pane, click in the **Tree Name** field and type PriceFacettedFilterTree.

2. Right-click on **Item 1** to open the **Tree Properties** pop up. Uncheck the checkbox next to **Show Expand/Collapse Icon**.

3. Click on **Item 1** and type Price. In the **Widget interactions and Notes** pane, click in the **Tree Node Name** field and type PriceFilter.

4. Click on **Item 1.1** and type View All. In the **Widget interactions and Notes** pane, click in the **Tree Node Name** field and type PriceFilterViewAll.

5. In the **Widget Properties and Style** pane, with the **Properties** tab selected scroll to **Tree Node** dropdown and perform the following steps:

    1. Under **Interaction Styles**, click on **MouseOver**

    2. Click on the checkbox next to **Fill Color**.

    3. Click on the down arrow next to the paint bucket (Fill Color) icon.

    4. In the # field, enter C9C9C9.

    5. Under **Interaction Styles**, click on **Selected**.

    6. Click on the checkbox next to **Fill Color**.

    7. Click on the down arrow next to the paint bucket (Fill Color) icon.

    8. In the # field, enter E4E4E4.

    9. Click on **OK**.

6. Click on **Item 1.2** and type $20.00 and Under. In the **Widget interactions and Notes** pane, click in the **Tree Node Name** field and type PriceFilter20Under.

7. Click on **Item 1.3** and type $50.00 and Under. In the **Widget interactions and Notes** pane, click in the **Tree Node Name** field and type PriceFilter50Under.

8. Right-click on **$50.00 and Under**, mouse over **Add** and click on **Add Sibling After**.

9. Click on **enter text…** and type $50.00 and Over. In the **Widget Interactions and Notes** pane, click in the **Tree Node Name** field and type PriceFilter50Over.

Adding Category facetted filtering

To add Category facetted filtering, from the **Widgets** pane, drag the **Tree** widget and place at coordinates (10,390). With the **Tree** widget selected, perform the following steps:

1. In the **Widget Interactions and Notes** pane, click in the **Tree Name** field and type CategoryFacettedFilterTree.

2. Right-click on **Item 1** to open the **Tree Properties** pop up. Uncheck the checkbox next to **Show Expand/Collapse Icon**.

3. Click on **Item 1** and type Category. In the **Widget Interactions and Notes** pane, click in the **Tree Node Name** field and type CategoryFilter.

4. Click on **Item 1.1** and type View All. In the **Widget Interactions and Notes** pane, click in the **Tree Node Name** field and type CategoryFilterViewAll.

5. In the **Widget Properties and Style** pane, with the **Properties** tab selected scroll to **Tree Node** dropdown and perform the following steps:

    1. Under **Interaction Styles**, click on **MouseOver**

    2. Click on the checkbox next to **Fill Color**.

    3. Click on the down arrow next to the paint bucket (Fill Color) icon.

    4. In the **#** field, enter C9C9C9.

    5. Under **Interaction Styles**, click on **Selected**

    6. Click on the checkbox next to **Fill Color**.

    7. Click on the down arrow next to the paint bucket (Fill Color) icon.

    8. In the **#** field, enter E4E4E4.

    9. Click on **OK**.

6. Click on **Item 1.2** and type Women. In the **Widget Interactions and Notes** pane, click in the **Tree Node Name** field and type CategoryFilterWomen.

7. Click on **Item 1.3** and type `Men`. In the **Widget interactions and Notes** pane, click in the **Tree Node Name** field and type `CategoryFilterMen`.

8. Right-click on **Men**, mouse over **Add** and click on **Add Sibling After**.

9. Click on **enter text...** and type `Kids`. In the **Widget interactions and Notes** pane, click in the **Tree Node Name** field and type `CategoryFilterKids`.

10. Right-click on **Kids**, mouse over **Add** and click on **Add Sibling After**.

11. Click on **enter text...** and type `Shoes`. In the **Widget Interactions and Notes** pane, click in the **Tree Node Name** field and type `CategoryFilterShoes`.

12. Right-click on **Shoes**, mouse over **Add** and click on **Add Sibling After**.

13. Click on **enter text...** and type `Accessories`. In the **Widget Interactions and Notes** pane, click in the **Tree Node Name** field and type `CategoryFilterAccessories`.

Designing Sorting and Pagination controls

To design sorting and pagination controls with the **CMS Repeater** master open in the design area, perform the following steps:

1. From the **Widgets** pane, drag the **Droplist** widget and place at coordinates (234,140). With the **Droplist** widget selected, perform the following steps:

    1. In the toolbar, change the value of **w** to `126` and **h** to `15`.

    2. In the **Widget interactions and Notes** pane, click in the **Droplist Name** field and type `SortByDroplist`.

    3. In the **Widget Properties and Style** pane, with the **Style** tab selected scroll to **Font** and change the font size to `11`.

    4. Right-click on the **Droplist** and click on **Edit List Items**. Click on the **Add Many** button and enter the following values (one per line):

        ◦ Newest
        ◦ Brand
        ◦ Price: Low to High
        ◦ Price: High to Low

- ° Click on **OK**.
- ° Click on the checkbox next to **Newest** to select as a default value and click on **OK**.

2. From the **Widgets** pane, drag the **Label** widget and place at coordinates (160,140). With the **Label** widget selected, perform the following steps:

   1. Type SORT BY: You will see **SORT BY:** displayed as text on the **Label** widget.
   2. In the toolbar, change the value of **w** to 74 and **h** to 15.
   3. In the **Widget Interactions and Notes** pane, click in the **Shape Name** field and type SortByLabel.
   4. Repeat step 2 placing **Label** widgets, coordinates, display text, toolbar changes (that is, **w**, **h** and **Hidden**) and **Shape Name**.

Coordinates	Text on label	Toolbar			Shape name
		w	**h**	**Hidden**	
(620,140)	1000	29	15		NumberOfItemsLabel
(652,140)	ITEMS	42	15		NumberOfItemsTextLabel
(762,140)	PAGE	38	15		PageLabel
(806,140)	1	8	15		Page1Link
(826,140)	2	8	15	Yes	Page2Link

 In the preceding table if column Hidden equals Yes, click on the checkbox next to **Hidden** in the toolbar.

3. To place the previous and next page rectangle widgets, from the **Widgets** pane, drag the **Rectangle** widget and place at coordinates (880,140). With the **Rectangle** widget selected, perform the following steps:

   1. Type <. You will see < displayed as text on the **Rectangle** widget.
   2. In the toolbar, change the value of **w** to 40 and **h** to 15.

3. In the **Widget interactions and Notes** pane, click in the **Shape Name** field and type `PreviousPage`.

4. From the **Widgets** pane, drag the **Rectangle** widget and place at coordinates (920,140). With the **Rectangle** widget selected, type >. You will see **>** displayed as text on the **Rectangle** widget.

5. In the toolbar, change the value of **w** to `40` and **h** to `15`.

6. In the **Widget Interactions and Notes** pane, click in the **Shape Name** field and type `NextPage`.

4. The **SetGlobalFilters Hot Spot** widget is used to remove and apply filters as well as force the Repeater to refresh Repeater items displayed.

 The **SetGlobalFilters Hot Spot** widget will not be interacted with or seen by the user of the prototype.

○ To place the **Hot Spot** widget, from the **Widgets** pane, drag the **Hot Spot** widget and place at coordinates (20,570). With the **Hot Spot** widget selected, in the **Widget Interactions and Notes** pane, click in the text field of the **Hot Spot Name** field and type `SetGlobalFilters`.

5. The SetDetailCrossSellFilters Hot Spot widget is used to remove and apply the Detail and Cross Sell filters as well as force the Repeater to refresh causing content to dynamically update on the Product Detail page. To place the **Hot Spot** widget, from the **Widgets** pane, drag the **Hot Spot** widget and place at coordinates (1010,180). With the **Hot Spot** widget selected, in the **Widget Interactions and Notes** pane, click in the **Hot Spot Footnote and Name** field and type `SetDetailCrossSellFilters`.

With facetted filtering, sorting, and pagination controls placed on the **CMS Repeater** master, we are ready to define the interactions.

Interactions for Facetted filtering, sorting, and pagination

To create interactions for facetted filtering, sorting, and pagination, we will first specify **Page Interactions** on the **CMS Repeater** master. Next, we will define interactions for the **CategoryRepeater**. Finally, we will define interactions for the facetted filtering, sorting, and pagination controls.

We will start by creating **Page Interactions** on the **CMS Repeater** master for the **OnPageLoad** event. Once complete, the **Page Properties** pane will look like this:

For the **OnPageLoad** event, the first six cases will be as follows:

- SetNumberOfItemsLabel
- SetCrossSellFilter
- NewestSort

- ShowPage2Link
- HidePage2Link
- ShowCatalog

In the **Masters** pane, double-click on the icon next to the **CMS Repeater** master to open in the design area. To create the **Page Interactions** on the **CMS Repeater** master for the **OnPageLoad** event, perform the steps mentioned in the upcoming sections.

Defining the SetNumberOfItemsLabel case

Under the design area in the **Page Properties** pane, click on the **Page Interactions** tab and double-click on the **OnPageLoad** event. A **Case Editor** dialog box will open. In the Case Description field on the **Case Editor** dialog, type `SetNumberOfItemLabel` and perform the steps mentioned in the upcoming sections.

Creating conditions

We need to add two conditions in the **SetRepeater** case.

Adding the first condition

Perform the following steps to create the condition:

1. Click on the **Add Condition** button.
2. In the **Condition Builder** dialog box, perform the following steps in the outlined condition box:
    1. In the first dropdown, select **value of variable**.
    2. In the second dropdown, select **ShowCatalog**.
    3. In the third dropdown, select **equals**.
    4. In the fourth dropdown, select **value**.
    5. In the text field, enter 0.

Adding the second condition

Perform the following steps to create the condition:

1. Click on the green plus sign to add a second condition.
2. In the **Condition Builder** dialog box, perform the following steps in the outlined condition box:
    1. In the first dropdown, select **value of variable**.
    2. In the second dropdown, select **ShowDetail**.

3. In the third dropdown, select **equals**.

4. In the fourth dropdown, select **value**.

5. In the text field, enter 0.

6. Click on **OK**.

Adding and configuring actions

To set the text on the **NumberOfItemsLabel** perform the following steps:

1. Under **Click to add actions**, scroll to the **Widgets** drop-down menu and click on **set the text**.

2. Under **Configure actions**, click on the checkbox next to **NumberOfItemsLabel**.

3. Under **set the text to**, click on the first dropdown and click on **value**.

4. Click on **fx**. An **Edit Text** dialog box will open.

5. Under **Local Variables**, click on the **Add Local Variable** link and perform the following steps:

    1. In the first text field, type LVAR1.

    2. In the second dropdown, select **widget**.

    3. In the third dropdown, select **CategoryRepeater**.

6. In the first textbox, replace the current text with [[LVAR1.itemCount]].

7. Click on **OK**.

Defining the SetCrossSellFilter case

To define the SetCrossSellFilter case, do the following:

Under the design area in the **Page Properties** pane, with the **Page Interactions** tab selected, double-click on the **OnPageLoad** event. A **Case Editor** dialog box will open. Within the **Case Editor** dialog in the **Case Description** field, type SetCrossSellFilter and perform the steps mentioned in the upcoming sections.

Create the condition

1. Click on the **Add Condition** button.

2. In the **Condition Builder** dialog box, perform the following steps in the outlined condition box:

    1. In the first dropdown, select **value of variable**.

    2. In the second dropdown, select **SKU_CrossSell1**.

    3. In the third dropdown, select **equals**.

    4. In the fourth dropdown, select **value**.

    5. In the text field, enter `Initialize`.

3. Click on **OK**.

Create the actions

1. To set the variable value of the **SKU_CrossSell1** item, perform the following steps:

    1. Under **Click to add actions**, scroll to the **Variables** drop-down menu and click on **set variable value**.

    2. Under **Configure actions** in the **Select the variables to set** section, click on the checkbox next to **SKU_CrossSell1**.

    3. Under **Configure actions** in the **Set variable to** section, select **value** in the first drop-down menu and enter `0` in the text field.

2. To toggle the **SetDetailCrossSellFilters** and cause the **Repeater** to reload, perform the following steps:

    1. Under **Click to add actions**, scroll to the **Widgets** drop-down menu. Under the **Show/Hide** drop-down menu, click on **Toggle Visibility**.

    2. Under **Configure actions**, in the **Select the widgets to hide/show** section, click on the checkbox next to **SetDetailCrossSellFilters**.

3. Click on **OK**.

4. Under the **OnPageLoad** event, right-click on the **SetCrossSellFilter** case and click on **Toggle IF/ELSE IF**.

Defining the NewestSort case

To define the NewestSort case, do the following:

Under the design area in the **Page Properties** pane, click on the **Page Interactions** tab and double-click on the **OnPageLoad** event. A **Case Editor** dialog box will open. Within the **Case Editor** dialog in the **Case Description** field, type NewestSort and perform the steps mentioned in the upcoming sections.

Create the conditions

To add the first condition, perform the following steps:

- Click on the **Add Condition** button.
- In the **Condition Builder** dialog box, perform the following steps in the outlined condition box:

    1. In the first dropdown, select **value of variable**.
    2. In the second dropdown, select **ShowCatalog**.
    3. In the third dropdown, select **equals**.
    4. In the fourth dropdown, select **value**.
    5. In the text field, enter 0.

To add the second condition, perform the following steps:

- Click on the green plus sign to add a second condition.
- In the **Condition Builder** dialog box, perform the following steps in the outlined condition box:

    1. In the first dropdown, select **value of variable**.
    2. In the second dropdown, select **ShowDetail**.
    3. In the third dropdown, select **equals**.
    4. In the fourth dropdown, select **value**.
    5. In the text field, enter 0.
    6. Click on **OK**.

Create the actions

1. To set the Brand, Price, and Category Filter's View All option to true, perform the following steps:

    1. Under **Click to add actions**, scroll to the **Widgets** drop-down menu. Under the **set selected/Checked** drop-down, click on **Selected**.

2. Under **Configure actions**, in the **Select the widgets to set selected state** section, click on the checkboxes next to **BrandFilterViewAll**, **PriceFilterViewAll**, and **CategoryFilterViewAll**.

2. To add Sort Newest to the Repeater, perform the following steps:

   1. Under **Click to add actions**, scroll to the **Repeaters** drop-down menu and click on **Add Sort**.

   2. Under **Configure actions**, in the **Select the repeaters to add sorting** section, click on the checkbox next to **CategoryRepeater**.

   3. In the **Name:** text field, type Newest.

   4. In the **Property:** dropdown, select **StockDate**.

   5. In the **Sort as:** dropdown, select **Date – YYYY-MM-DD**.

   6. In the **Order:** dropdown, select **Descending**.

3. Click on **OK**.

4. Under the **OnPageLoad** event, right-click on the **NewestSort** case and click on **Toggle IF/ELSE IF**.

Defining the ShowPage2Link case

To define the ShowPage2Link case, under the design area in the **Page Properties** pane, click on the **Page Interactions** tab and double-click on the **OnPageLoad** event. A **Case Editor** dialog box will open. Within the **Case Editor** dialog in the **Case Description** field, type ShowPage2Link and perform the steps mentioned in the upcoming sections.

Create the conditions

To add the first condition, perform the following steps:

- Click on the **Add Condition** button.

- In the **Condition Builder** dialog box, perform the following steps in the outlined condition box:

   1. In the first dropdown, select **text on widget**.

   2. In the second dropdown, select **NumberOfItemsLabel**.

   3. In the third dropdown, select **is greater than**.

   4. In the fourth dropdown, select **value**.

   5. In the text field, enter 8.

To add the second condition, perform the following steps:

- Click on the green plus sign to add a second condition.
- In the **Condition Builder** dialog box, perform the following steps in the outlined condition box:
  1. In the first dropdown, select **value of variable**.
  2. In the second dropdown, select **ShowCatalog**.
  3. In the third dropdown, select **equals**.
  4. In the fourth dropdown, select **value**.
  5. In the text field, enter 0.

To add the third condition, perform the following steps:

- Click on the green plus sign to add a third condition.
- In the **Condition Builder** dialog box, perform the following steps in the outlined condition box:
  1. In the first dropdown, select **value of variable**.
  2. In the second dropdown, select **ShowDetail**.
  3. In the third dropdown, select **equals**.
  4. In the fourth dropdown, select **value**.
  5. In the text field, enter 0.
  6. Click on **OK**.

Create the action

1. To show the **Page2Link** case perform the following steps:
   1. Under **Click to add actions**, scroll to the **Widgets** drop-down menu. Under the **Set Show/Hide** dropdown, click on **Show**.
   2. Under **Configure actions**, click on the checkbox next to **Page2Link**.

2. Click on **OK**.

3. Under the **OnPageLoad** event, right-click on the **ShowPage2Link** case and click on **Toggle IF/ELSE IF**.

Defining the HidePage2Link case

To define the HidePage2Link case, under the design area in the **Page Properties** pane, click on the **Page Interactions** tab and double-click on the **OnPageLoad** event. A **Case Editor** dialog box will open. Within the **Case Editor** dialog in the **Case Description** field, type HidePage2Link and perform the steps mentioned in the upcoming sections.

Create the conditions

To add the first condition, perform the following steps:

- Click on the **Add Condition** button.
- In the **Condition Builder** dialog box, perform the following steps in the outlined condition box:

    1. In the first dropdown, select **text on widget**.
    2. In the second dropdown, select **NumberOfItemsLabel**.
    3. In the third dropdown, select **is less than**.
    4. In the fourth dropdown, select **value**.
    5. In the text field, enter 8.

To add the second condition, perform the following steps:

- Click on the green plus sign to add a second condition.
- In the **Condition Builder** dialog box, perform the following steps in the outlined condition box:

    1. In the first dropdown, select **value of variable**.
    2. In the second dropdown, select **ShowCatalog**.
    3. In the third dropdown, select **equals**.
    4. In the fourth dropdown, select **value**.
    5. In the text field, enter 0.

To add the third condition, perform the following steps:

- Click on the green plus sign to add a third condition.
- In the **Condition Builder** dialog box, perform the following steps in the outlined condition box:

    1. In the first dropdown, select **value of variable**.
    2. In the second dropdown, select **ShowDetail**.
    3. In the third dropdown, select **equals**.
    4. In the fourth dropdown, select **value**.
    5. In the text field, enter 0.
    6. Click on **OK**.

Create the action

1. To Hide the **Page2Link** case perform the following steps:

   1. Under **Click to add actions**, scroll to the **Widgets** drop-down menu. Under the **Set Show/Hide** dropdown, click on **Hide**.

   2. Under **Configure actions**, click on the checkbox next to **Page2Link**.

2. Click on **OK**.

Defining the ShowCatalog case

To define the ShowCatalog case, under the design area in the **Page Properties** pane, click on the **Page Interactions** tab and double-click on the **OnPageLoad** event. A **Case Editor** dialog box will open. Within the **Case Editor** dialog in the **Case Description** field, type ShowCatalog and perform the steps mentioned in the upcoming sections.

Create the condition

1. Click on the **Add Condition** button.

2. In the **Condition Builder** dialog box, perform the following steps in the outlined condition box:

   1. In the first dropdown, select **value of variable**.

   2. In the second dropdown, select **ShowCatalog**.

   3. In the third dropdown, select **equals**.

   4. In the fourth dropdown, select **value**.

   5. In the text field, enter 0.

3. Click on **OK**.

Create the actions

1. To bring to front the CatalogDynamicPanel, perform the following steps:

   1. Under **Click to add actions**, scroll to the **Widgets** drop-down menu. Under the **Bring to Front/Back** dropdown, click on on **Bring to Front**.

   2. Under **Configure actions**, click on the checkbox next to **CatalogDynamicPanel**.

2. To show the CatalogDynamicPanel, perform the following steps:

   1. Under **Click to add actions**, scroll to the **Widgets** drop-down menu. Under the **Set Show/Hide** dropdown, click on on **Show**.

   2. Under **Configure actions**, click on the checkbox next to **CatalogDynamicPanel**.

3. Click on **OK**.

4. Under the **OnPageLoad** event, right-click on the **ShowCatalog** case and click on **Toggle IF/ELSE IF**.

With the **Page Interactions** for the **OnPageLoad** event defined on the **CMS Repeater** master, we are now ready to define interactions for the facetted filters.

Defining Facetted Filtering interactions

To keep track of the current state of each facetted filter, we will use the global variables **BrandFilter**, **PriceFilter**, and **CategoryFilter**. These variables start with an initial Default value of 0. When the user clicks on a node on the **BrandFilter**, **PriceFilter**, or **CategoryFilter** Tree widget, the corresponding variable and filter value is set prior to Toggling Visibility of the **SetGlobalFilters Hot Spot**. Toggling Visibility of the hotspot triggers the **OnShow** or **OnHide** event.

When the **OnShow** or **OnHide** event is triggered, all filters are first removed. Next, new filters are set based on the values stored in the **BrandFilter**, **PriceFilter**, and **CategoryFilter** global variables.

Finally, because the **SetGlobalFilters Hot Spot** widget changed state (that is, visibility was toggled), the **Repeater** reloads and displays the filtered **Repeater Dataset** items as specified by Repeater item interactions. Filtered **Repeater Dataset** items are then shown on the Repeater item as the Repeater iterates through the selected items from the **Repeater Dataset**.

To define interactions for nodes on the **BrandFilter**, **PriceFilter**, and **CategoryFilter** Tree widgets, open the **CMS Repeater** master in the design area and perform the steps mentioned in the upcoming sections.

Defining BrandFilter, PriceFilter, and CategoryFilter interactions

To define interactions for the first indented node on the **BrandFilter**, click on the BrandFilterViewAll node in the design area on the BrandFacettedFilterTree. Perform the steps given next.

In the **Widget Interactions and Notes** pane, double-click on the **OnClick** event. In the **Case Description** field, type SetBrandFilterViewAll. To create the actions, do the following:

- To set variable value for the **BrandFilter** label, perform the following steps:
  1. Under **Click to add actions**, scroll to the **Variables** drop-down menu and click on on **set variable value**.
  2. Under **Configure actions** in the **Select the variables to set** section, click on the checkbox next to **BrandFilter**.
  3. Under **Configure actions**, in the **Set variable to** section, select **value** in the first drop-down menu and enter None in the text field.

- To toggle the **SetDetailCrossSellFilters** and cause the **Repeater** to reload, perform the following steps:
  1. Under **Click to add actions**, scroll to the **Widgets drop-down** menu. Under the **Show/Hide** drop-down menu, click on **Toggle Visibility**.
  2. Under **Configure actions**, in the **Select the widgets to hide/show** section, click on the checkbox next to **SetDetailCrossSellFilters**.

- Click on **OK**.

Repeat the preceding step four more times to define the interactions for the remaining indented nodes on the BrandFacettedFilterTree using the following table:

BrandFilter node	Case description	Set variable value
BrandFilterAFashionLTD	SetBrandFilterA	A Fashion LTD
BrandFilterBFashionLTD	SetBrandFilterB	B Fashion LTD
BrandFilterCFashionLTD	SetBrandFilterC	C Fashion LTD
BrandFilterDFashionLTD	SetBrandFilterD	D Fashion LTD

To define interactions for the indented nodes on the **PriceFilter**, click on each indented node in the design area on the PriceFacettedFilterTree, repeating step 1 four more times to define the interactions using the following table:

PriceFilter node	Case description	Set variable	Set variable value
PriceFilterViewAll	SetPriceFilterViewAll	PriceFilter	None
PriceFilter20Under	SetPriceFilter20Under	PriceFilter	20Under
PriceFilter50Under	SetPriceFilter50Under	PriceFilter	50Under
PriceFilter50Over	SetPriceFilter50Over	PriceFilter	50Over

To define interactions for the indented nodes on the **CategoryFilter**, click on each indented node in the design area on the CategoryFacettedFilterTree, repeating step 1 six more times to define the interactions using the following table:

CategoryFilter node	Case description	Set variable	Set variable value
CategoryFilterViewAll	SetCategoryFilterViewAll	CategoryFilter	None
CategoryFilterWomen	SetCategoryFilterWomen	CategoryFilter	Women
CategoryFilterMen	SetCategoryFilterMen	CategoryFilter	Men
CategoryFilterKids	SetCategoryFilterKids	CategoryFilter	Kids
CategoryFilterShoes	SetCategoryFilterShoes	CategoryFilter	Shoes
CategoryFilterAccesories	SetCategoryFilterAccessories	CategoryFilter	Accessories

With the interactions for nodes on the **BrandFilter**, **PriceFilter**, and **CategoryFilter** Tree widgets defined, we are now ready to remove old filters from the **CMS Repeater** and set the new filters using the SetGlobalFilters hotspot. Next we will define cases for the **SetGlobalFilters Hot Spot**.

Defining Cases for our SetGlobalFilters hotspot

Since Toggling Visibility triggers the **SetGlobalFilters Hot Spot** interactions, we will have 18 identical cases defined for both **OnShow** and **OnHide** events. The following screenshot shows a complete set of cases for the **OnShow** event:

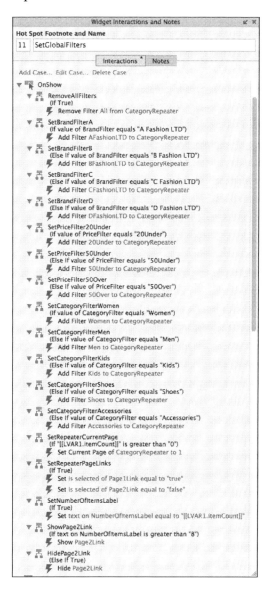

To define the filters set with the **SetGlobalFilters Hot Spot**, open the **CMS Repeater** master in the design area In the design area, click on on the **SetGlobalFilters Hot Spot** at coordinates (20,570). Perform the steps mentioned in the upcoming sections.

Defining the RemoveAllFilters case

In the **Widget Interactions and Notes** pane, double-click on the **OnShow** event. A **Case Editor** dialog box will open. Within the **Case Editor** dialog in the **Case Description** field, type RemoveAllFilters and create the actions by performing the following steps:

1. To remove all current filters, perform the following steps:

    1. Under **Click to add actions**, scroll to the **Repeaters** drop-down menu and click on on **Remove Filter**.

    2. Under **Configure actions**, in the **Select the repeaters to remove filters** section click on the checkbox next to **CategoryRepeater**.

    3. Click on the checkbox next to **Remove all filters**.

2. Click on **OK**.

Defining the SetBrandFilterA case

In the **Widget interactions and Notes** pane, double-click on the **OnShow** event. A **Case Editor** dialog box will open. Within the **Case Editor** dialog in the **Case Description** field, type SetBrandFilterA and perform the steps mentioned in the upcoming sections.

Create the condition

1. Click on the **Add Condition** button.

2. In the **Condition Builder** dialog box, perform the following steps in the outlined condition box:

    1. In the first dropdown, select **value of variable**.

    2. In the second dropdown, select **BrandFilter**.

    3. In the third dropdown, select **equals**.

    4. In the fourth dropdown, select **value**.

    5. In the text field, enter A Fashion LTD.

3. Click on **OK**.

Create the action

1. To add filter to **A FashionLTD** to the Repeater, perform the following steps:

    1. Under **Click to add actions**, scroll to the **Repeaters** drop-down menu and click on **Add Filter**.

    2. Under **Configure actions**, in the **Select the repeaters to add filters** section, click on the checkbox next to **CategoryRepeater**.

3. In the **Name:** text field, type `AFashionLTD`.

4. In the **Rule:** text field, type `[[Item.ItemBrand == 'A Fashion LTD']]`.

2. Click on **OK**.

3. Under the **OnShow** event, right-click on on the **SetBrandFilterA** case and click on **Toggle IF/ELSE IF**.

Defining additional Set Filter cases

Repeat the steps in the *Defining the SetBrandFilterA case* section 11 more times to define interactions for additional cases for the **SetGlobalFilters Hot Spot** using the following table:

Case description	Condition text field	Action name	Action rule	Toggle IF/ELSE IF
SetBrandFilterB	B Fashion LTD	BFashionLTD	[[Item.ItemBrand == 'B Fashion LTD']]	
SetBrandFilterC	C Fashion LTD	CFashionLTD	[[Item.ItemBrand == 'C Fashion LTD']]	
SetBrandFilterD	D Fashion LTD	DFashionLTD	[[Item.ItemBrand == 'D Fashion LTD']]	
SetPriceFilter20Under	20Under	20Under	[[Item.ItemPrice <= 20.00]]	Yes
SetPriceFilter50Under	50Under	50Under	[[Item.ItemPrice <= 50.00]]	
SetPriceFilter50Over	50Over	50Over	[[Item.ItemPrice >= 50.00]]	
SetCategoryFilterWomen	Women	Women	[[Item.ItemCategory == 'Women']]	Yes
SetCategoryFilterMen	Men	Men	[[Item.ItemCategory == 'Men']]	
SetCategoryFilterKids	Kids	Kids	[[Item.ItemCategory == 'Kids']]	
SetCategoryFilterShoes	Shoes	Shoes	[[Item.ItemCategory == 'Shoes']]	
SetCategoryFilterAccessories	Accessories	Accessories	[[Item.ItemCategory == 'Accessories']]	

> In the preceding table below, if column **Toggle IF/ELSE IF** equals Yes do the following, in the **Widgets Interactions and Notes** pane under the **OnShow** or **OnHide** event, right-click on on the corresponding **Case Description**, and click on **Toggle IF/ELSE IF**.

With all of the **SetFilter** cases defined, we are now ready to define the **SetRepeaterCurrentPage** case.

Defining the SetRepeaterCurrentPage case

In the **Widget interactions and Notes** pane, double-click on the **OnShow** event. A **Case Editor** dialog box will open. Within the **Case Editor** dialog in the **Case Description** field, type `SetRepeaterCurrentPage` and perform the steps mentioned in the upcoming sections.

Create the condition

Click on the **Add Condition** button. In the **Condition Builder** dialog box, perform the following steps in the outlined condition box:

1. In the first dropdown, select `value`
2. Next to the second field, click on **fx**. An **Edit Text** dialog box will open. Under **Local Variables,** click on the **Add Local Variable** link and perform the following steps:
    1. In the first text field, type `LVAR1`.
    2. In the second dropdown, select **widget**.
    3. In the third dropdown, select **CategoryRepeater**.
    4. In the first textbox, replace the current text with `[[LVAR1. itemCount]]`.
    5. Click on **OK**.
3. In the third dropdown, select **is greater than**.
4. In the fourth dropdown, select **value**.
5. In the text field, enter `0`.
6. Click on **OK**.

Create the action

1. To set current page of the Repeater, perform the following steps:

    1. Under **Click to add actions**, scroll to the **Repeaters** drop-down menu and click on **set current page**.

    2. Under **Configure actions**, in the **Select the repeaters to set current page** section, click on the checkbox next to **CategoryRepeater**.

    3. In the **Select the page:** drop-down, click on `Value`.

    4. In the **Page #** text field, type `1`.

2. Click on **OK**.

3. Under the **OnShow** event, right-click on the **SetRepeaterCurrentPage** case and click on **Toggle IF/ELSE IF**.

Defining the SetRepeaterPageLinks case

In the **Widget interactions and Notes** pane, double-click on the **OnShow** event. A **Case Editor** dialog box will open. Within the **Case Editor** dialog in the **Case Description** field, type `SetRepeaterPageLinks` and perform the steps mentioned in the upcoming sections.

Create the actions

1. To set selected the **Page1Link** case, perform the following steps:

    1. Under **Click to add actions**, scroll to the **Widgets** drop-down menu and under **set selected/Checked**, click on **Selected**.

    2. Under **Configure actions**, in the **Select the widgets to set selected state** section, click on the checkbox next to **Page1Link**.

    3. In the **Set selected state to:** drop-down click on `Value`.

    4. In the second dropdown, click on `true`.

2. To set not selected the **Page2Link** case, perform the following steps:

    1. Under **Click to add actions**, scroll to the **Widgets** drop-down menu; and under **set selected/Checked**, click on **Not Selected**.

    2. Under **Configure actions**, in the **Select the widgets to set selected state** section, click on the checkbox next to **Page2Link**.

    3. In the **Set selected state to:** drop-down, click on `Value`.

    4. In the second dropdown, click on `false`.

3. Click on **OK**.

4. Under the **OnShow** event, right-click on the **SetRepeaterPageLinks** case and click on **Toggle IF/ELSE IF**.

Defining the SetNumberOfItemsLabel case

In the **Widget interactions and Notes** pane, double-click on the **OnShow** event. A **Case Editor** dialog box will open. Within the **Case Editor** dialog in the **Case Description** field, type `SetRepeaterPageLinks` and perform the steps mentioned in the upcoming sections.

Create the action

To set the text on the **NumberOfItemsLabel**, perform the following steps:

1. Under **Click to add actions**, scroll to the **Widgets** drop-down menu and click on on **set the text**.

2. Under **Configure actions**, click on the checkbox next to **NumberOfItemsLabel**.

3. Under **set the text to**, click on the first dropdown and click on **value**.

4. Click on **fx**. An **Edit Text** dialog box will open.

5. Under **Local Variables** click on the **Add Local Variable** link and perform the following steps:

    1. In the first text field, type `LVAR1`.

    2. In the second dropdown, select **widget**.

    3. In the third dropdown, select **CategoryRepeater**.

6. In the first textbox, replace the current text with `[[LVAR1.itemCount]]`.

7. Click on **OK**.

8. Under the **OnShow** event, right-click on the **SetNumberOfItemsLabel** case and click on **Toggle IF/ELSE IF**.

Defining the ShowPage2Link case

In the **Widget interactions and Notes** pane, double-click on the **OnShow** event. A **Case Editor** dialog box will open. Within the **Case Editor** dialog in the **Case Description** field, type ShowPage2Link and perform the steps mentioned in the upcoming sections.

Create the condition

To add the first condition, perform the following steps:

1. Click on the **Add Condition** button.

2. In the **Condition Builder** dialog box, perform the following steps in the outlined condition box:

    1. In the first dropdown, select **text on widget**.
    2. In the second dropdown, select **NumberOfItemsLabel**.
    3. In the third dropdown, select **is greater than**.
    4. In the fourth dropdown, select **value**.
    5. In the text field, enter 8.
    6. Click on **OK**.

Create the action

To show the **Page2Link** perform the following steps:

1. Under **Click to add actions**, scroll to the **Widgets** drop-down menu. Under the **Set Show/Hide** dropdown, click on **Show**.

2. Under **Configure actions**, click on the checkbox next to **Page2Link**.

3. Click on **OK**.

4. Under the **OnPageLoad** event, right-click on the **ShowPage2Link** case and click on **Toggle IF/ELSE IF**.

Defining the HidePage2Link case

In the **Widget interactions and Notes** pane, double-click on the **OnShow** event. A **Case Editor** dialog box will open. Within the **Case Editor** dialog in the **Case Description** field, type `HidePage2Link` and perform the steps mentioned in the upcoming sections.

Create the action

1. To Hide the **Page2Link**, perform the following steps:

    1. Under **Click to add actions**, scroll to the **Widgets** drop-down menu. Under the **Set Show/Hide** drop-down, click on **Hide**.

    2. Under **Configure actions**, click on the checkbox next to **Page2Link**.

2. Click on **OK**.

Copying all OnShow cases to the OnHide event

To copy all cases from the **OnShow** event to the **OnHide** event, perform the following steps:

1. Under the **OnShow** event, perform the following steps:

    1. Click on the **RemoveAllFilters** case.

    2. Hold down the shift key, and click on on the last case, **HidePage2Link**. This selects all cases under the **OnShow** event.

    3. Right-click on it and click on **Copy**.

2. Right-click on the **OnHide** event and click on **Paste**. All cases from the **OnShow** event should now be visible under the **OnHide** event as well.

With interactions completed for the **SetGlobalFilters Hot Spot**, we are now ready to define interactions for sorting.

Creating sorting interactions

For sorting options, recall we defined four list options: **Newest, Brand, Price: Low to High**, and **Price: High to Low**. When the user interacts with the **SortByDropList** and changes the selection, the **OnSelectionChange** event is triggered. Once complete, the **Widget Interactions and Notes** pane for the **SortByDropList** will look like this:

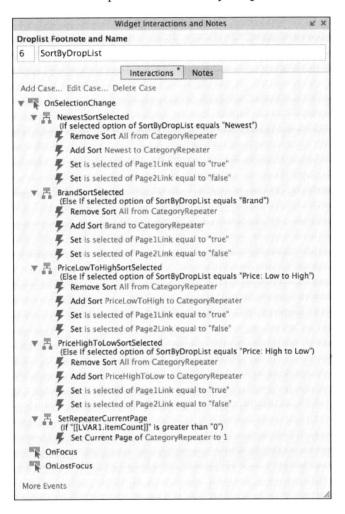

We will define four cases that will first set the appropriate sort and then set the current page of the Repeater.

Defining the NewestSortSelected case

With the **CMS Repeater** master open in the design area, perform the following steps:

In the design area, click on on the **SortByDropList** at coordinates (234,140). In the **Widget Interactions and Notes** pane, double-click on the **OnSelectionChange** event. A **Case Editor** dialog box will open. Within the **Case Editor** dialog in the **Case Description** field, type NewestSortSelected and perform the steps mentioned in the upcoming sections.

Create the condition

1. Click on the **Add Condition** button.

2. In the **Condition Builder** dialog box, perform the following steps in the outlined condition box:

    1. In the first dropdown, select **Selected option of**.

    2. In the second dropdown, select **SortByDropList**.

    3. In the third dropdown, select **equals**.

    4. In the fourth dropdown, select **option**.

    5. In the fifth dropdown, select **Newest**.

3. Click on **OK**.

Create the actions

1. To remove all current sorting, perform the following steps:

    1. Under **Click to add actions**, scroll to the **Repeaters** drop-down menu and click on on **Remove Sort**.

    2. Under **Configure actions** in the **Select the repeaters to remove filters** section, click on the checkbox next to **CategoryRepeater**.

    3. Click on the checkbox next to **Remove all sorting**.

2. To add sort newest to the **Repeater**, perform the following steps:

    1. Under **Click to add actions**, scroll to the **Repeaters** drop-down menu and click on **Add Sort**.

    2. Under **Configure actions** in the **Select the repeaters to add sorting** section, click on the checkbox next to **CategoryRepeater**.

    3. In the **Name:** text field, type Newest.

4. In the **Property:** dropdown, select **StockDate**.

5. In the **Sort as:** dropdown, select **Date – YYYY-MM-DD**.

6. In the **Order:** dropdown, select **Descending**.

3. To set selected the **Page1Link**, perform the following steps:

   1. Under **Click to add actions**, scroll to the **Widgets** drop-down menu, and under **set selected/Checked**, click on **Selected**.

   2. Under **Configure actions**, in the **Select the widgets to set selected state** section, click on the checkbox next to **Page1Link**.

   3. In the **Set selected state to:** drop-down, click on `Value`.

   4. In the second dropdown, click on `true`.

4. To set not selected the **Page2Link**, perform the following steps:

   1. Under **Click to add actions**, scroll to the **Widgets** drop-down menu, and under **set selected/Checked**, click on **Not Selected**.

   2. Under **Configure actions** in the **Select the widgets to set selected state** section, click on the checkbox next to **Page2Link**.

   3. In the **Set selected state to:** drop-down, click on `Value`.

   4. In the second dropdown, click on `false`.

5. Click on **OK**.

Defining additional Sort Selected cases

Repeat the steps in the *Defining the NewestSortSelected case* section three more times to define interactions for additional cases on the **SortByDropList** using the following table:

Case description	Condition for fifth drop-down	Action			
		Name:	Property:	Sort as:	Order:
BrandSortSelected	Brand	Brand	ItemBrand	Text	Ascending
PriceLowToHighSortSelected	Price: Low to High	PriceLowToHigh	ItemPrice	Number	Ascending
PriceHighToLowSortSelected	Price: High to Low	PriceHighToLow	ItemPrice	Number	Ascending

With the additional Sort Selected cases defined, we are now ready to define the SetRepeaterCurrentPage case.

Defining the SetRepeaterCurrentPage case

In the **Widget interactions and Notes** pane, double-click on the **OnShow** event. A **Case Editor** dialog box will open. Within the **Case Editor** dialog in the **Case Description** field, type `SetRepeaterCurrentPage` and perform the steps mentioned in the upcoming sections.

Create the condition

Click on the **Add Condition** button. In the **Condition Builder** dialog box, perform the following steps in the outlined condition box:

- In the first dropdown, select **value**
- Next to the second field, click on **fx**. An **Edit Text** dialog box will open. Under **Local Variables**, click on the **Add Local Variable** link and perform the following steps:

    1. In the first text field, type `LVAR1`.
    2. In the second dropdown, select **widget**.
    3. In the third dropdown, select **CategoryRepeater**.

- In the first textbox, replace the current text with `[[LVAR1.itemCount]]`.
- Click on **OK**.
    - In the third dropdown, select **is greater than**.
    - In the fourth dropdown, select **value**.
    - In the text field, enter `0`.

- Click on **OK**.

Create the action

1. To set the current page of the Repeater, perform the following steps:

    1. Under **Click to add actions**, scroll to the **Repeaters** drop-down menu and click on **set current page**.
    2. Under **Configure actions** in the **Select the repeaters to set current page** section, click on the checkbox next to **CategoryRepeater**.
    3. In the **Select the page:** dropdown, click on `Value`.
    4. In the **Page #** text, field type `1`.

2. Click on **OK**.

3. Under the **OnShow** event, right-click on the **SetRepeaterCurrentPage** case and click on **Toggle IF/ELSE IF**.

With interactions completed for sorting, we are now ready to define interactions for pagination.

Enabling pagination

For pagination interactions, we will define **OnClick** events for **Page1Link**, **Page2Link**, **PreviousPage**, and **NextPage** widgets. With the **CMS Repeater** master open in the design area, perform the steps mentioned in the upcoming sections.

Defining the Page1Link OnClick event

To define the **OnClick** event for the **Page1link** case, do the following:

In the design area, click on the **Page1Link** at coordinates (806,140). In the **Widget interactions and Notes** pane, double-click on the **OnClick** event. In the **Case Editor** dialog, perform the steps mentioned in the upcoming sections.

Create the actions

1. To set the current page of the Repeater to page 1, perform the following steps:

    1. Under **Click to add actions**, scroll to the **Repeaters** drop-down menu and click on **set current page**.

    2. Under **Configure actions** in the **Select the repeaters to set current page** section, click on the checkbox next to **CategoryRepeater**.

    3. In the **Select the page:** drop-down, click on `Value`.

    4. In the **Page #** text field, type `1`.

2. To set selected the **Page1Link**, perform the following steps:

    1. Under **Click to add actions**, scroll to the **Widgets** drop-down menu, and under **set selected/Checked**, click on **Selected**.

    2. Under **Configure actions** in the **Select the widgets to set selected state** section, click on the checkbox next to **Page1Link**.

    3. In the **Set selected state to:** drop-down, click on `Value`.

    4. In the second dropdown, click on `true`.

3. To set not selected the **Page2Link**, perform the following steps:

    1. Under **Click to add actions**, scroll to the **Widgets** drop-down menu, and under **set selected/Checked**, click on **Not Selected**.

    2. Under **Configure actions** in the **Select the widgets to set selected state** section, click on the checkbox next to **Page2Link**.

    3. In the **Set selected state to:** drop-down, click on Value.

    4. In the second dropdown, click on false.

4. Click on **OK**.

Defining the Page2Link OnClick event

To define the **OnClick** event for the **Page2Link**, do the following:

In the design area, click on the **Page2Link** at coordinates (826,140). In the **Widget Interactions and Notes** pane, double-click on the **OnClick** event. A **Case Editor** dialog box will open. In the **Case Editor** dialog, perform the steps mentioned in upcoming section:

Create the actions

1. To set the current page of the **Repeater** to page 2, perform the following steps:

    1. Under **Click to add actions**, scroll to the **Repeaters** drop-down menu and click on **set current page**.

    2. Under **Configure actions** in the **Select the repeaters to set current page** section, click on the checkbox next to **CategoryRepeater**.

    3. In the **Select the page:** drop-down, click on Value.

    4. In the **Page #** text field, type 2.

2. To set selected the **Page2Link**, perform the following steps:

    1. Under **Click to add actions**, scroll to the **Widgets** drop-down menu, and under **set selected/Checked**, click on **Selected**.

    2. Under **Configure actions** in the **Select the widgets to set**

    3. **selected state** section, click on the checkbox next to **Page2Link**.

    4. In the **Set selected state to:** dropdown, click on Value.

    5. In the second dropdown, click on true.

3. To set not selected the **Page1Link**, perform the following steps:

    1. Under **Click to add actions**, scroll to the **Widgets** drop-down menu and under **set selected/Checked**, click on **Not Selected**.

    2. Under **Configure actions** in the **Select the widgets to set selected state** section, click on the checkbox next to **Page1Link**.

    3. In the **Set selected state to:** drop-down, click on `Value`.

    4. In the second dropdown, click on `false`.

4. Click on **OK**.

Defining the PreviousPage OnClick event

To define the **OnClick** events for the **PreviousPage** widget, click on on the **PreviousPage** widget at coordinates (880,140) in the design area. Next we will define three cases: SetRepeaterCurrentPage, PageIndexPage1, and NotPage1.

Defining the SetRepeaterCurrentPage case

In the **Widget Interactions and Notes** pane, double-click on the **OnClick** event. A **Case Editor** dialog box will open. Within the **Case Editor** dialog in the **Case Description** field, type `SetRepeaterCurrentPage`, create the action, and perform the following steps:

1. To set the current page of the Repeater to **Previous**, perform the following steps:

    1. Under **Click to add actions**, scroll to the **Repeaters** drop-down menu and click on **set current page**.

    2. Under **Configure actions** in the **Select the repeaters to set current page** section, click on the checkbox next to **CategoryRepeater**.

    3. In the **Select the page:** drop-down, click on `Previous`.

2. Click on **OK**.

Defining the PageIndexPage1 case

In the **Widget interactions and Notes** pane, double-click on the **OnClick** event. A **Case Editor** dialog box will open. Within the **Case Editor** dialog in the **Case Description** field, type `PageIndexPage1` and, perform the steps mentioned in upcoming sections.

Create the condition

Click on the **Add Condition** button. In the **Condition Builder** dialog box, perform the following steps in the outlined condition box:

1. In the first dropdown, select **value**.
2. Next to the second field, click on **fx**. An **Edit Text** dialog box will open. Under **Local Variables**, click on the **Add Local Variable** link and perform the following steps:
   1. In the first text field, type LVAR1.
   2. In the second dropdown, select **widget**.
   3. In the third dropdown, select **CategoryRepeater**.
   4. In the first textbox, replace the current text with [[LVAR1. itemCount]].
   5. Click on **OK**.
3. In the third dropdown, select **equals**.
4. In the fourth dropdown, select **value**.
5. In the text field, enter 1.
6. Click on **OK**.

Create the actions

1. To set selected the **Page1Link**, perform the following steps:
   1. Under **Click to add actions**, scroll to the **Widgets** drop-down menu, and under **set selected/Checked**, click on **Selected**.
   2. Under **Configure actions** in the **Select the widgets to set selected state** section, click on the checkbox next to **Page1Link**.
   3. In the **Set selected state to:** drop-down, click on Value.
   4. In the second dropdown, click on true.
2. To set not selected the **Page2Link**, perform the following steps:
   1. Under **Click to add actions**, scroll to the **Widgets** drop-down menu, and under **set selected/Checked**, click on **Not Selected**.
   2. Under **Configure actions** in the **Select the widgets to set selected state** section, click on the checkbox next to **Page2Link**.

3. In the **Set selected state to:** drop-down, click on `Value`.

4. In the second dropdown, click on `false`.

3. Click on **OK**.

4. Under the **OnClick** event, right-click on the **PageIndexPage1** case and click on **Toggle IF/ELSE IF**.

Defining the NotPage1 case

In the **Widget Interactions and Notes** pane, double-click on the **OnClick** event. A **Case Editor** dialog box will open. Within the **Case Editor** dialog in the **Case Description** field, type `NotPage1`, and perform the steps mentioned in the upcoming sections.

Create the condition

Click on the **Add Condition** button. In the **Condition Builder** dialog box, perform the following steps in the outlined condition box:

1. In the first dropdown, select **value**.

2. Next to the second field, click on **fx**. An **Edit Text** dialog box will open. Under **Local Variables**, click on the **Add Local Variable** link and perform the following steps:

   1. In the first text field, type `LVAR1`.

   2. In the second dropdown, select **widget**.

   3. In the third dropdown, select **CategoryRepeater**.

   4. In the first textbox, replace the current text with `[[LVAR1.itemCount]]`.

   5. Click on **OK**.

3. In the third dropdown, select **equals**.

4. In the fourth dropdown, select **value**.

5. In the text field enter `2`.

6. Click on **OK**.

Create the actions

1. To set selected the **Page2Link**, perform the following steps:

    1. Under **Click to add actions**, scroll to the **Widgets** drop-down menu, and under **set selected/Checked**, click on **Selected**.

    2. Under **Configure actions** in the **Select the widgets to set selected state** section, click on the checkbox next to **Page2Link**.

    3. In the **Set selected state to:** dropdown, click on `Value`.

    4. In the second dropdown, click on `true`.

2. To set not selected the **Page1Link**, perform the following steps:

    1. Under **Click to add actions**, scroll to the **Widgets** drop-down menu, and under **set selected/Checked**, click on **Not Selected**.

    2. Under **Configure actions** in the **Select the widgets to set selected state** section, click on the checkbox next to **Page1Link**.

    3. In the **Set selected state to:** drop-down, click on `Value`.

    4. In the second dropdown, click on `false`.

3. Click on **OK**.

Creating the NextPage OnClick events

To create the **OnClick** events for the **NextPage** widget, click on on the **PreviousPage** widget at coordinates (920,140) in the design area Next we will define three cases: SetRepeaterCurrentPage, PageIndexPage1, and NotPage1.

Defining the SetRepeaterCurrentPage case

To define the SetRepeaterCurrentPage case, perform the following steps:

In the **Widget interactions and Notes** pane, double-click on the **OnClick** event. A **Case Editor** dialog box will open. Within the **Case Editor** dialog in the **Case Description** field, type `SetRepeaterCurrentPage`.

Create the action

To set current page of the Repeater to **Next**, perform the following steps:

1. Under **Click to add actions**, scroll to the **Repeaters** drop-down menu and click on **set current page**.

2. Under **Configure actions** in the **Select the repeaters to set current page** section, click on the checkbox next to **CategoryRepeater**.

3. In the **Select the page:** dropdown, click on `Next`.

Defining the PageIndexPage2 case

To define the PageIndexPage2 case, double-click on the **OnClick** event in the **Widget interactions and Notes** pane. A **Case Editor** dialog box will open. In the **Case Editor** dialog in the **Case Description** field, type `PageIndexPage2` and perform the steps mentioned in the upcoming sections.

Create the condition

Click on the **Add Condition** button. In the **Condition Builder** dialog box, perform the following steps in the outlined condition box:

1. In the first dropdown, select **value**
2. Next to the second field, click on **fx**. An **Edit Text** dialog box will open. Under **Local Variables**, click on the **Add Local Variable** link and perform the following steps:
   1. In the first text field, type `LVAR1`.
   2. In the second dropdown, select **widget**.
   3. In the third dropdown, select **CategoryRepeater**.
   4. In the first textbox, replace the current text with `[[LVAR1.pageIndex]]`.
   5. Click on **OK**.

3. In the third dropdown, select **equals**.
4. In the fourth dropdown, select **value**.
5. In the text field, enter `2`.
6. Click on **OK**.

Create the actions

1. To set selected the **Page2Link**, perform the following steps:
   1. Under **Click to add actions**, scroll to the **Widgets** drop-down menu, and under **set selected/Checked**, click on **Selected**.
   2. Under **Configure actions** in the **Select the widgets to set selected state** section, click on the checkbox next to **Page2Link**.
   3. In the **Set selected state to:** dropdown, click on `Value`.
   4. In the second dropdown, click on `true`.

2. To set not selected the **Page1Link**, perform the following steps:

   1. Under **Click to add actions**, scroll to the **Widgets** drop-down menu, and under **set selected/Checked**, click on **Not Selected**.

   2. Under **Configure actions** in the **Select the widgets to set selected state** section, click on the checkbox next to **Page1Link**.

   3. In the **Set selected state to:** dropdown, click on `Value`.

   4. In the second dropdown, click on `false`.

3. Click on **OK**.

4. Under the **OnClick** event, right-click on on the **PageIndexPage2** case and click on **Toggle IF/ELSE IF**.

With Repeater item widgets placed and the **Repeater Dataset** defined, we are now ready to create the Catalog and Detail Dynamic Panels with interactions.

Summary

Using a single Repeater widget, we created a Dynamic Content Management System (CMS). This CMS provides content for the Catalog, Category, and Detail pages. You learned how to apply Faceted Filtering, Sorting, and Pagination on the **Repeater Dataset**.

In the next chapter, we will complete interactions for the SetDetailCrossSellFilter Hot Spot widget. We will build the interactive Category page and use the Header, CMS Repeater and Footer masters with dynamic panels to create the Product and Detail pages.

Self-test questions

- What was the first step we took prior to designing our Catalog Repeater?

- How many parts does a Repeater have and what are the parts typically known as?

- Explain how a Repeater operates.

- How many Repeaters did we use for the Catalog, Category and Product Detail designs and what were the name(s) of the Repeater(s)?

- For the Repeater on the CMS Repeater master, how many columns did the Repeater Dataset have?

- How did we group the columns for the Category Repeater's Dataset?

- Name the widgets on the Repeater item for the Category Repeater.

- What are the minimum and maximum Cross Sell Items that our Category Repeater is designed to utilize?

- For the ItemImageRepeater when an Item Image is clicked, what Global Variables are set prior to showing Product Details?

- When an Item Image is clicked, what action defined in the ItemImageClicked case causes the ItemImageRepeater to reload?

5
Product Pages and Interactions

With the Catalog Repeater in place on the **CMS Repeater** master, we are now ready to place masters on the **Category**, **Catalog**, and **Product** pages as well as complete any remaining interactions.

In this chapter, you will learn about:

- Enhancing Masters, Interactions, and Design
    - Augmenting our CMS Repeater master
    - Completing our Header master

- Designing our Category page
- Designing our Catalog page
    - Creating the Design and Interactions for our Catalog page

- Defining the OnPageLoad event for the Catalog page
    - Building the CatalogDynamicPanel

- Enabling a Catalog with Cross-Sell state
- Completing the Item Detail Design
- Creating a Cross-Sell Design
- Defining Cross-Sell Interactions
- Enabling Social Media Interactions

Enhancing masters, interactions, and design

Before designing the **Category**, **Catalog**, and **Product** pages, there are a few remaining widgets and interactions that need to be added to the **CMS Repeater** master and **Header** master. We will complete the **CMS Repeater** master by adding Catalog and Product Dynamic Panels as well as by creating the interactions for the **SetDetailCrossSellFilter** Hot Spot widget. We will then add interactions to the **Header** master's HzMenu widget enabling the **OnClick** event for each menu item.

Augmenting our CMS Repeater master

Our **CMS Repeater** master leverages a single Repeater to dynamically update the Catalog, Category and Product Detail designs. We will first add Dynamic Panels to facilitate the Category, and Product Detail designs. Next, since we have defined interactions for the **CMS Repeater**, we also need to add additional interactions for the **SetDetailCrossSellFilter Hot Spot**. Once the Dynamic Panels have been placed and the **SetDetailCrossSellFilter** hotspot interactions have been specified, we will update the main menu interactions on the **Header** master.

Crafting our Catalog and Product dynamic panels

Dynamic Panels can be used to hide and swap content. We will add a **CatalogDynamicPanel** and a **DetailDynamicPanel** to our **CMS Repeater** master enabling the Catalog and Product Detail designs to be leveraged from the same master.

To place the **CatalogDynamicPanel** and the **DetailDynamicPanel** on the **CMS Repeater** master, open the **CMS Repeater** master in the design area and perform the following steps:

1. From the **Widgets** pane, drag the **Dynamic Panel** widget and place at coordinates (0,140). With the **Dynamic Panel** widget selected, perform the following steps:

    1. In the toolbar, change the value of **w** to 960, **h** to 824 and click on the checkbox next to **Hidden**.

2. In the **Widget Interactions and Notes** pane, click in the **Dynamic Panel Name** field and type `CatalogDynamicPanel`.

3. In the **Widget Manager** pane, slow double-click on the **State** name **State1** and rename to `CatalogWithCrossSell`.

2. From the Widgets pane, drag the **Dynamic Panel** widget and place at coordinates (94,130). With the **Dynamic Panel** widget selected, perform the following steps:

1. In the toolbar, change the value of **w** to `930`, **h** to `700` and click on the checkbox next to **Hidden**.

2. In the **Widget Interactions and Notes** pane, click in the **Dynamic Panel Name** field and type `DetailDynamicPanel`.

3. In the **Widget Manager** pane, slow double-click on the **State** name **State1** and rename to `ItemDetailWithCrossSell`.

With the **CatalogDynamicPanel** and **DetailDynamicPanel** placed on our **CMS Repeater** master, we are now ready to complete the remaining interactions for the DetailCrossSellFilter.

Creating DetailCrossSellFilter interactions

Our **CMS Repeater** master leverages a single Repeater to dynamically update the Catalog, Category and Product Detail designs. We have defined all interactions for the CMS Repeater except for the **SetDetailCrossSellFilter Hot Spot**. Once these interactions have been specified, we will then be ready to update the main menu interactions on the **Header** master.

The **SetDetailCrossSellFilter** hotspot widget is used to remove and apply the Detail and Cross-Sell filters on the **CategoryRepeater**. Toggling visibility of the Hot Spot forces the Repeater to refresh. Once the Repeater has refreshed, content is then dynamically updated on the Product Detail page. Since Toggling visibility triggers the **SetGlobalFilters Hot Spot** interactions, we will have five identical cases defined for both **OnShow** and **OnHide** events. The following screenshot shows a complete set of cases for the **OnShow** event:

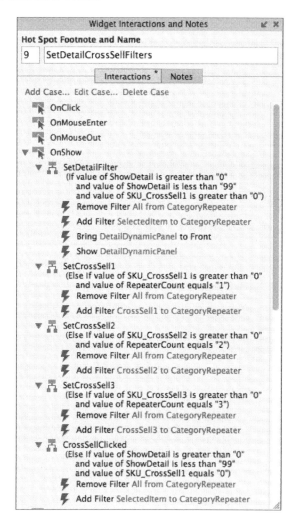

To define the filters set with the **SetDetailCrossSellFilter Hot Spot,** open the **CMS Repeater** master in the design area and create the cases mentioned in the upcoming sections.

Defining the SetDetailCrossSellFilter case

In the design area, click on the **SetDetailCrossSellFilter Hot Spot** at coordinates (1010,180).

In the **Widget Interactions and Notes** pane, double-click on the **OnShow** event. A **Case Editor** dialog box will open. Within the **Case Editor** dialog in the **Case Description** field, type `SetDetailFilter` and perform the steps mentioned in the upcoming sections.

Create the conditions

To add the first condition, perform the following steps:

1. Click on the **Add Condition** button.
2. In the **Condition Builder** dialog box, perform the following steps in the outlined condition box:
   1. In the first dropdown, select **value of variable**.
   2. In the second dropdown, select **ShowDetail**.
   3. In the third dropdown, select **is greater than**.
   4. In the fourth dropdown, select **value**.
   5. In the text field, enter `0`.

To add the second condition, perform the following steps:

1. Click on the green plus sign to add a second condition.
2. In the **Condition Builder** dialog box, perform the following steps in the outlined condition box:
   1. In the first dropdown, select **value of variable**.
   2. In the second dropdown, select **ShowDetail**.
   3. In the third dropdown, select **is less than**.
   4. In the fourth dropdown, select **value**.
   5. In the text field, enter `99`.

To add the third condition perform the following steps:

1. Click on the green plus sign to add a third condition.
2. In the **Condition Builder** dialog box, perform the following steps in the outlined condition box:
    1. In the first dropdown, select **value of variable**.
    2. In the second dropdown, select **SKU_CrossSell1**.
    3. In the third dropdown, select **is greater then**.
    4. In the fourth dropdown, select **value**.
    5. In the text field, enter 0.
    6. Click on **OK**.

Create the actions

To remove all filters, perform the following steps:

1. Under **Click to add actions**, scroll to the **Repeaters** drop-down menu and click on **Remove Filter**.
2. Under **Configure actions**, in the **Select the repeaters to remove filters** section click on the checkbox next to **CategoryRepeater**.
3. Click on the checkbox next to **Remove all filters**.

To add the **SelectedItem** filter to the Repeater, perform the following steps:

1. Under **Click to add actions**, scroll to the **Repeaters** drop-down menu and click on **Add Filter**.
2. Under **Configure actions**, in the **Select the repeaters to add filters** section, click on the checkbox next to **CategoryRepeater**.
3. In the **Name:** text field, type AFashionLTD.
4. In the **Rule:** text field, type [[Item.SKU == ShowDetail].

To bring to front the **DetailDynamicPanel** widget, perform the following steps:

1. Under **Click to add actions**, scroll to the **Widgets** drop-down menu, and in the **Bring to Front/Back** drop-down menu, click on **Bring to Front**.
2. Under **Configure actions**, in the **Select the widgets to send to back or bring to front** section, click on the checkbox next to **DetailDynamicPanel**.
3. Next to **Order**, click on the radio button next to **Bring to Front**.

To show the **DetailDynamicPanel**, perform the following steps:

1. Under **Click to add actions**, scroll to the **Widgets** drop-down menu, and in the **Show/Hide** drop-down menu, click on **Show**.

2. Under **Configure actions**, in the **Select the widgets to hide/show** section, click on the checkbox next to **DetailDynamicPanel**.

3. Next to **Visibility**, click on the radio button next to **Show**.

4. Click on **OK**.

Defining the SetCrossSell1 case

In the **Widget Interactions and Notes** pane, double-click on the **OnShow** event. A **Case Editor** dialog box will open. Within the **Case Editor** dialog in the **Case Description** field, type `SetCrossSell1` and perform the steps mentioned in the upcoming sections.

Create the conditions

To add the first condition, perform the following steps:

1. Click on the **Add Condition** button.

2. In the **Condition Builder** dialog box, perform the following steps in the outlined condition box:

    1. In the first dropdown, select **value of variable**.

    2. In the second dropdown, select the condition variable name **SKU_CrossSell1**.

    3. In the third dropdown, select **is greater than**.

    4. In the fourth dropdown, select **value**.

    5. In the text field, enter the condition value `0`.

To add the second condition, perform the following steps:

1. Click on the green plus sign to add a second condition.

2. In the **Condition Builder** dialog box, perform the following steps in the outlined condition box:

    1. In the first dropdown, select **value of variable**.

    2. In the second dropdown, select the condition variable name **RepeaterCount**.

    3. In the third dropdown, select **equals**.

4. In the fourth dropdown, select **value**.

5. In the text field, enter the condition value 1.

6. Click on **OK**.

Create the actions

To remove all filters, perform the following steps:

1. Under **Click to add actions**, scroll to the **Repeaters** drop-down menu and click on **Remove Filter**.

2. Under **Configure actions**, in the **Select the repeaters to remove filters** section click on the checkbox next to **CategoryRepeater**.

3. Click on the checkbox next to **Remove all filters**.

To add filter to the Repeater, perform the following steps:

1. Under **Click to add actions**, scroll to the **Repeaters** drop-down menu and click on **Add Filter**.

2. Under **Configure actions**, in the **Select the repeaters to add filters** section, click on the checkbox next to **CategoryRepeater**.

3. In the **Name:** text field, type the action name CrossSell1.

4. In the **Rule:** text field, type the action rule [[Item.SKU == SKU_ CrossSell1]].

5. Click on **OK**.

Defining the CrossSell2 and CrossSell3 cases

Repeat the steps mentioned in *Defining the SetCrossSell1 case* section two more times to define interactions for additional cases on the **SetDetailCrossSellFilter** Hot Spot using the following table:

Case description	Condition	Condition variable name	Condition value	Action name	Action rule
SetCrossSell2	First	SKU_CrossSell2	0	CrossSell2	[[Item.SKU == SKU_CrossSell2]]
	Second	RepeaterCount	2		
SetCrossSell3	First	SKU_CrossSell3	0	CrossSell3	[[Item.SKU == SKU_CrossSell3]]
	Second	RepeaterCount	3		

Defining the CrossSellClicked case

In the **Widget Interactions and Notes** pane, double-click on the **OnShow** event. A **Case Editor** dialog box will open. Within the **Case Editor** dialog in the **Case Description** field, type `CrossSellClicked` and perform the steps mentioned in the upcoming sections.

Create the conditions

To add the first condition, perform the following steps:

1. Click on the **Add Condition** button.
2. In the **Condition Builder** dialog box, perform the following steps in the outlined condition box:
    1. In the first dropdown, select **value of variable**.
    2. In the second dropdown, select **ShowDetail**.
    3. In the third dropdown, select **is greater than**.
    4. In the fourth dropdown, select **value**.
    5. In the text field, enter `0`.

To add the second condition, perform the following steps:

1. Click on the green plus sign to add a second condition.
2. In the **Condition Builder** dialog box, perform the following steps in the outlined condition box:
    1. In the first dropdown, select **value of variable**.
    2. In the second dropdown, select **ShowDetail**.
    3. In the third dropdown, select **is less than**.
    4. In the fourth dropdown, select **value**.
    5. In the text field, enter `99`.

To add the third condition, perform the following steps:

1. Click on the green plus sign to add a third condition.
2. In the **Condition Builder** dialog box, perform the following steps in the outlined condition box:
    1. In the first dropdown, select **value of variable**.
    2. In the second dropdown, select **SKU_CrossSell1**.
    3. In the third dropdown, select **equals**.

4. In the fourth dropdown, select **value**.

5. In the text field, enter 0.

6. Click on **OK**.

Create the actions

To remove all filters, perform the following steps:

1. Under **Click to add actions**, scroll to the **Repeaters** drop-down menu and click on **Remove Filter**.

2. Under **Configure actions**, in the **Select the repeaters to remove filters** section, click on the checkbox next to **CategoryRepeater**.

3. Click on the checkbox next to **Remove all filters**.

To add the **SelectedItem** filter to the Repeater, perform the following steps:

1. Under **Click to add actions**, scroll to the **Repeaters** drop-down menu and click on **Add Filter**.

2. Under **Configure actions**, in the **Select the repeaters to add filters** section, click on the checkbox next to **CategoryRepeater**.

3. In the **Name:** text field, type SelectedItem.

4. In the **Rule:** text field, type [[Item.SKU == ShowDetail]].

5. Click on **OK**.

With interactions completed for the **SetDetailCrossSellFilter** Hot Spot, we are now ready to define interactions for the main menu on the **Header** master.

Copying all OnShow cases to the OnHide event

To copy all cases from the **OnShow** event to the **OnHide** event, perform the following steps:

1. Under the **OnShow** event, perform the following steps:

   1. Click on the **SetDetailFilter** case.

   2. Hold down the *Shift* key, and click on the last case, **CrossSellClicked**. This selects all cases under the **OnShow** event.

   3. Right-click on it and click on **Copy**.

2. Right-click on the **OnHide** event and click on **Paste**. All cases from the **OnShow** event should now be visible under the **OnHide** event as well.

Completing our Header master

To complete our **Header** master, we will need to add interactions to the main menu named **HzMenu**. When a user clicks on a menu item, the **ShowCatalog** Global Variable is set to a corresponding Category value and the **Catalog** page is opened in the current window.

Defining main menu interactions

After a menu item is clicked, the **OnClick** event sets the ShowCatalog Global Variable. The following table lists Category names and values:

Category name	Category value
Women	1
Men	2
Kids	3
Shoes	4
Accessories	5

To define the interactions for the **HzMenu** on the **Header** master, in the **Masters** pane double-click on the **Header** master. The **Header** master will open in the design area.

1. In the design area, click on the **HzMenu** at coordinates (240,80) and in the **Widget Properties and Style** pane, with the **Properties** tab selected, scroll to **Tree Node** dropdown and perform the following steps:

2. Under **Interaction Styles**, click on **MouseOver**.

3. Click on the checkbox next to **Fill Color**.

4. Click on the down arrow next to the Paint Bucket (Fill Color) icon.

5. In the # field, enter C9C9C9.

6. Click off of the drop-down menu to close.

7. Click on **OK**.

Click on the first menu item **Woman**. With the menu item named **HZMenuWoman** selected, double-click on the **OnClick** event and perform the following steps to create the actions:

1. In the **Case Description** field, type `HzMenuWomanClicked`.

2. To set the variable value for **ShowCatalog**, perform the following steps:

    1. Under **Click to add actions**, scroll to the **Variables** drop-down menu and click on **Set Variable Value**.

    2. Under **Configure actions**, in the **Select the variables to set** section, click on the checkbox next to **ShowCatalog**.

    3. Under **Configure actions**, in the **Set variable to** section, in the first drop-down menu select **value** and enter variable value `1`.

3. To open the **Catalog** page in the current window, perform the following steps:

    1. Under **Click to add actions**, scroll to the **Links** drop-down menu. Under the **Open Link** drop-down menu, click on **Current Window**.

    2. Under **Configure actions**, with the **Link to a page in this design** radio button selected, in the **Sitemap**, click on the **Catalog** page.

    3. Click on **OK**.

Repeat step 2 four more times to define interactions for additional cases on the remaining **HzMenu** items using the following table:

Menu item name	Action set variable name
HzMenuMen	2
HzMenuKids	3
HzMenuShoes	4
HzMenuAccessories	5

With the main menu interactions completed on the **Header** master, we are now ready to design and define interactions for the **Category** page.

Designing our Category page

The **Category** page comprises the **Header**, **CMS Repeater**, and **Footer** masters.
The **Category Repeater** item on the **CMS Repeater** master is used to populate
the **Category Product** grid. Items displayed on the grid are based on results
from the Faceted Filtering and Sorting of the **Repeater Dataset**.

Once completed, our **Category** page will look like this:

To build the **Category** page, we will first place the **Header**, **CMS Repeater**,
and **Footer** masters. Next, we will define the **OnPageLoad** interaction to
initialize variables.

Creating the design and interactions for our Category page

To create the **Category** page, perform the following steps:

1. In the **Sitemap** pane, double-click on the **Category** page to open it in the design area. In the **Masters** pane, click on the **Header** master. While holding down
   the mouse button, drag the **Header** master and drop it at any location on the wireframe.

2. In the **Masters** pane, click on the **CMS Repeater** master. While holding down the mouse button, drag the **CMS Repeater** master and drop it at any location on the wireframe. In the **Widget Interactions and Notes** pane, in the **CMS Repeater** name field, type `CatalogRepeaterMaster`.

3. In the **Masters** pane, click on the **Footer** master. While holding down the mouse button, drag the **Footer** master and place at coordinates (10,970).

With the design complete for the **Category** page, we are now ready to define the **OnPageLoad** interaction.

Defining the OnPageLoad event for the Category page

There will be a single case for the OnPageLoad event. Define the OnPageLoad interaction with the **Category** page still open in the design area by performing the steps mentioned in the upcoming sections.

Defining the InitializeVars case

Under the design area in the **Page Properties** pane, click on the **Page Interactions** tab and double-click on the **OnPageLoad** event. A **Case Editor** dialog box will open. Within the **Case Editor** dialog box in the **Case Description** field, type `InitializeVars` and perform the steps mentioned in the upcoming sections.

Create the conditions

To add the first condition, perform the following steps:

1. Click on the **Add Condition** button.

2. In the **Condition Builder** dialog box, perform the following steps in the outlined condition box:

    1. In the first dropdown, select **value of variable**.

    2. In the second dropdown, select **ShowDetail**.

    3. In the third dropdown, select **equals**.

    4. In the fourth dropdown, select **value**.

    5. In the text field, enter 0.

    6. Click on **OK**.

Create the actions

To set the variable value of the **BrandFilter**, **PriceFilter**, and **CategoryFilter** items, perform the following steps:

1. Under **Click to add actions**, scroll to the **Variables** drop-down menu and click on **Set Variable Value**.

2. Under **Configure actions**, in the **Select the variables to set** section, click on the checkbox next to **SKU_CrossSell2**.

3. Under **Configure actions**, in the **Set variable to** section, select **value** in the first drop-down menu and enter 0 in the text field.

4. Under **Configure actions**, in the **Select the variables to set** section, click on the checkbox next to **SKU_CrossSell3**.

5. Under **Configure actions**, in the **Set variable to** section, select **value** in the first drop-down menu and enter 0 in the text field.

6. Under **Configure actions**, in the **Select the variables to set** section, click on the checkbox next to **ShowDetail**.

7. Under **Configure actions**, in the **Set variable to** section, select **value** in the first drop-down menu and enter 0 in the text field.

8. Under **Configure actions**, in the **Select the variables to set** section, click on the checkbox next to **RepeaterCount**.

9. Under **Configure actions**, in the **Set variable to** section, select **value** in the first drop-down menu and enter 0 in the text field.

10. Click on **OK**.

With the **Category** page completed, we are now ready to design the **Catalog** page.

Designing our Catalog page

The Catalog page comprises the **Header**, **CMS Repeater**, and **Footer** masters. The **CatalogDynamicPanel** on the **CMS Repeater** master is used to build the Catalog Image template. Images displayed on the template are determined by the value of **ShowCatalog**. If the value of **ShowCatalog** is greater then 0, then on page load the **CMS Repeater** master will bring the **CatalogDynamicPanel** to the front and show the Dynamic Panel.

Once completed, our **Category** page will look like this:

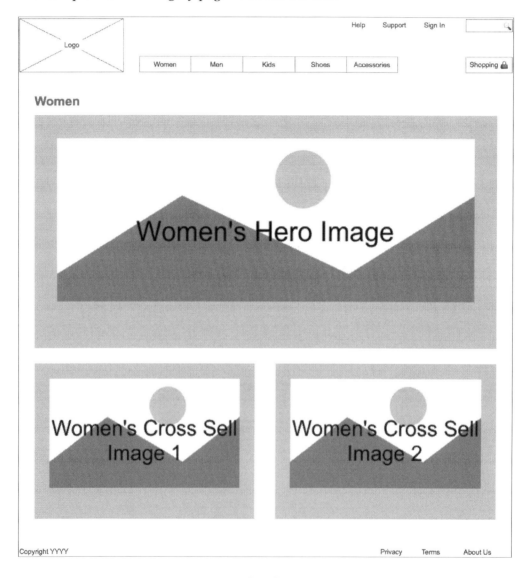

To design the **Catalog** page, we will first place the **Header**, **CMS Repeater**, and **Footer** masters. Next we will define the **OnPageLoad** interaction to initialize the variables.

Creating the Design and Interactions for our Catalog page

To design the **Catalog** page, perform the following steps:

1. In the **Sitemap** pane, double-click on the **Catalog** page to open in the design area.

2. In the **Masters** pane, click on the **Header** master. While holding down the mouse button, drag the **Header** master and drop it at any location on the wireframe.

3. In the **Masters** pane, click on the **CMS Repeater** master. While holding down the mouse button, drag the **CMS Repeater** master and drop it at any location on the wireframe. Perform the following:

   ◦ In the **Widget Interactions and Notes** pane, type `CatalogRepeaterMaster` in the **CMS Repeater Name** field.

4. In the **Masters** pane, click on the **Footer** master. While holding down the mouse button, drag the **Footer** master and place at coordinates (10,990).

With the design complete for the **Catalog** page, we are now ready to define the **OnPageLoad** interaction. There will be a total of three cases for the **OnPageLoad** event. Once completed, the **Page Properties** page will look like this:

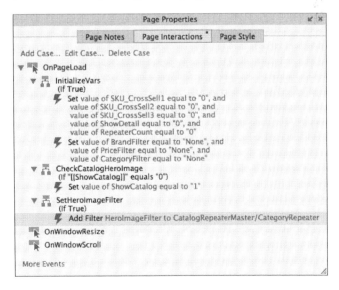

Defining the OnPageLoad event for the Catalog page

To define the **OnPageLoad** interaction, with the **Catalog** page still open in the design area, perform the steps mentioned in the upcoming sections.

Defining the InitializeVars case

Under the design area in the **Page Properties** pane, click on the **Page Interactions** tab and double-click on the **OnPageLoad** event. A **Case Editor** dialog box will open. Within the **Case Editor** dialog box, in the **Case Description** field, type InitializeVars and perform the steps mentioned in the upcoming sections.

Create the conditions

To add the first condition, perform the following steps:

1. Click on the **Add Condition** button.
2. In the **Condition Builder** dialog box, perform the following steps in the outlined condition box:

    1. In the first dropdown, select **value of variable**.
    2. In the second dropdown, select **SKU_CrossSell1**.
    3. In the third dropdown, select **equals**.
    4. In the fourth dropdown, select **value**.
    5. In the text field, enter 0.

To add the second condition, perform the following steps:

1. Click on the green plus sign to add a second condition.
2. In the **Condition Builder** dialog box, perform the following steps in the outlined condition box:

    1. In the first dropdown, select **value of variable**.
    2. In the second dropdown, select **SKU_CrossSell2**.
    3. In the third dropdown, select **equals**.
    4. In the fourth dropdown, select **value**.
    5. In the text field, enter 0.

To add the third condition, perform the following steps:

1. Click on the green plus sign to add a third condition.
2. In the **Condition Builder** dialog box, perform the following steps in the outlined condition box:

    1. In the first dropdown, select **value of variable**.
    2. In the second dropdown, select **SKU_CrossSell3**.
    3. In the third dropdown, select **equals**.
    4. In the fourth dropdown, select **value**.
    5. In the text field, enter 0.

To add the fourth condition, perform the following steps:

1. Click on the green plus sign to add a fourth condition.
2. In the **Condition Builder** dialog box, perform the following steps in the outlined condition box:

    1. In the first dropdown, select **value of variable**.
    2. In the second dropdown, select **ShowDetail**.
    3. In the third dropdown, select **equals**.
    4. In the fourth dropdown, select **value**.
    5. In the text field, enter 0.

To add the fifth condition, perform the following steps:

1. Click on the green plus sign to add a fifth condition.
2. In the **Condition Builder** dialog box, perform the following steps in the outlined condition box:

    1. In the first dropdown, select **value of variable**.
    2. In the second dropdown, select **RepeaterCount**.
    3. In the third dropdown, select **equals**.
    4. In the fourth dropdown, select **value**.
    5. In the text field, enter 0.
    6. Click on **OK**.

Create the actions

To set the variable value of the **BrandFilter**, **PriceFilter**, and **CategoryFilter** items perform the following steps:

1. Under **Click to add actions**, scroll to the **Variables** drop-down menu and click on **Set Variable Value**.

2. Under **Configure actions**, in the **Select the variables to set** section, click on the checkbox next to **BrandFilter**.

3. Under **Configure actions**, in the **Set variable to** section, select **value** in the first drop-down menu select and enter None in the text field.

4. Under **Configure actions**, in the **Select the variables to set** section, click on the checkbox next to **PriceFilter**.

5. Under **Configure actions**, in the **Set variable to** section, select **value** in the first drop-down menu and enter None in the text field.

6. Under **Configure actions**, in the **Select the variables to set** section, click on the checkbox next to **CategoryFilter**.

7. Under **Configure actions**, in the **Set variable to** section, select **value** in the first drop-down menu and enter None in the text field.

8. Click on **OK**.

Defining the CheckCatalogHeroImage case

Under the design area in the **Page Properties** pane, with the **Page Interactions** tab selected, double-click on the **OnPageLoad** event. A **Case Editor** dialog box will open. Within the **Case Editor** dialog in the **Case Description** field, type CheckCatalogHeroImage and perform the steps mentioned in the upcoming sections.

Create the condition

1. Click on the **Add Condition** button.

2. In the **Condition Builder** dialog box, perform the following steps in the outlined condition box:

   1. In the first dropdown, select **value of variable**.

   2. In the second dropdown, select **ShowCatalog**.

   3. In the third dropdown, select **equals**.

   4. In the fourth dropdown, select **value**.

   5. In the text field, enter 0.

3. Click on **OK**.

Create the action

1. To set the variable value of the **ShowCatalog** item perform the following steps:

    1. Under **Click to add actions**, scroll to the **Variables** drop-down menu and click on **Set Variable Value**.

    2. Under **Configure actions**, in the **Select the variables to set** section, click on the checkbox next to **ShowCatalog**.

    3. Under **Configure actions**, in the **Set variable to** section, select **value** in the first drop-down menu and enter 1 in the text field.

2. Click on **OK**.

3. Under the **OnPageLoad** event, right-click on the **SetCrossSellFilter** case and click on **Toggle IF/ELSE IF**.

Defining the SetHeroImageFilter case

Under the design area in the **Page Properties** pane, click on the **Page Interactions** tab and double-click on the **OnPageLoad** event. A **Case Editor** dialog box will open. Within the **Case Editor** dialog box in the **Case Description** field, type `SetHeroImageFilter` and perform the steps given in the following section.

Create the action

1. To add the filter, HeroImageFilter, to the Repeater, perform the following steps:

    1. Under **Click to add actions**, scroll to the **Repeaters** drop-down menu and click on **Add Filter**.

    2. Under **Configure actions**, in the **Select the repeaters to add filters** section, click on the checkbox next to **CategoryRepeater**.

    3. In the **Name:** text field, type `HeroImageFilter`.

    4. In the **Rule:** text field, type `[[Item.SKU == ShowCatalog]]`

2. Click on **OK**.

3. Under the **OnPageLoad** event, right-click on the **NewestSort** case and click on **Toggle IF/ELSE IF**.

With the **OnPageLoad** interaction for the **Catalog** page completed, we are now ready to finish the **CatalogDynamicPanel**.

Building the CatalogDynamicPanel

To complete the **CatalogDynamicPanel**, we will need to rename **State1**, place widgets, and define interactions.

Enabling a CatalogWithCrossSell state

To update the **CategoryDynamicPanel** on the **CMS Repeater** master, we will place widgets on the **CatalogWithCrossSell** state and define interactions for those widgets.

Designing the CatalogDynamicPanel

To start our design, we will first place the **CatalogBackground** and **CatalogHeadline** on the **CatalogDynamicPanel**. Open the **CMS Repeater** master in the design area. In the **Widget Manager**, under the **CatalogDynamicPanel**, click on the state icon two times to open the **CatalogWithCrossSell** state in the design area.

To place the CatalogBackground on the **CatalogDynamicPanel** state, perform the following steps:

1. From the **Widget** pane, drag the **Rectangle** widget and place at coordinates (10,0). With the **Rectangle** widget selected, perform the following steps:

    1. In the toolbar, change the value of **w** to 950 and **h** to 824.

    2. In the **Widget Interactions and Notes** pane, click in the **Shape Name** field and type CatalogBackground.

    3. In the **Widget Properties and Style** pane, scroll to **Borders, Lines, + Fills** with the **Style** tab selected and click on the down arrow next to the second dropdown Line Width icon . In the drop-down menu, click on none to indicate no line.

To place the **CatalogHeadline** on the **CatalogDynamicPanel** state, perform the following steps:

1. From the **Widget** pane, drag the **Heading 2** widget and place at coordinates (39,10). With the **Heading 2** widget selected, perform the following steps:

    1. In the toolbar, change the value of **w** to 892.

    2. In the **Widget Interactions and Notes** pane, click in the **Shape Name** field and type CatalogHeadline.

    3. In the **Widget Properties and Style** pane, scroll to **Font** with the **Style** tab selected and click on the down arrow next to the A (Text Color) icon. In the drop-down menu, in the **#** text field enter 797979.

Next we will place the **CatalogHeroImage** on the **CatalogDynamicPanel** state.

Creating the CatalogHeroImage with interactions

To place and define interactions for the **CatalogHeroImage** on the
CatalogDynamicPanel state, from the **Widget** pane, drag the **Image** widget
and place at coordinates (39,49). With the **Image** widget selected, perform
the following steps:

1. In the toolbar, change the value of **w** to 892 and **h** to 432.

2. In the **Widget Interactions and Notes** pane, click in the **Image Name** field
   and type CatalogHeroImage.

3. In the **Widget Interactions and Notes** pane, double-click on the **OnClick**
   event. In the **Case Description** field, type CatalogHeroImageClicked.

Create the actions

1. To set the variable values for **SetCategory**, perform the following steps:

   1. Under **Click to add actions**, scroll to the **Variables** drop-down menu
      and click on **Set Variable Value**.

   2. Under **Configure actions** in the **Select the variables to set** section,
      click on the checkbox next to **SetCategory**.

   3. Under **Configure actions**, in the **Set variable to** section, in the first
      drop-down menu select **value of variable** and in the second drop-
      down menu select **ShowCatalog**.

2. To set the variable value for **ShowCatalog**, **SKU_CrossSell1**, and **SKU_
   CrossSell2** items, perform the following steps:

   1. Under **Click to add actions**, scroll to the **Variables** drop-down menu
      and click on **Set Variable Value**.

   2. Under **Configure actions** in the **Select the variables to set** section,
      click on the checkbox next to **ShowCatalog**.

   3. Under **Configure actions** in the **Set variable to** section, select **value**
      in the first drop-down menu and enter 0 in the text field.

   4. Under **Configure actions** in the **Select the variables to set** section,
      click on the checkbox next to **SKU_CrossSell1**.

   5. Under **Configure actions** in the **Set variable to** section, select **value**
      in the first drop-down menu and enter 0 in the text field.

6. Under **Configure actions** in the **Select the variables to set** section, click on the checkbox next to **SKU_CrossSell2**.

7. Under **Configure actions** in the **Set variable to** section, select **value** in the first drop-down menu and enter 0 in the text field.

3. To open the **Category** page in the current window, perform the following steps:

    1. Under **Click to add actions**, scroll to the **Links** drop-down menu. Under the **Open Link** drop-down menu, click on **Current Window**.

    2. Under **Configure actions**, with the **Link to a page in this design** radio button selected, in the **Sitemap** click on the **Category** page.

4. Click on **OK**.

Creating the CrossSell1_Image with interactions

To place and define interactions for the **CrossSell1_Image** on the **CatalogDynamicPanel** state, from the **Widget** pane, drag the **Image** widget and place at coordinates (39,509). With the **Image** widget selected, perform the following steps:

1. In the toolbar, change the value of **w** to 426 and **h** to 288.

2. In the **Widget Interactions and Notes** pane, click in the **Image Name** field and type CrossSell1_Image.

3. In the **Widget Interactions and Notes** pane, double-click on the **OnClick** event.

4. In the **Case Description** field, type CrossSell1_Image_Clicked.

Create the actions

To set the variable value for the **ShowDetail** item, perform the following steps:

1. Under **Click to add actions**, scroll to the **Variables** drop-down menu and click on **Set Variable Value**.

2. Under **Configure actions**, in the **Select the variables to set** section, click on the checkbox next to **ShowDetail**.

3. Under **Configure actions** in the **Set variable to** section, select **value of variable** in the first drop-down menu and **SKU_CrossSell1** in the second drop-down menu.

To set the variable values for **ShowCatalog**, **SKU_CrossSell1**, and **SKU_CrossSell2** items, perform the following steps:

1. Under **Click to add actions**, scroll to the **Variables** drop-down menu and click on **Set Variable Value**.

2. Under **Configure actions** in the **Select the variables to set** section, click on the checkbox next to **ShowCatalog**.

3. Under **Configure actions** in the **Set variable to** section, select **value** in the first drop-down menu and enter 0 in the text field.

4. Under **Configure actions** in the **Select the variables to set** section, click on the checkbox next to **SKU_CrossSell1**.

5. Under **Configure actions** in the **Set variable to** section, select **value** in the first drop-down menu and enter Initialize in the text field.

6. Under **Configure actions** in the **Select the variables to set** section, click on the checkbox next to **SKU_CrossSell2**.

7. Under **Configure actions** in the **Set variable to** section, select **value** in the first drop-down menu and enter 0 in the text field.

To open the **Category** page in the current window, perform the following steps:

1. Under **Click to add actions**, scroll to the **Links** drop-down menu. Under the **Open Link** drop-down menu, click on **Current Window**.

2. Under **Configure actions**, with the **Link to a page in this design** radio button selected, in the **Sitemap** click on the **Category** page.

3. Click on **OK**.

Creating the CrossSell2_Image with interactions

To place and define interactions for the **CrossSell2_Image** on the **CatalogDynamicPanel** state, from the **Widget** pane, drag the **Image** widget and place at coordinates (505,509). With the **Image** widget selected, perform the following steps:

1. In the toolbar, change the value of **w** to 426 and **h** to 288.

2. In the **Widget Interactions and Notes** pane, click in the **Image Name** field and type CrossSell2_Image.

3. In the **Widget Interactions and Notes** pane, double-click on the **OnClick** event.

4. In the **Case Description** field, type CrossSell2_Image_Clicked.

Create the actions

To set the variable value for the **ShowDetail** item, perform the following steps:

1. Under **Click to add actions**, scroll to the **Variables** drop-down menu and click on **Set Variable Value**.

2. Under **Configure actions**, in the **Select the variables to set** section, click on the checkbox next to **ShowDetail**.

3. Under **Configure actions**, in the **Set variable to** section, select **value of variable** in the first drop-down menu and **SKU_CrossSell2** in the second drop-down menu.

To set the variable values for **ShowCatalog**, **SKU_CrossSell1**, and **SKU_CrossSell2** items, perform the following steps:

1. Under **Click to add actions**, scroll to the **Variables** drop-down menu and click on **Set Variable Value**.

2. Under **Configure actions** in the **Select the variables to set** section, click on the checkbox next to **ShowCatalog**.

3. Under **Configure actions** in the **Set variable to** section, select **value** in the first drop-down menu and enter 0 in the text field.

4. Under **Configure actions** in the **Select the variables to set** section, click on the checkbox next to **SKU_CrossSell1**.

5. Under **Configure actions** in the **Set variable to** section, select **value** in the first drop-down menu and enter 0 in the text field.

6. Under **Configure actions**, in the **Select the variables to set** section, click on the checkbox next to **SKU_CrossSell2**.

7. Under **Configure actions**, in the **Set variable to** section, select **value** in the first drop-down menu and enter Initialize in the text field.

To open the **Category** page in the current window, perform the following steps:

1. Under **Click to add actions**, scroll to the **Links** drop-down menu. Under the **Open Link** drop-down menu, click on **Current Window**.

2. Under **Configure actions**, with the **Link to a page in this design** radio button selected, click on the **Category** page in the **Sitemap**.

3. Click on **OK**.

With the **Catalog** page as well as the **CategoryDynamicPanel** on the **CMS Repeater** master complete, we are now ready to design the Product Detail page.

Making our DetailDynamicPanel

By showing the **DetailDynamicPanel** widget (which is part of the Category Repeater built from the **CMS Repeater** master) on the **Category** page, a dynamic Product Detail page is created. The **DetailDynamicPanel** on the **CMS Repeater** master is used to build the Detail Image template. Images displayed on the template are determined by the value of ShowDetail. When the user clicks on the **ItemImageRepeater**, **ShowDetail** and the **SKU_CrossSell[1-3]** variables are set. Then the visibility of the **DetailCrossSellFilter** is toggled. Toggling visibility of the **DetailCrossSellFilter** triggers the **SelectedItem** filter to be set and the **DetailDynamicPanel** widget to be brought to the front and shown. The Repeater **OnItemLoad** event updates the **HeroImageDetail** and additional widgets as specified by the **SetDetail** case. The **RepeaterCount** variable is incremented and the visibility of the **DetailCrossSellFilter** is again toggled. This process is repeated to populate additional Cross-Sell Images and their corresponding widgets.

 There must be at least one and no more then three Cross-Sell SKUs defined in the **CMS Repeater** master dataset.

Once completed, the **DetailDynamicPanel** item shown on the **Category** page will look like this:

To complete the **DetailDynamicPanel**, we will need to rename **State1**, place widgets, and define interactions.

Enabling the ItemDetailWithCrossSell state

To update the **DetailDynamicPanel** on the **CMS Repeater** master, we will place widgets on the **ItemDetailWithCrossSell** state and define interactions for those widgets.

Completing the Item Detail design

To complete the design of Item Detail widgets on the **ItemDetailWithCrossSell** state, with the **CMS Repeater** master open in the design area in the **Widget Manager** pane, double-click the **ItemDetailWithCrossSell** state icon under the **DetailDynamicPanel** to open it in the design area.

From the **Widgets** pane, drag the **Image** widget and place at coordinates (0,0). With the **Image** widget selected, perform the following steps:

1. In the toolbar, change the value of **w** to `930` and **h** to `690`.
2. In the **Widget Interactions and Notes** pane, click in the **Shape Name** field and type `ItemDetailBackground`.
3. In the **Widget Properties and Style** pane, with the **Style** tab selected scroll to **Borders, Lines, + Fills** and perform the following step:

   1. Click on the down arrow next to the second dropdown Line Width icon. In the drop-down menu, click on **none** to indicate no line.

4. From the **Widgets** pane, drag the Image widget and place at coordinates (25,10). With the **Image** widget selected, perform the following:

   1. In the toolbar, change the value of **w** to `595` and **h** to `370`.
   2. In the **Widget Interactions and Notes** pane, click in the **Shape Name** field and type `HeroImageDetail`.

From the **Widgets** pane, drag the **Heading 2** widget and place at coordinates (650,10). With the **Heading 2** widget selected, perform the following:

- In the toolbar, change the value of **w** to 173 and **h** to 18.

- In the **Widget Interactions and Notes** pane, click in the **Shape Name** field and type ItemBrandDetail.

- In the **Widget Properties and Style** pane, scroll to **Font** with the **Style** tab selected and change the font size to 16.

From the **Widgets** pane, drag the **Label** widget and place at coordinates (650,35). With the **Label** widget selected, perform the following:

- Type Description that could take up to two lines.. You will see the error message displayed on the **Label** widget.

- In the toolbar, change the value of **w** to 173 and **h** to 30.

- In the **Widget Interactions and Notes** pane, click in the **Shape Name** field and type ItemDescriptionDetail.

From the **Widgets** pane, drag the **Label** widget and place at coordinates (650,80). With the **Label** widget selected, perform the following:

- Type $. You will see the text displayed on the **Label** widget.

- In the toolbar, change the value of **w** to 15 and **h** to 15.

- In the **Widget Interactions and Notes** pane, click in the **Shape Name** field and type CurrencySymbolDetail.

From the **Widgets** pane, drag the **Label** widget and place at coordinates (665,80). With the **Label** widget selected, perform the following:

- Type ###.##. You will see the text displayed on the **Label** widget.

- In the toolbar, change the value of **w** to 158 and **h** to 15.

- In the **Widget Interactions and Notes** pane, click in the **Shape Name** field and type ItemPriceDetail.

From the Widgets pane, drag the **Rectangle** widget and place at coordinates (650,115). With the **Rectangle** widget selected, perform the following:

- Type `Add to Shopping`. You will see the text displayed as text on the **Rectangle** widget.

 You can also add an image icon displaying a shopping bag icon. For example an image of a handbag emoji 👜 sized to 20 x 20 pixels could be used. The handbag emoji as well as other useful emojis can be found at `http://emojipedia.org`.

- In the toolbar, change the value of **w** to `140` and **h** to `30`.
- In the **Widget Interactions and Notes** pane, click in the **Shape Name** field and type `AddToShoppingButton`.

From the **Widgets** pane, drag the **Paragraph** widget and place at coordinates (650,170). With the **Paragraph** widget selected, perform the following:

- In the toolbar, change the value of **w** to `220` and **h** to `180`.
- In the **Widget Interactions and Notes** pane, click in the **Shape Name** field and type `ItemDetailFullDescription`.

From the **Widgets** pane, drag the **Label** widget and place at coordinates (650,367). With the **Label** widget selected, perform the following:

- Type `Share:`. You will see the error message displayed on the **Label** widget.
- In the toolbar, change the value of **w** to `40` and **h** to `15`.
- In the **Widget Interactions and Notes** pane, click in the **Shape Name** field and type `SocialShareLabel`.

From the **Widgets** pane, drag the **Image** widget and place at coordinates (698,362). With the **Image** widget selected, perform the following:

- In the toolbar, change the value of **w** to `24` and **h** to `24`.
- In the **Widget Interactions and Notes** pane, click in the **Shape Name** field and type `TwitterShareLink`.
- Double-click on the **TwitterShareLink** image widget in the design area and select the file with the Twitter icon.

If you need social share icons, sample images and code downloads are available at http://www.packtpub.com/learning-axure-rp-interactive-prototypes. To download, click on the support tab and then the **Download now** button.

From the **Widgets** pane, drag the **Image** widget and place at coordinates (726,362). With the **Image** widget selected, perform the following:

- In the toolbar, change the value of **w** to 24 and **h** to 24.
- In the **Widget Interactions and Notes** pane, click in the **Shape Name** field and type PinterestShareLink.
- Double-click on the **PinterestShareLink** image widget in the design area and select the file with the Pinterest icon.

From the **Widgets** pane, drag the **Image** widget and place at coordinates (760,365). With the **Image** widget selected, perform the following:

- In the toolbar, change the value of **w** to 18 and **h** to 18.
- In the **Widget Interactions and Notes** pane, click in the **Shape Name** field and type FacebookShareLink.
- Double-click on the **FacebookShareLink** image widget in the design area and select the file with the Facebook icon.

From the **Widgets** pane, drag the **Horizontal Line** widget and place at coordinates (25,400). With the **Horizontal Line** widget selected, perform the following:

- In the toolbar, change the value of **w** to 842.
- In the **Widget Interactions and Notes** pane, click in the **Horizontal Line Name** field and type HzLine.

With the Item Detail widgets placed on the **ItemDetailWithCrossSell** state, we are now ready to place the Cross-Sell widgets on the **ItemDetailWithCrossSell** state.

Creating a Cross-Sell design

To complete the design of the Cross-Sell widgets on the **ItemDetailWithCrossSell** state, we will place three sets of Cross-Sell widgets (that is CrossSell1, CrossSell2, and CrossSell3). There will always be one Cross-Sell item defined in the CMS Repeater dataset, so CrossSell1 will always be visible. The second and third sets are hidden by default and will be shown only if there are additional CrossSell defined in the CMS **Repeater Dataset**.

Placing our CrossSell1 widgets on the ItemDetailWithCrossSell state

To start the design of the Cross-Sell widgets on the **ItemDetailWithCrossSell** state, we will first place widgets for CrossSell1. With the **CMS Repeater** master open in the **design area**, perform the following steps:

1. In the **Widget Manager** pane, under the **DetailDynamicPanel** double-click on the **ItemDetailWithCrossSell** state icon to open it in the **design area**.

2. From the **Widgets** pane, drag the **Heading 2** widget and place at coordinates (25,420). With the **Heading 2** widget selected, perform the following:
    ○ In the toolbar, change the value of **w** to 173 and **h** to 18.
    ○ In the **Widget Interactions and Notes** pane, click in the **Shape Name** field and type AlsoConsiderHeadline.
    ○ In the **Widget Properties and Style** pane, with the **Style** tab selected scroll to **Font** and change the font size to 16.

3. From the **Widgets** pane, drag the **Image** widget and place at coordinates (20,450). With the **Image** widget selected, perform the following:
    ○ In the toolbar, change the value of **w** to 173 and **h** to 173.
    ○ In the **Widget Interactions and Notes** pane, click in the **Shape Name** field and type ItemImageCrossSell1.

4. From the Widgets pane, drag the **Heading 2** widget and place at coordinates (20,630). With the **Heading 2** widget selected, perform the following:
    ○ In the toolbar, change the value of **w** to 173 and **h** to 18.
    ○ In the **Widget Interactions and Notes** pane, click in the **Shape Name** field and type ItemBrandCrossSell1.
    ○ In the **Widget Properties and Style** pane, with the **Style** tab selected scroll to **Font** and change the font size to 16.

5. From the **Widgets** pane, drag the **Label** widget and place at coordinates (20,650). With the **Label** widget selected, perform the following:

    ○ Type `Description that could take up to two lines..` You will see the error message displayed on the **Label** widget.

    ○ In the toolbar, change the value of **w** to `173` and **h** to `30`.

    ○ In the **Widget Interactions and Notes** pane, click in the **Shape Name** field and type `ItemDescriptionCrossSell1`.

6. From the **Widgets** pane, drag the **Label** widget and place at coordinates (20,685). With the **Label** widget selected, perform the following:

    ○ Type `$`. You will see the text displayed on the **Label** widget.

    ○ In the toolbar change the value of **w** to `15` and **h** to `15`.

    ○ In the **Widget Interactions and Notes** pane, click in the **Shape Name** field and type `CurrencySymbolCrossSell1`.

7. From the **Widgets** pane, drag the **Label** widget and place at coordinates (35,685). With the **Label** widget selected, perform the following:

    ○ Type `###.##`. You will see the text displayed on the **Label** widget.

    ○ In the toolbar, change the value of **w** to `158` and **h** to `15`.

    ○ In the **Widget Interactions and Notes** pane, click in the **Shape Name** field and type `ItemPriceCrossSell1`.

Placing our CrossSell2 widgets on the ItemDetailWithCrossSell state

To place CrossSell2 widgets on the **ItemDetailWithCrossSell** state, with the **CMS Repeater** master open in the design area, perform the following steps:

1. From the **Widgets** pane, drag the **Image** widget and place at coordinates (233,450). With the **Image** widget selected, perform the following:

    ○ In the toolbar, change the value of **w** to `173`, **h** to `173` and click on the checkbox next to **Hidden**.

    ○ In the **Widget Interactions and Notes** pane, click in the **Shape Name** field and type `ItemImageCrossSell2`.

2. From the **Widgets** pane, drag the **Heading 2** widget and place at coordinates (233,630). With the **Heading 2** widget selected, perform the following:

   ° In the toolbar, change the value of **w** to `173`, **h** to `18` and click on the checkbox next to **Hidden**.

   ° In the **Widget Interactions and Notes** pane, click in the **Shape Name** field and type `ItemBrandCrossSell2`.

   ° In the **Widget Properties and Style** pane, with the **Style** tab selected, scroll to **Font** and change the font size to `16`.

3. From the **Widgets** pane, drag the **Label** widget and place at coordinates (233,650). With the **Label** widget selected, perform the following:

   ° Type `Description that could take up to two lines..` You will see the error message displayed on the **Label** widget.

   ° In the toolbar, change the value of **w** to `173`, **h** to `30` and click on the checkbox next to **Hidden**.

   ° In the **Widget Interactions and Notes** pane, click in the **Shape Name** field and type `ItemDescriptionCrossSell2`.

4. From the **Widgets** pane, drag the **Label** widget and place at coordinates (233,685). With the **Label** widget selected, perform the following:

   ° Type `$`. You will see the text displayed on the **Label** widget.

   ° In the toolbar, change the value of **w** to `15`, **h** to `15` and click on the checkbox next to **Hidden**.

   ° In the **Widget Interactions and Notes** pane, click in the **Shape Name** field and type `CurrencySymbolCrossSell2`.

5. From the **Widgets** pane, drag the **Label** widget and place at coordinates (248,685). With the **Label** widget selected, perform the following:

   ° Type `###.##`. You will see the text displayed on the **Label** widget.

   ° In the toolbar, change the value of **w** to `158`, **h** to `15` and click on the checkbox next to **Hidden**.

   ° In the **Widget Interactions and Notes** pane, click in the **Shape Name** field and type `ItemPriceCrossSell2`.

Placing our CrossSell3 widgets on the ItemDetailWithCrossSell state

To place CrossSell3 widgets on the **ItemDetailWithCrossSell** state, with the **CMS Repeater** master open in the design area, perform the following steps:

1. From the **Widgets** pane, drag the **Image** widget and place at coordinates (447,450). With the **Image** widget selected, perform the following:

    ° In the toolbar, change the value of **w** to 173, **h** to 173 and click on the checkbox next to **Hidden**.

    ° In the **Widget Interactions and Notes** pane, click in the **Shape Name** field and type ItemImageCrossSell3.

2. From the **Widgets** pane, drag the **Heading 2** widget and place at coordinates (447,630). With the **Heading 2** widget selected, perform the following:

    ° In the toolbar, change the value of **w** to 173, **h** to 18 and click on the checkbox next to **Hidden**.

    ° In the **Widget Interactions and Notes** pane, click in the **Shape Name** field and type ItemBrandCrossSell3.

    ° In the **Widget Properties and Style** pane, with the **Style** tab selected scroll to **Font** and change the font size to 16.

3. From the **Widgets** pane, drag the **Label** widget and place at coordinates (447,650). With the **Label** widget selected, perform the following:

    ° Type Description that could take up to two lines.. You will see the error message displayed on the **Label** widget.

    ° In the toolbar, change the value of **w** to 173, **h** to 30 and click on the checkbox next to **Hidden**.

    ° In the **Widget Interactions and Notes** pane, click in the **Shape Name** field and type ItemDescriptionCrossSell3.

4. From the **Widgets** pane, drag the **Label** widget and place at coordinates (447,685). With the **Label** widget selected, perform the following:

    ° Type $. You will see the text displayed on the **Label** widget.

    ° In the toolbar, change the value of **w** to 15, **h** to 15 and click on the checkbox next to **Hidden**.

      ◦ In the **Widget Interactions and Notes** pane, click in the **Shape Name** field and type `CurrencySymbolCrossSell3`.

5. From the **Widgets** pane, drag the **Label** widget and place at coordinates (462,685). With the **Label** widget selected, perform the following:

      ◦ Type `###.##`. You will see the text displayed on the **Label** widget.

      ◦ In the toolbar, change the value of **w** to `158`, **h** to `15` and click on the checkbox next to **Hidden**.

      ◦ In the **Widget Interactions and Notes** pane, click in the **Shape Name** field and type `ItemPriceCrossSell3`.

With the design of the Cross-Sell widgets completed, we are now ready to define the Cross-Sell and social media interactions.

Defining Cross-Sell interactions

First we will define interactions for each **ItemImageCrossSell[1-3]** widget. Next we will define the social media interactions for the three social media Share Links (that is Twitter, Pinterest, and Facebook).

Creating the ItemImageCrossSell1 widget interaction

To create the interaction for **ItemImageCrossSell1**, with the **CMS Repeater** master in the design area, perform the following steps:

1. In the **Widget Manager** pane, under the **DetailDynamicPanel** double-click on the **ItemDetailWithCrossSell** state icon to open it in the design area.

2. Click on **ItemImageCrossSell1** at coordinates (20,450).

3. Within the **Widget Interactions and Notes** pane, double-click on the **OnClick** event.

4. In the **Case Description** field, type `ItemImageCrossSell1Clicked`.

Create the actions

To set the variable value for **ShowDetail**, perform the following steps:

1. Under **Click to add actions**, scroll to the **Variables** drop-down menu and click on **Set Variable Value**.

2. Under **Configure actions** in the **Select the variables to set** section, click on the checkbox next to **ShowDetail**.

3. Under **Configure actions** in the **Set variable to** section, select **value** in the first drop-down menu and enter `[[SKU_CrossSell1]]` in the text field.

To set the variable values for **SKU_CrossSell1**, **SKU_CrossSell2**, and **SKU_CrossSell3**, perform the following steps:

1. Under **Click to add actions**, scroll to the **Variables** drop-down menu and click on **Set Variable Value**.

2. Under **Configure actions** in the **Select the variables to set** section, click on the checkbox next to **SKU_CrossSell1**.

3. Under **Configure actions** in the **Set variable to** section, select **value** in the first drop-down menu and enter 0 in the text field.

4. Under **Configure actions** in the **Select the variables to set** section, click on the checkbox next to **SKU_CrossSell2**.

5. Under **Configure actions** in the **Set variable to** section, select **value** in the first drop-down menu and enter 0 in the text field.

6. Under **Configure actions** in the **Select the variables to set** section, click on the checkbox next to **SKU_CrossSell3**.

7. Under **Configure actions** in the **Set variable to** section, select **value** in the first drop-down menu and enter 0 in the text field.

To hide all CrossSell2 and CrossSell3 widgets, perform the following steps:

1. Under **Click to add actions**, scroll to the **Widgets** drop-down menu. Under the **Set Show/Hide** dropdown, click on **Hide**.

2. Under **Configure actions**, click on the checkboxes next to the following widgets:

   ○ **ItemImageCrossSell2**

   ○ **ItemBrandCrossSell2**

   ○ **ItemDescriptionCrossSell2**

   ○ **ItemPriceCrossSell2**

   ○ **CurrencySymbolCrossSell2**

   ○ **ItemImageCrossSell3**

   ○ **ItemBrandCrossSell3**

   ○ **ItemDescriptionCrossSell3**

   ○ **ItemPriceCrossSell3**

   ○ **CurrencySymbolCrossSell3**

3. Click on **OK**.

To toggle the **SetDetailCrossSellFilters** and cause the Repeater to reload, perform the following steps:

1. Under **Click to add actions**, scroll to the **Widgets** drop-down menu. Under the **Show/Hide** drop-down menu, click on **Toggle Visibility**.

2. Under **Configure actions**, in the **Select the widgets to hide/show** section, click on the checkbox next to **SetDetailCrossSellFilters**.

3. Click on **OK**.

Creating the ItemImageCrossSell2 widget interaction

To create the interaction, perform the following steps for **ItemImageCrossSell2** with the **CMS Repeater** master in the design area:

1. Click on **ItemImageCrossSell2** at coordinates (233,450).

2. In the **Widget Interactions and Notes** pane, double-click on the **OnClick** event.

3. In the **Case Description** field, type `ItemImageCrossSell2Clicked`.

Create the actions

To set the variable value for **ShowDetail**, perform the following steps:

1. Under **Click to add actions**, scroll to the **Variables** drop-down menu and click on **Set Variable Value**.

2. Under **Configure actions** in the **Select the variables to set** section, click on the checkbox next to **ShowDetail**.

3. Under **Configure actions** in the **Set variable to** section, select **value** in the first drop-down menu and enter `[[SKU_CrossSell2]]` in the text field.

To set the variable values for **SKU_CrossSell1**, **SKU_CrossSell2**, and **SKU_CrossSell3**, perform the following steps:

1. Under **Click to add actions**, scroll to the **Variables** drop-down menu and click on **Set Variable Value**.

2. Under **Configure actions** in the **Select the variables to set** section, click on the checkbox next to **SKU_CrossSell1**.

3. Under **Configure actions** in the **Set variable to** section, select **value** in the first drop-down menu and enter `0` in the text field.

4. Under **Configure actions** in the **Select the variables to set** section, click on the checkbox next to **SKU_CrossSell2**.

5. Under **Configure actions** in the **Set variable to** section, select **value** in the first drop-down menu and enter 0 in the text field.

6. Under **Configure actions** in the **Select the variables to set** section, click on the checkbox next to **SKU_CrossSell3**.

7. Under **Configure actions** in the **Set variable to** section, select **value** in the first drop-down menu and enter 0 in the text field.

To hide all CrossSell2 and CrossSell3 widgets, perform the following steps:

1. Under **Click to add actions**, scroll to the **Widgets** drop-down menu. Under the **Set Show/Hide** dropdown, click on **Hide**.

2. Under **Configure actions**, click on the checkboxes next to the following widgets:
   - **ItemImageCrossSell2**
   - **ItemBrandCrossSell2**
   - **ItemDescriptionCrossSell2**
   - **ItemPriceCrossSell2**
   - **CurrencySymbolCrossSell2**
   - **ItemImageCrossSell3**
   - **ItemBrandCrossSell3**
   - **ItemDescriptionCrossSell3**
   - **ItemPriceCrossSell3**
   - **CurrencySymbolCrossSell3**

3. Click on **OK**.

To toggle the **SetDetailCrossSellFilters** and cause the **Repeater** to reload, perform the following steps:

1. Under **Click to add actions**, scroll to the **Widgets** drop-down menu. Under the **Show/Hide** drop-down menu, click on **Toggle Visibility**.

2. Under **Configure actions**, in the **Select the widgets to hide/show** section, click on the checkbox next to **SetDetailCrossSellFilters**.

3. Click on **OK**.

Creating the ItemImageCrossSell3 widget interaction

To create the interaction for **ItemImageCrossSell3** with the **CMS Repeater** master in the design area, click on **ItemImageCrossSell3** at coordinates (447,450) and perform the following steps:

1. In the **Widget Interactions and Notes** pane, double-click on the **OnClick** event.

2. In the **Case Description** field, type `ItemImageCrossSell3Clicked`.

Create the actions

To set the variable value for **ShowDetail**, perform the following steps:

1. Under **Click to add actions**, scroll to the **Variables** drop-down menu and click on **Set Variable Value**.

2. Under **Configure actions** in the **Select the variables to set** section, click on the checkbox next to **ShowDetail**.

3. Under **Configure actions** in the **Set variable to** section, select **value** in the first drop-down menu and enter `[[SKU_CrossSell3]]` in the text field.

To set the variable values for **SKU_CrossSell1**, **SKU_CrossSell2**, and **SKU_CrossSell3**, perform the following steps:

1. Under **Click to add actions**, scroll to the **Variables** drop-down menu and click on **Set Variable Value**.

2. Under **Configure actions**, in the **Select the variables to set** section, click on the checkbox next to **SKU_CrossSell1**.

3. Under **Configure actions**, in the **Set variable to** section, select **value** in the first drop-down menu and enter `0` in the text field.

4. Under **Configure actions**, in the **Select the variables to set** section, click on the checkbox next to **SKU_CrossSell2**.

5. Under **Configure actions**, in the **Set variable to** section, select **value** in the first drop-down menu and enter `0` in the text field.

6. Under **Configure actions**, in the **Select the variables to set** section, click on the checkbox next to **SKU_CrossSell3**.

7. Under **Configure actions**, in the **Set variable to** section, select **value** in the first drop-down menu and enter `0` in the text field.

To hide all CrossSell2 and CrossSell3 widgets, perform the following steps:

1. Under **Click to add actions**, scroll to the **Widgets** drop-down menu. Under the **Set Show/Hide** dropdown, click on **Hide**.

2. Under **Configure actions**, click on the checkboxes next to the following widgets:
   ○ **ItemImageCrossSell2**
   ○ **ItemBrandCrossSell2**
   ○ **ItemDescriptionCrossSell2**
   ○ **ItemPriceCrossSell2**
   ○ **CurrencySymbolCrossSell2**
   ○ **ItemImageCrossSell3**
   ○ **ItemBrandCrossSell3**
   ○ **ItemDescriptionCrossSell3**
   ○ **ItemPriceCrossSell3**
   ○ **CurrencySymbolCrossSell3**

3. Click on **OK**.

To toggle the **SetDetailCrossSellFilters** and cause the **Repeater** to reload, perform the following steps:

1. Under **Click to add actions**, scroll to the **Widgets** drop-down menu. Under the **Show/Hide** drop-down menu, click on **Toggle Visibility**.

2. Under **Configure actions**, in the **Select the widgets to hide/show** section, click on the checkbox next to **SetDetailCrossSellFilters**.

3. Click on **OK**.

With the design of the Cross-Sell interactions completed, we are now ready to define the social media interactions for the three social media Share Links (that is, Twitter, Pinterest, and Facebook).

Enabling social media interactions

For social media interactions, our goal is to enable each social media link and allow the user to experience the social sharing flow for the corresponding social media platform. To generate the social share link, we will use the Share Link Generator available for free at `http://www.sharelinkgenerator.com`.

We will use a test link to generate the share links and not an actual link to prototype.

Creating the Twitter share link interaction

To create the interaction for **TwitterShareLink** with the **CMS Repeater** master in the design area, perform the following steps:

1. In the **Widget Manager** pane, under the **DetailDynamicPanel** double-click on the **ItemDetailWithCrossSell** state icon to open in the design area. Click on **TwitterShareLink** at coordinates (698,362).

2. In the **Widget Interactions and Notes** pane, double-click on the OnClick event. In the **Case Description** field, type `TwitterShareLinkClicked`.

Create the actions

To open a pop-up window enabling the user to post a tweet on Twitter, perform the following steps:

1. Under **Click to add actions**, click on the **Links** drop-down menu. Now, click on the **Open Link** drop-down menu and then on **Popup Window**.

2. Under **Configure actions**, with the **Link to an external url or file** radio button selected, enter the following in the hyperlink text field: `https://twitter.com/home?status=Check%20out%20this%20Awesome%20Find!%20http://bit.ly/AxureRPIntProtos%20`

3. Click on **OK**.

Creating the Pinterest share link interaction

To create the interaction for **PinterestShareLink**, with the **CMS Repeater** master in the design area and in the **Widget Manager** pane, double-click on the **ItemDetailWithCrossSell** state icon under the **DetailDynamicPanel** to open it in the design area and perform the following steps:

1. Click on **PinterestShareLink** at coordinates(726,362).

2. In the **Widget Interactions and Notes** pane, double-click on the **OnClick** event.

3. In the **Case Description** field, type `PinterestShareLinkClicked`.

Create the actions

To open a pop-up window enabling the user to post a pin on Pinterest, perform the following steps:

1. Under **Click to add actions**, click on the **Links** drop-down menu. Now, click on the **Open Link** drop-down menu and then on **Popup Window**.

2. Under **Configure actions**, with the **Link to an external url or file** radio button selected, enter the following in the hyperlink text field:

   ```
   https://pinterest.com/pin/create/button/?url=http://www.
   packtpub.com/axure-rp-prototyping-cookbook/book&media=http://
   www.packtpub.com/sites/default/files/7989OT_Axure%2520RP%2
   520Prototyping%2520Cookbook.jpg&description=Check%20out%20
   this%20Awesome%20Find!%20%0Ahttp://www.packtpub.com/axure-rp-
   prototyping-cookbook/book
   ```

3. Click on **OK**.

Creating the Facebook share link interaction

To create the interaction for **FacebookShareLink**, with the **CMS Repeater** master in the design area and in the **Widget Manager** pane, double-click on the **ItemDetailWithCrossSell** state icon under the **DetailDynamicPanel** to open in the design area and perform the following steps:

1. Click on **FacebookShareLink** at coordinates (760,365).

2. In the **Widget Interactions and Notes** pane, double-click on the **OnClick** event.

3. In the **Case Description** field, type `FacebookShareLinkClicked`.

Create the actions

To open a pop-up window enabling the user to post an update on Facebook, perform the following steps:

1. Under **Click to add actions**, click on the **Links** drop-down menu. Now, click on the **Open Link** drop-down menu and then on **Popup Window**.

2. Under **Configure actions**, with the **Link to an external url or file** radio button selected, enter the following in the hyperlink text field:

3. ```
   https://www.facebook.com/sharer/sharer.php?u=http://bit.ly/
   AxureRPIntProtos
   ```

4. Click on **OK**.
   ```

Summary

We first completed the **CMS Repeater** master by adding Catalog and Product Dynamic Panels as well as interactions for the **SetDetailCrossSellFilter** Hot Spot widget. We also updated the **Header** master's **HzMenu** widget to enable an OnClick event for each menu item. Finally, we designed the **Category**, **Catalog**, and **Product** pages.

In the next chapter, we will enable Search and create a dynamic Search Results page.

Self-test questions

- What enhancements were needed to complete the CMS Repeater master?
- What is the SetDetailCrossSellFilter Hot Spot widget used for?
- What happens when the visibility of the SetDetailCrossSellFilter Hot Spot is toggled?
- What happens when a user clicks a menu item in the main menu on the Header master?
- When we built the Category page, what were the first things we placed?
- What actions did we define for the Category Page OnPageLoad event?
- Which Social Media channels did we enable interactions for on the ItemDetailWithCrossSell state of the Detail Dynamic Panel?

6
Search and Search Results

With the Category, Catalog, and Product page designs complete, we are ready to enable the Search functionality and build the Search Results page. We will design a Search Results page that utilizes a Header, Footer, and Repeater Item defined on the **CMS Repeater** master. We will then enable the search by adding search interactions to the Header master, and we will update the SetGlobalFilters Hot Spot to filter the results.

In this chapter, we will learn about:

- Enabling Search for the CMS Repeater master
- Designing our Search Results Page
- Specifying Search Interactions

Enabling search for the CMS Repeater master

Since we have done an excellent job of architecting our **CMS Repeater** master, adding the search functionality will be much easier! We will start by designing our Search Results page and defining the **OnPageLoad** interaction.

Designing our Search Results page

To design our Search Results page, we will first place the **Header**, **CMS Repeater**, and **Footer** masters, as well as add a `SearchTerm` variable. Next, we will define the **OnPageLoad** interaction to initialize the variables. Once completed, our Search Results page will look like the following:

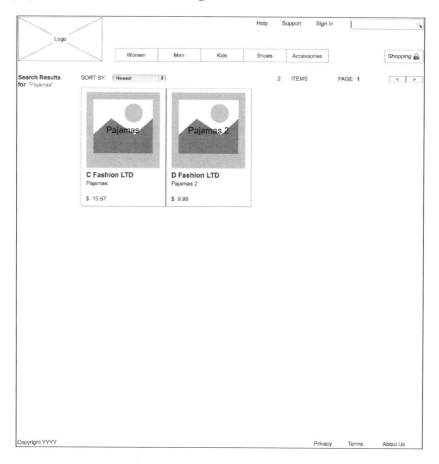

To create the Search Results page, perform the following steps:

1. In the **Sitemap** pane, double-click on the **Search** page to open in the Design Area.

2. From the **Masters** pane, drag-and-drop the **Header** master at any location on the wireframe.

3. From the **Masters** pane, drag-and-drop the **CMS Repeater** master at any location on the wireframe. In the **Widget Interactions and Notes** pane in the **CMS Repeater Name** field, type `SearchRepeaterMaster`.

4. In the **Masters** pane, click on the **Footer** master. While holding down the mouse button, drag the **Footer** master and place it at the coordinates (10,970).

5. In the **Widgets** pane, click on the **Label** widget. While holding down the mouse button, drag the **Label** widget and place it at the coordinates (10,139). With the **Label** widget selected, perform the following steps:

   ° Type `Search Results for`. You will see the message displayed on the **Label** widget.

   ° In the toolbar, change the value of **w** to `110` and **h** to `32`.

   ° In the **Widget Interactions and Notes** pane, click on the **Shape Name** field and type `SearchResultsHeading`.

   ° In the **Widget Properties and Style** pane, with the **Style** tab selected, scroll to **Font**, click on the **B** icon to select bold, and change the font size to `14`.

6. In the **Widgets** pane, click on the **Label** widget. While holding down the mouse button, drag the **Label** widget and place it at the coordinates (34,156). With the **Label** widget selected, perform the following steps:

   ° In the toolbar, change the value of **w** to `116` and **h** to `42`.

   ° In the **Widget Interactions and Notes** pane, click in the **Shape Name** field and type `SearchTermLabel`.

   ° In the **Widget Properties and Style** pane, with the **Style** tab selected, scroll to **Font** and perform the following steps:

   Click on the down arrow next to the A (Text Color) icon. In the dropdown menu, in the # text field enter `FF6600`.

7. To add the SearchTerm Global Variable, perform the following steps:

   ° In the main menu, click on **Project** and then on **Global Variables…**.

   ° In the **Global Variables** dialog, click on the green **+** sign and type `SearchTerm`.

   ° Click on **OK**.

Since we are leveraging the current design of the Repeater Item for the **CMS Repeater** master, we have completed the Search Results page design. With the design complete, we are ready to define the OnPageLoad interaction.

Developing page interactions

With the Search Results page still open in the Design Area, perform the following steps.

Defining the Initialize Search case

Under the Design Area in the Page Properties pane, click on the **Page Interactions** tab and double-click on the **OnPageLoad** event. A **Case Editor** dialog box will open. Within the **Case Editor** dialog in the **Case Name** field, type InitializeSearch, and perform the following steps.

Creating the actions

To Hide the Brand, Price, and Category Facetted Filter Tree widgets, perform the following steps:

1. Under **Click to add actions**, scroll to the **Widgets** drop-down menu. Under the **Set Show/Hide** dropdown, click on **Hide**.

2. Under **Configure actions**, click on the checkboxes next to the following widgets:

    ° BrandFacettedFilterTree

    ° PriceFacettedFilterTree

    ° CategoryFacettedFilterTree

To set the text on the SearchTermLabel, perform the following steps:

1. Under **Click to add actions**, scroll to the **Widgets** drop-down menu and click on **Set Text**.

2. Under **Configure actions**, in the section **Select the widgets to set text**, click on the checkbox next to **SearchTermLabel**.

3. Under **Configure actions**, in the section **Set text to**, in the first drop-down menu, select value, and in the text field, enter " [[SearchTerm]] ".

To Toggle the SetGlobalFilters and cause the **Repeater** to reload, perform the following steps:

1. Under **Click to add actions**, scroll to the **Widgets** drop-down menu. Under the Show/Hide drop-down menu, click on **Toggle Visibility**.

2. Under **Configure actions**, in the section **Select the widgets to hide/show**, click on the checkbox next to **SetGlobalFilters**.

3. Click on **OK**.

With the Search page design complete, we are now ready to specify search interactions.

Specifying Search interactions

To facilitate the Search functionality in the **Header** master, we will create an **OnClick** event on the SearchRectangleExpanded widget for the Expanded State of the ExpandingSearchDP Dynamic Panel. The **OnClick** event will set the SearchTerm Global Variable and open the Search page in the current window. We are now ready to add the Search functionality to the **Header** master.

Supporting the Search functionality in the Header master

1. We will activate the Search functionality by utilizing the SearchRectangleClicked OnClick interaction. To update the **OnClick** event on the SearchRectangleExpanded widget for the **Header** master, in the **Masters** pane, double-click on the **Header** master. The **Header** master will open in the Design Area. Perform the following steps:

2. In the **Widget Manager** pane, under the **ExpandingSearchDP**, double-click on the **Expanded** State to open it in the design area.

3. In the Design Area, click on the SearchRectangleExpanded widget.

4. In the **Widget Interactions and Notes** pane, double-click on the **OnClick** event.

5. In the **Case Name** field, type `SearchRectangleClicked`.

Creating the actions

To set the variable value for SearchTerm, perform the following steps:

1. Under **Click to add actions**, scroll to the **Variables** drop-down menu and click on **Set Variable Value**.

2. Under **Configure actions**, in the section **Select the variables to set**, click on the checkbox next to **SearchTerm**.

3. Under **Configure actions**, in the section **Set variable to**, in the first drop-down menu select **text on widget**, and in the second drop-down menu, select **SearchTextFieldExpanded**.

4. To open the Search page in the current window, perform the following steps:

5. Under **Click to add actions**, scroll to the **Links** drop-down menu. Under the **Open Link** drop-down menu, click on **Current Window**.

6. Under **Configure actions**, with the **Link to a page in this design** radio button selected, in the **Sitemap**, click on the **Search** page.

7. Click on **OK**.

With the Search functionality enabled for the Header master, we are ready to add the SetSearchFiltering case to the SetGlobalFilters Hot Spot.

Adding the SetSearchFilter to the SetGlobalFilters Hot Spot

We are now ready to add the SetSearchFilter. A filter based on the SearchTerm Global Variable will be added to the SearchRepeaterMaster. We will look for matches of the SearchTerm in the following columns of the Data Set:

- ItemCategory
- ItemBrand
- ItemDescription

Each of the three expressions for our query will be evaluated using the Boolean OR (||) operator. We will also use the toLowerCase() function. The toLowerCase() function allows us to return both upper and lower case results when performing the query. Once completed, the query string will look as follows:

```
[[Item.ItemCategory.toLowerCase().indexOf(SearchTerm.toLowerCase())
>= 0 || Item.ItemBrand.toLowerCase().indexOf(SearchTerm.
toLowerCase()) >= 0 || Item.ItemDescription.toLowerCase().
indexOf(SearchTerm.toLowerCase()) >= 0]]
```

Updating the SetGlobalFilters Hot Spot with the SetSearchFilter case

To update the SetGlobalFilters Hot Spot with the SetSearchFilter case, perform the following steps:

1. In the **Masters** pane, double-click on the **CMS Repeater** master to open it in the Design Area.

2. In the Design Area, click on the SetGlobalFilters Hot Spot at the coordinates (20,570).

3. In the **Widget Interactions and Notes** pane, double-click on the **OnShow** event. A **Case Editor** dialog box will open. Within the **Case Editor** dialog, in the **Case Name** field, type SetSearchFilter and perform the following steps.

Creating the condition

1. Click on the **Add Condition** button.

2. In the **Condition Builder** dialog box, in the outlined condition box, perform the following steps:

    1. In the first dropdown, select **length of variable value**.

    2. In the second dropdown, select **SearchTerm**.

    3. In the third dropdown, select **is greater than**.

    4. In the fourth dropdown, select **value**.

    5. In the text field, enter 0.

    6. Click on **OK**.

Creating the actions

To add a SearchFilter to the **Repeater**, perform the following steps:

1. Under **Click to add actions**, scroll to the **Repeaters** drop-down menu and click on **Add Filter**.

2. Under **Configure actions**, in the section **Select the repeaters to add filters**, click on the checkbox next to **CategoryRepeater**.

3. In the **Name:** text field, type SearchFilter.

4. In the **Rule:** text field, type the following:

```
[[Item.ItemCategory.toLowerCase().indexOf(SearchTerm.
toLowerCase()) >= 0 || Item.ItemBrand.toLowerCase().
indexOf(SearchTerm.toLowerCase()) >= 0 || Item.ItemDescription.
toLowerCase().indexOf(SearchTerm.toLowerCase()) >= 0]]
```

 For the rule (that is, query) to work correctly, you must make sure that there are no extra spaces or hidden characters (such as carriage returns and the like) in the statement.

5. Click on **OK**.

6. Under the **OnShow** event, click on the **SetSearchFilter** case and click on **Toggle IF/ELSE IF**.

7. Under the **OnShow** event, right-click on the **SetSearchFilter** case. While holding down the mouse button, drag the **SetSearchFilter** case to be the second case between the **RemoveAllFilters** case and the **SetBrandFilterA** case.

8. Right-click on the **SetSearchFilter** case and click on **Copy**.

9. In the **Widgets Interaction and Notes** pane, scroll to the **OnHide** event.

10. Under the **OnHide** event, right-click on the **RemoveAllFilters** event and click on **Paste**. You should now see the **SetSearchFilter** case added as the second case between the **RemoveAllFilters** case and the **SetBrandFilterA** case.

Summary

In this chapter, we enhanced the Header and **CMS Repeater** masters, thereby enabling Search, and quickly designed a Search Results page. We added a Search Filter with the user-entered term to our **CMS Repeater** master. We then showed the resultant Data Set with the Repeater Item to complete our Search page.

In the next chapter, we will complete the design and interactions for our Shopping Cart.

Self-test questions

*   What Global Variable did we add to support Search?

*   Which Masters did we use to build the Search page?

*   How did we facilitate the Search functionality in the Header master?

*   What filter did we have to add to the SetGlobalFilters Hot Spot?

*   Which columns of the Data Set did we search for matches of our SearchTerm variable?

7

The Shopping Bag Functionality and Interactions

Many e-commerce sites leverage a shopping bag or shopping cart. This functionality allows customers to add, update, and remove items prior to finalizing their purchase.

With the Search functionality added to our prototype, we are now ready to create a Shopping Bag page with interactions. We will design a Shopping Bag page that utilizes a Header, Footer, and Repeater item, as defined on a new Shopping Bag Repeater master.

In this chapter, we will learn about:

- Designing our Shopping Bag Repeater
- Defining the Shopping Bag Repeater master
- MyShoppingBagRepeater OnItemLoad event interactions
- MyShoppingBagRepeater item OnClick interactions
- Viewing our Shopping Bag page
- Designing our Shopping Bag page

Designing our Shopping Bag Repeater

Our first step is to decide which content we will need in order to leverage the Shopping Bag design. We will create a new Shopping Bag Repeater master, adding the appropriate columns to support our Shopping Bag. When a user adds an item to the Shopping Bag, the Repeater dataset is updated with the appropriate data. When the user clicks on the link to view the Shopping Bag, the Shopping Bag page loads, and using the Repeater item design for the Shopping Bag Repeater, the current contents of the Shopping Bag is displayed. The user can then update or delete items in the Shopping Bag prior to entering the CheckOut flow.

Defining the Shopping Bag Repeater

We will now define a new Shopping Bag Repeater master based on the Content Management System Repeater master. When a user adds an item to the **Shopping Bag**, data for that item is copied from the CMS Repeater master to the Shopping Bag Repeater master. The Shopping Bag Repeater master will also update the Quantity and SubTotal columns.

To create the Shopping Bag Repeater master, perform the following steps:

1. In the **Masters** pane, click on the **Add Master** icon. Slow-click the master labeled **New Master 1**, type `Shopping Bag Repeater`, and press *Enter*.

2. In the **Masters** pane, right-click on the icon next to **CMS Repeater** master, hover over **Drop Behavior**, and click on **Lock to Master Location**.

3. In the **Masters** pane, double-click on the icon next to the **Shopping Bag Repeater** master to open in the **design area**.

Designing the Shopping Bag Repeater

We are now ready to place the CheckOut Call To Action widgets and the **Repeater** widget on the Repeater item.

Creating the CheckOut Call widget

To place the CheckOut Call To Action widgets, perform the following steps:

1. From the **Widgets** pane, drag the **Rectangle** widget and place it at the coordinates (760,140). With the **Rectangle** widget selected, perform the following steps:

   1. In the toolbar, change the value of **w** to `200` and **h** to `100`.

   2. In the **Widget Interactions and Notes** pane, click on the **Shape Name** field and type `CheckOutBackground`.

2. From the **Widgets** pane, drag the **Label** widget and place it at the coordinates (772,149). With the **Label** widget selected, perform the following steps:

   1. Type `Subtotal:`. You will see the text displayed on the **Label** widget.

   2. In the toolbar, change the value of **w** to `53` and **h** to `16`.

   3. In the **Widget Interactions and Notes** pane, click on the **Shape Name** field and type `BagSubTotalLabel`.

   4. In the **Widget Properties and Style** pane, with the **Style** tab selected, scroll to **Font** and change the font size to `14`.

3. From the **Widgets** pane, drag the **Label** widget and place it at the coordinates (835,154). With the **Label** widget selected, perform the following steps:

    1. Type 0. You will see the text displayed on the **Label** widget.

    2. In the toolbar, change the value of **w** to 9 and **h** to 9.

    3. In the **Widget Interactions and Notes** pane, click on the **Shape Name** field and type BagNumOfItemsLabel.

    4. In the **Widget Properties and Style** pane, with the **Style** tab selected, scroll to **Font** and change the font size to 8.

4. From the **Widgets** pane, drag the **Label** widget and place it at the coordinates (845,154). With the **Label** widget selected, perform the following steps:

    1. Type ITEMS. You will see the text displayed on the **Label** widget.

    2. In the toolbar, change the value of **w** to 42 and **h** to 9.

    3. In the **Widget Interactions and Notes** pane, click on the **Shape Name** field and type BagNumOfItemsTextLabel.

    4. In the **Widget Properties and Style** pane, with the **Style** tab selected, scroll to **Font** and change the font size to 8.

5. From the **Widgets** pane, drag the **Label** widget and place it at the coordinates (890,150). With the **Label** widget selected, perform the following steps:

    1. Type $. You will see the text displayed as text on the **Label** widget.

    2. In the toolbar, change the value of **w** to 15 and **h** to 15.

    3. In the **Widget Interactions and Notes** pane, click on the **Shape Name** field and type BagCurrencySymbol.

6. From the **Widgets** pane, drag the **Label** widget and place it at the coordinates (905,150). With the **Label** widget selected, perform the following steps:

    1. Type ###.##. You will see the text displayed on the **Label** widget.

    2. In the toolbar, change the value of **w** to 65 and **h** to 15.

    3. In the **Widget Interactions and Notes** pane, click on the **Shape Name** field and type BagSubTotal.

7. From the **Widgets** pane, drag the **Button Shape** widget and place it at the coordinates (790,185). With the **Button Shape** widget selected, perform the following steps:

   1. Type Check Out. You will see the text displayed on the **Button Shape** widget.

   2. In the toolbar, change the value of **w** to 140 and **h** to 30.

   3. In the **Widget Interactions and Notes** pane, click on the **Shape Name** field and type CheckOutButton.

8. From the **Masters** pane, drag the **Footer** master and place it at coordinates (10,555). In the **Widget Interactions and Notes** pane, in the **Footer Name** field, type ShoppingBagFooter.

Creating the Repeater widget

To place the **Repeater** widget, perform the following steps:

1. From the **Widgets** pane, drag the **Repeater** widget and place it at the coordinates (10,260).

2. In the **Widget Interactions and Notes** pane, click on the **Repeater Footnote and Name** field and type MyShoppingBagRepeater.

Next, we will place widgets on the Repeater item.

Placing widgets on the Repeater item

To adjust and place widgets on the Repeater item, perform the following steps:

1. Double-click on the **MyShoppingBagRepeater** Repeater to open the Repeater item in the design area.

2. In the design area, click on the Repeater item at the coordinates (0,0). Perform the following steps:

   1. In the toolbar, change the value of **w** to 720 and **h** to 220.

   2. In the **Widget Interactions and Notes** pane, click on the **Shape Name** field and type BagItemBackground.

3. From the **Widgets** pane, drag the **Image** widget and place it at the coordinates (13,24). With the **Image** widget selected, perform the following steps:

   1. In the toolbar, change the value of **w** to 173 and **h** to 173.

   2. In the **Widget Interactions and Notes** pane, click on the **Shape Name** field and type BagItemImageRepeater.

4. From the **Widgets** pane, drag the **Heading 2** widget and place it at the coordinates (220,27). With the **Heading 2** widget selected, perform the following steps:

    1. In the toolbar, change the value of **w** to 173 and **h** to 18.

    2. In the **Widget Interactions and Notes** pane, click on the **Shape Name** field and type BagItemBrandRepeater.

    3. In the **Widget Properties and Style** pane, with the **Style** tab selected, scroll to **Font** and change the font size to 16.

5. From the **Widgets** pane, drag the **Label** widget and place it at the coordinates (220,47). With the **Label** widget selected, perform the following steps:

    1. Type Description that could take up to two lines.. You will see the text displayed on the **Label** widget.

    2. In the toolbar, change the value of **w** to 173 and **h** to 30.

    3. In the **Widget Interactions and Notes** pane, click on the **Shape Name** field and type BagItemDescriptionRepeater.

6. From the **Widgets** pane, drag the **Label** widget and place it at the coordinates (220,88). With the **Label** widget selected, perform the following steps:

    1. Type Color:. You will see the text displayed on the **Label** widget.

    2. In the toolbar, change the value of **w** to 35 and **h** to 15.

    3. In the **Widget Interactions and Notes** pane, click on the **Shape Name** field and type BagItemColorLabel.

7. From the **Widgets** pane, drag the **Droplist** widget and place it at the coordinates (260,85). With the **Droplist** widget selected, perform the following steps:

    1. In the toolbar, change the value of **w** to 110 and **h** to 22.

    2. In the **Widget Interactions and Notes** pane, click on the **Shape Name** field and type ColorDroplist.

    3. Right-click on the **Droplist** widget and click on **Edit List Items**. Click on the **Add Many** button and enter the following values (one per line):

       - Black
       - White
       - Blue
       - Red

    4. Click on **OK**.

8. From the **Widgets** pane, drag the **Label** widget and place it at the coordinates (220,120). With the **Label** widget selected, perform the following steps:

    1. Type `Size:`. You will see the text displayed on the **Label** widget.

    2. In the toolbar, change the value of **w** to `31` and **h** to `15`.

    3. In the **Widget interactions and Notes** pane, click on the **Shape Name** field and type `BagItemSizeLabel`.

9. From the **Widgets** pane, drag the **Droplist** widget and place it at the coordinates (260,117). With the **Droplist** widget selected, perform the following steps:

    1. In the toolbar, change the value of **w** to `110` and **h** to `22`.

    2. In the **Widget interactions and Notes** pane, click on the **Shape Name** field and type `SizeDroplist`.

    3. Right-click on the **Droplist** widget and click on **Edit List Items**. Click on the **Add Many** button and enter the following values (one per line):

       - Small
       - Medium
       - Large

    4. Click on **OK**.

10. From the **Widgets** pane, drag the **Label** widget and place it at the coordinates (220,152). With the **Label** widget selected, perform the following steps:

    1. Type `SKU:`. You will see the text displayed on the **Label** widget.

    2. In the toolbar, change the value of **w** to `25` and **h** to `11`.

    3. In the **Widget Interactions and Notes** pane, click on the **Shape Name** field and type `BagItemSKUTextLabel`.

    4. In the **Widget Properties and Style** pane, with the **Style** tab selected, scroll to **Font** and change the font size to `10`.

11. From the **Widgets** pane, drag the **Label** widget and place it at the coordinates (260,152). With the **Label** widget selected, perform the following steps:

    1. Type `1`. You will see the text displayed on the **Label** widget.

    2. In the toolbar, change the value of **w** to `7` and **h** to `11`.

3. In the **Widget Interactions and Notes** pane, click on the **Shape Name** field and type `BagItemSKULabel`.

4. In the **Widget Properties and Style** pane, with the **Style** tab selected, scroll to **Font** and change the font size to `10`.

12. From the **Widgets** pane, drag the **Label** widget and place it at the coordinates (220,187). With the **Label** widget selected, perform the following steps:

    1. Type `Remove Item`. You will see the text displayed on the **Label** widget.

    2. In the toolbar, change the value of **w** to `62` and **h** to `11`.

    3. In the **Widget Interactions and Notes** pane, click on the **Shape Name** field and type `RemoveItemLabel`.

    4. In the **Widget Properties and Style** pane, with the **Style** tab selected, scroll to **Font** and change the font size to `10`.

13. From the **Widgets** pane, drag the **Label** widget and place it at the coordinates (420,28). With the **Label** widget selected, perform the following steps:

    1. Type `Price:`. You will see the text displayed on the **Label** widget.

    2. In the toolbar, change the value of **w** to `35` and **h** to `15`.

    3. In the **Widget Interactions and Notes** pane, click on the **Shape Name** field and type `BagItemPriceLabel`.

14. From the **Widgets** pane, drag the **Label** widget and place it at the coordinates (460,28). With the **Label** widget selected, perform the following steps:

    1. Type `$`. You will see the text displayed as text on the **Label** widget.

    2. In the toolbar, change the value of **w** to `15` and **h** to `15`.

    3. In the **Widget Interactions and Notes** pane, click on the **Shape Name** field and type `BagItemCurrencySymbolRepeater`.

15. From the **Widgets** pane, drag the **Label** widget and place it at the coordinates (475,28). With the **Label** widget selected, perform the following steps:

    1. Type `###.##`. You will see the text displayed on the **Label** widget.

    2. In the toolbar, change the value of **w** to `65` and **h** to `15`.

    3. In the **Widget Interactions and Notes** pane, click on the **Shape Name** field and type `BagItemPriceRepeater`.

16. From the **Widgets** pane, drag the **Label** widget and place it at the coordinates (540,28). With the **Label** widget selected, perform the following steps:

    1. Type `Qty:`. You will see the text displayed on the **Label** widget.

    2. In the toolbar, change the value of **w** to `26` and **h** to `15`.

    3. In the **Widget Interactions and Notes** pane, click on the **Shape Name** field and type `BagItemQtyLabel`.

17. From the **Widgets** pane, drag the **Text Field** widget and place it at the coordinates (570,23). With the **Text Field** widget selected, perform the following steps:

    1. Type `1`. You will see the text displayed on the **Text Field** widget.

    2. In the toolbar, change the value of **w** to `50` and **h** to `25`.

    3. In the **Widget Interactions and Notes** pane, click on the **Shape Name** field and type `BagItemQtyTextField`.

18. From the **Widgets** pane, drag the **Button Shape** widget and place it at the coordinates (640,20). With the **Button Shape** widget selected, perform the following steps:

    1. Type `Update`. You will see the text displayed on the **Button Shape** widget.

    2. In the toolbar, change the value of **w** to `60` and **h** to `30`.

    3. In the **Widget Interactions and Notes** pane, click on the **Shape Name** field and type `UpdateLineItemButton`.

With the Repeater item widgets placed, we are ready to define the Repeater Dataset.

Defining the Repeater dataset

To create and name the 11 columns of the Repeater dataset, with the Repeater item still open in the design area, perform the following steps:

- Under the design area in the **Repeater** pane, click on the **Repeater dataset** tab. To define the Repeater Dataset, do the following:

    1. Double-click on **Column0** and type `SKU` to rename it.

    2. Double-click on **Add Column** 10 times, renaming each column as follows:

Repeater column name
ItemImage
ItemBrand
ItemDescription
ItemPrice
SKU_CrossSell1
SKU_CrossSell2
SKU_CrossSell3
ItemColor
ItemSize
ItemQty

With widgets placed on the Shopping Bag Repeater master and columns for the Repeater dataset identified, we are now ready to define the Shopping Bag Repeater item interactions.

MyShoppingBagRepeater OnItemLoad event interactions

You will start by defining interactions for the MyShoppingBagRepeater OnItemLoad event. Once completed, the OnItemLoad event will have a total of three cases, and the MyShoppingBagRepeater Widget interactions pane will look like this:

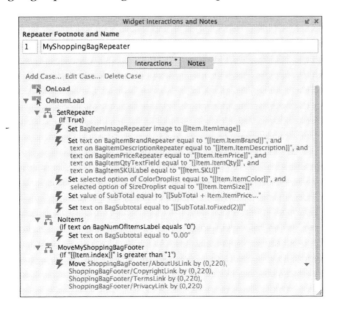

Defining the SetRepeater case

To create the interactions on the MyShoppingBagRepeater for the SetRepeater case, open the Shopping Bag Repeater master in the design area, click on the MyShoppingBagRepeater at the coordinates (10,260), and do the following:

In the **Widget Interactions and Notes** pane, click on the **Interactions** tab and double-click on the **OnItemLoad** event. A **Case Editor** dialog box will open. Within the **Case Editor** dialog in the **Case Description** field, type SetRepeater, and perform the steps given in the following sections.

Create the actions

To Set the Image on BagItemImageRepeater, perform the following steps:

1. Under **Click to add actions**, scroll to the **Widgets** drop-down menu and click on **Set Image**.

2. Under **Configure actions**, in the section **Select the image widgets to set the image**, click the checkbox next to **BagItemImageRepeater**.

3. Under **Configure actions**, in the section **Default**, in the first drop-down menu, select **value** and enter [[Item.ItemImage]] in the text field.

To set the text on the BagItemBrandRepeater, BagItemDescriptionRepeater, BagItemPriceRepeater, BagItemQtyTextField, and BagItemSKULabel, perform the following steps:

1. Under **Click to add actions**, scroll to the **Widgets** drop-down menu and click on **Set Text**.

2. Under **Configure actions**, in the section **Select the widgets to set text**, click on the checkbox next to **BagItemBrandRepeater**.

3. Under **Configure actions**, in the section **Set variable to**, in the first drop-down menu, select **value** and enter [[Item.ItemBrand]] in the text field.

4. Under **Click to add actions**, scroll to the **Widgets** drop-down menu and click on **Set Text**.

5. Under **Configure actions**, in the section **Select the widgets to set text**, click on the checkbox next to **BagItemDescriptionRepeater**.

6. Under **Configure actions**, in the section **Set variable to**, in the first drop-down menu, select **value** and enter [[Item.ItemDescription]] in the text field.

7. Under **Configure actions**, in the section **Select the widgets to set text**, click on the checkbox next to **BagItemPriceRepeater**.

8. Under **Configure actions**, in the section **Set variable to**, in the first drop-down menu, select **value** and enter `[[Item.ItemPrice]]` in the text field.

9. Under **Configure actions**, in the section **Select the widgets to set text**, click on the checkbox next to **BagItemQtyTextField**.

10. Under **Configure actions**, in the section **Set variable to**, in the first drop-down menu, select **value** and enter `[[Item.ItemQty]]` in the text field.

11. Under **Configure actions**, in the section **Select the widgets to set text**, click on the checkbox next to **BagItemSKULabel**.

12. Under **Configure actions**, in the section **Set variable to**, in the first drop-down menu, select **value** and enter `[[Item.SKU]]` in the text field.

To set the Selected List Option for the ColorDroplist and SizeDroplist, perform the following steps:

1. Under **Click to add actions**, scroll to the **Widgets** drop-down menu and click on **Set Selected List Option**.

2. Under **Configure actions**, in the section **Select the widgets to set selected option**, click on the checkbox next to **ColorDroplist**.

3. In the **Set selected state to:** dropdown, click on **Value**.

4. In the text field, type `[[Item.ItemColor]]`.

5. Under **Configure actions**, in the section **Select the widgets to set selected option**, click on the checkbox next to **SizeDroplist**.

6. In the **Set selected state to:** dropdown, click **Value**.

7. In the text field, type `[[Item.ItemSize]]`.

To set the variable value for SubTotal, perform the following steps:

1. Under **Click to add actions**, scroll to the **Variables** drop-down menu and click on **Set Variable Value**.

2. Under **Configure actions**, in the section **Select the variables to set**, click on the checkbox next to **SubTotal**.

3. Under **Configure actions**, in the section **Set variable to**, in the first drop-down menu, select **value** and then enter the following in the text field: `[[SubTotal + Item.ItemPrice * Item.ItemQty]]`.

To set the text on BagSubTotal, perform the following steps:

1. Under **Click to add actions**, scroll to the **Widgets** drop-down menu and click on **Set Text**.

2. Under **Configure actions**, in the section **Select the widgets to set text**, click on the checkbox next to **BagSubTotal**.

3. Under **Configure actions**, in the section **Set variable to**, in the first drop-down menu, select **value** and then enter `[[SubTotal.toFixed(2)]]` in the text field.

4. Click on **OK**.

Next, we will define the NoItems case.

Defining the NoItems case

To create the interactions on the MyShoppingBagRepeater for the NoItems case, open the Shopping Bag Repeater master in the design area, click on the MyShoppingBagRepeater at the coordinates (10,260), and perform the steps given in the following sections.

Create the condition

In the **Widget Interactions and Notes** pane, click on the **Interactions** tab and double-click on the **OnItemLoad** event. A **Case Editor** dialog box will open. In the **Case Editor** dialog, perform the following steps:

• In the **Case Description** field, type `NoItems`.

• Click on the **Add Condition** button.

• In the **Condition Builder** dialog box, in the outlined condition box, perform the following steps:

 1. In the first dropdown, select **value of variable**.

 2. In the second dropdown, select **BagNumOfItemsLabel**.

 3. In the third dropdown, select **equals**.

 4. In the fourth dropdown, select **value**.

 5. In the text field, enter `0`.

 6. Click on **OK**.

Create the action

To set the text on BagSubTotal, perform the following steps:

1. Under **Click to add actions**, scroll to the **Widgets** drop-down menu and click on **Set Text**.

2. Under **Configure actions**, in the section **Select the widgets to set text**, click on the checkbox next to **BagSubTotal**.

3. Under **Configure actions**, in the section **Set variable to**, in the first drop-down menu, select **value** and enter 0.00 in the text field.

4. Click on **OK**.

5. Under the **OnPageLoad** event, right-click on the **NoItems** case and click on **Toggle IF/ELSE IF**.

Next, we will define the MoveMyShoppingBagFooter case.

Defining the MoveMyShoppingBagFooter case

When a new Repeater item is displayed on our Shopping Bag page, we will want to move the Footer by 220 pixels. To create the interactions on the MyShoppingBagRepeater for the MoveMyShoppingBagFooter case, open the Shopping Bag Repeater master, click on the MyShoppingBagRepeater at the coordinates (10,260) in the design area, and perform the steps given in the following sections.

Create the condition

In the **Widget Interactions and Notes** pane, click on the **Interactions** tab and double-click on the **OnItemLoad** event. A **Case Editor** dialog box will open. In the **Case Editor** dialog, perform the following steps:

1. In the **Case Description** field, type MoveMyShoppingBagFooter.

2. Click on the **Add Condition** button.

3. In the **Condition Builder** dialog box, in the outlined condition box, perform the following steps:

    1. In the first dropdown, select **value**.
    2. In the second dropdown, type [[Item.index]].
    3. In the third dropdown, select **is greater than**.
    4. In the fourth dropdown, select **value**.
    5. In the text field, enter 1.
    6. Click on **OK**.

Create the action

To move the Footer widgets, perform the following steps:

1. Under **Click to add actions**, scroll to the **Widgets** drop-down menu and click on **Move**.
2. Under **Configure actions**, in the section **Select the widgets to move**, under the **ShoppingBagFooter** dropdown, click on the checkbox next to **AboutUsLink**.
3. Under **Configure actions**, in the section **Move**, in the first drop-down menu, select **by**, and in the **y:** field, enter 220 in the text field.
4. Under **Configure actions**, in the section **Select the widgets to move**, under the **ShoppingBagFooter** dropdown, click on the checkbox next to **CopyrightLink**.
5. Under **Configure actions**, in the section **Move**, in the first drop-down menu, select **by**, and in the **y:** field, enter 220 in the text field.
6. Under **Configure actions**, in the section **Select the widgets to move**, under the **ShoppingBagFooter** dropdown, click on the checkbox next to **TermsLink**.
7. Under **Configure actions**, in the section **Move**, in the first drop-down menu, select **by**, and in the **y:** field, enter 220 in the text field.
8. Under **Configure actions**, in the section **Select the widgets to move**, under the **ShoppingBagFooter** dropdown, click on the checkbox next to **PrivacyLink**.
9. Under **Configure actions**, in the section **Move**, in the first drop-down menu, select **by**, and in the **y:** field, enter 220 in the text field.
10. Click on **OK**.
11. Under the **OnPageLoad** event, right-click on the **MoveMyShoppingBagFooter** case and click on **Toggle IF/ELSE IF**.

With the **MyShoppingBag OnItemLoad** interactions defined, we are now ready to define interactions for the **MyShoppingBagRepeater** item.

MyShoppingBagRepeater item OnClick interactions

The MyShoppingBagRepeater Repeater item supports the following events:

- An OnClick event on the BagItemImageRepeater Image widget
- An OnClick event on the RemoveItemLabel Label widget
- An OnClick event on the UpdateLineItem Button widget

We will now define the **OnClick** events for each of the three widgets.

Adding an OnClick event to the BagItemImageRepeater

The BagItemImageRepeater widget's OnClick event leverages a single case called ItemImageClicked. We will now add the interactions.

Defining the ItemImageClicked Case

With the Shopping Bag Repeater master opened in the design area, double-click on the MyShoppingBagRepeater at the coordinates (10,260). The MyShoppingBagRepeater will open in the design area. With the MyShoppingBagRepeater opened in the design area, click on the BagItemImageRepeater at the coordinates (13,24) and do the following:

In the **Widget Interactions and Notes** pane, click on the **Interactions** tab and double-click on the **OnClick** event. A **Case Editor** dialog box will open. Within the **Case Editor** dialog in the **Case Description** field, type `ItemImageClicked`, and perform the steps given in the following sections.

Create the actions

To set the variable value for SubTotal, perform the following steps:

1. Under **Click to add actions**, scroll to the **Variables** drop-down menu and click on **Set Variable Value**.

2. Under **Configure actions**, in the section **Select the variables to set**, click on the checkbox next to **SubTotal**.

3. Under **Configure actions**, in the section **Set variable to**, in the first drop-down menu, select **value** and enter `0` in the text field.

To set the variable value for ShowDetail, perform the following steps:

1. Under **Click to add actions**, scroll to the **Variables** drop-down menu and click on **Set Variable Value**.

2. Under **Configure actions**, in the section **Select the variables to set**, click on the checkbox next to **ShowDetail**.

3. Under **Configure actions**, in the section **Set variable to**, in the first drop-down menu, select **value** and enter `[[Item.SKU]]` in the text field.

To set the variable value for SKU_CrossSell1, SKU_CrossSell2, and SKU_CrossSell3, perform the following steps:

1. Under **Click to add actions**, scroll to the **Variables** drop-down menu and click on **Set Variable Value**.

2. Under **Configure actions**, in the section **Select the variables to set**, click on the checkbox next to **SKU_CrossSell1**.

3. Under **Configure actions**, in the section **Set variable to**, in the first drop-down menu, select **value** and enter `[[Item.SKU_CrossSell1]]` in the text field.

4. Under **Configure actions**, in the section **Select the variables to set**, click on the checkbox next to **SKU_CrossSell2**.

5. Under **Configure actions**, in the section **Set variable to**, in the first drop-down menu, select **value** and enter `[[Item.SKU_CrossSell2]]` in the text field.

6. Under **Configure actions**, in the section **Select the variables to set**, click on the checkbox next to **SKU_CrossSell3**.

7. Under **Configure actions**, in the section **Set variable to**, in the first drop-down menu, select **value** and enter `[[Item.SKU_CrossSell3]]` in the text field.

To open the **Category** page in the current window, perform the following steps:

1. Under **Click to add actions**, scroll to the **Links** drop-down menu. Under the **Open Link** drop-down menu, click on **Current Window**.

2. Under **Configure actions**, with the **Link to a page in this design** Radio Button selected, in the **Sitemap**, click on the **Category** page.

3. Click on **OK**.

Next, we will add an **OnClick** event on the **RemoveItemLabel** widget.

Adding an OnClick event to the RemoveItemLabel

The RemoveItemLabel widget's **OnClick** event leverages two cases called RemoveItemLabelClicked and NoItems. We will now create the cases and add the interactions.

Defining the RemoveItemLabelClicked Case

With the MyShoppingBagRepeater still open in the design area, click on the RemoveItemLabel at the coordinates (220,187) and perform the following steps.

Create the actions

In the **Widget Interactions and Notes** pane, click on the **Interactions** tab and double-click on the **OnClick** event. A **Case Editor** dialog box will open. Within the **Case Editor** dialog in the **Case Description** field, type `RemoveItemLabelClicked` and perform the following steps:

To set the variable value for SubTotal, perform the following steps:

1. Under **Click to add actions**, scroll to the **Variables** drop-down menu and click on **Set Variable Value**.

2. Under **Configure actions**, in the section **Select the variables to set**, click on the checkbox next to **SubTotal**.

3. Under **Configure actions**, in the section **Set variable to**, in the first drop-down menu, select **value** and enter 0 in the text field.

To delete rows from the Repeater, perform the following steps:

1. Under **Click to add actions**, scroll to the **Repeaters** drop-down menu, click on the **Datasets** dropdown and then on **Delete Rows**.

2. Under **Configure actions**, in the section **Select the repeaters to delete their items from**, click the checkbox next to **MyShoppingBagRepeater**.

3. Under **Configure actions**, in the section **Select the repeaters to delete their items from**, click on the radio button next to **This**.

To move the Footer widgets, perform the following steps:

1. Under **Click to add actions**, scroll to the **Widgets** drop-down menu and click on **Move**.

2. Under **Configure actions**, in the section **Select the widgets to move**, under the **ShoppingBagFooter** dropdown, click on the checkbox next to **AboutUsLink**.

3. Under **Configure actions**, in the section **Move**, in the first drop-down menu, select **by**, and in the **y:** field, enter -220 in the text field.

4. Under **Configure actions**, in the section **Select the widgets to move**, under the **ShoppingBagFooter** dropdown, click on the checkbox next to **CopyrightLink**.

5. Under **Configure actions**, in the section **Move**, in the first drop-down menu, select **by**, and in the **y:** field, enter -220 in the text field.

6. Under **Configure actions**, in the section **Select the widgets to move**, under the **ShoppingBagFooter** dropdown, click on the checkbox next to **TermsLink**.

7. Under **Configure actions**, in the section **Move**, in the first drop-down menu, select **by**, and in the **y:** field, enter `-220` in the text field.

8. Under **Configure actions**, in the section **Select the widgets to move**, under the **ShoppingBagFooter** dropdown, click on the checkbox next to **PrivacyLink**.

9. Under **Configure actions**, in the section **Move**, in the first drop-down menu, select **by**, and in the **y:** field, enter `-220` in the text field.

10. Click on **OK**.

To set the text on BagNumOfItemsLabel, perform the following steps:

1. Under **Click to add actions**, scroll to the **Widgets** drop-down menu and click on **Set Text**.

2. Under **Configure actions**, in the section **Select the widgets to set text**, click on the checkbox next to **BagItemBrandRepeater**.

3. Under **Configure actions**, in the section **Set variable to**, in the first drop-down menu, select **value**. Beside the **value** text field, click on **fx** to open the **Edit Value** dialog box. In the **Edit Value** dialog box, under **Insert Variable or Function...**, type `[[LVAR1.itemcount]]`. Beneath **Local Variables**, under **Add Local Variable**, in the text field, type `LVAR1`. In the first dropdown, select **value of variable**. In the second dropdown, select **MyShoppingBagRepeater**.

4. Click on **OK**.

Next, we will define the NoItems case for the **OnClick** event on the **RemoveItemLabel** widget.

Defining the NoItems Case

With the MyShoppingBagRepeater still open in the design area, perform the following steps.

Create the condition

Click on the MyShoppingBagRepeater. In the **Widget Interactions and Notes** pane, click on the **Interactions** tab and double-click on the **OnItemLoad** event. A **Case Editor** dialog box will open. Within the **Case Editor** dialog in the **Case Description** field, type `NoItems` and perform the following steps:

1. Click on the **Add Condition** button.

2. In the **Condition Builder** dialog box, in the outlined condition box, perform the following steps:

    1. In the first dropdown, select **value of variable**.

2. In the second dropdown, select **BagNumOfItemsLabel**.

3. In the third dropdown, select **equals**.

4. In the fourth dropdown, select **value**.

5. In the text field, enter 0.

6. Click on **OK**.

Create the action

To set the text on BagSubTotal, perform the following steps:

1. Under **Click to add actions**, scroll to the **Widgets** drop-down menu and click on **Set Text**.

2. Under **Configure actions**, in the section **Select the widgets to set text**, click on the checkbox next to **BagSubTotal**.

3. Under **Configure actions**, in the section **Set variable to**, in the first drop-down menu, select **value** and enter 0.00 in the text field.

4. Click on **OK**.

5. Under the **OnPageLoad** event, right-click on the **NoItems** case and click on **Toggle IF/ELSE IF**.

Next, we will add an **OnClick** event on the **UpdateLineItemButton** label widget.

Adding an OnClick event to the UpdateLineItemButton

The UpdateLineItemButton widget's **OnClick** event leverages three cases called UpdateButtonClicked, QtyZero, and NoItems. We will now create the cases and add the interactions.

Defining the UpdateButtonClicked Case

With the **MyShoppingBagRepeater** still open in the design area, click on the **UpdateLineItemButton** at the coordinates (640,20) and perform the following steps.

Create the actions

In the **Widget Interactions and Notes** pane, click on the **Interactions** tab and double-click on the **OnClick** event. A **Case Editor** dialog box will open. Within the **Case Editor** dialog in the **Case Description** field, type UpdateButtonClicked and perform the following:

To set the variable value for SubTotal, perform the following steps:

1. Under **Click to add actions**, scroll to the **Variables** drop-down menu and click on **Set Variable Value**.

2. Under **Configure actions**, in the section **Select the variables to set**, click on the checkbox next to **SubTotal**.

3. Under **Configure actions**, in the section **Set variable to**, in the first drop-down menu, select **value** and enter 0 in the text field.

Updating ItemColor, ItemSize, and ItemQty on the current row of the Repeater

To update ItemColor, ItemSize, and ItemQty on the current row of the Repeater, perform the following steps:

Under **Click to add actions**, scroll to the **Repeaters** drop-down menu, click on the **Datasets** dropdown, and click on **Update Rows**. Under **Configure actions**, in the section **Select the repeaters to update their rows**, perform the following steps:

1. Click on the checkbox next to **MyShoppingBagRepeater**.

2. Click on the radio button next to **This**.

3. Click on the **Select Column** dropdown and then on **ItemColor**. **ItemColor** will be displayed under the **Column** heading.

4. Under the **Value** heading, click on the row next to **ItemColor** and then click on **fx**. An **Edit Value** dialog box will open.

5. Under **Local Variables**, click on the **Add Local Variable** link and perform the following steps:

   1. In the first text field, type ColorSelection.

   2. In the second dropdown, select **selected option of**.

   3. In the third dropdown, select **ColorDroplist**.

   4. In the first textbox, replace the current text with [[ColorSelection]].

   5. Click on **OK**.

6. Click on the **Select Column** dropdown and then click on **ItemSize**. **ItemSize** will be displayed under the **Column** heading.

7. Under the **Value** heading, click on the row next to **ItemSize** and click on **fx**. An **Edit Value** dialog box will open.

8. Under **Local Variables**, click on the **Add Local Variable** link and perform the following steps:

    1. In the first text field, type `SizeSelection`.

    2. In the second dropdown, select **selected option of**.

    3. In the third dropdown, select **SizeDroplist**.

    4. In the first textbox, replace the current text with `[[SizeSelection]]`.

    5. Click on **OK**.

9. Click on the **Select Column** dropdown and then click on **ItemQty**. **ItemQty** will be displayed under the **Column** heading.

10. Under the **Value** heading, click on the row next to **ItemQty** and click on **fx**. An **Edit Value** dialog box will open.

11. Under **Local Variables**, click on the **Add Local Variable** link and perform the following steps:

    1. In the first text field, type `QtySelection`.

    2. In the second dropdown, select **text on widget**.

    3. In the third dropdown, select **BagItemQtyTextField**.

    4. In the first textbox, replace the current text with `[[QtySelection]]`.

    5. Click **OK**.

12. Click on **OK**.

Next, we will define the **QtyZero** case for the **OnClick** event on the **UpdateLineItemButton** widget.

Defining the QtyZero Case

With the **MyShoppingBagRepeater** still open in the design area, click on the **UpdateLineItemButton** at the coordinates (640,20) and perform the following steps.

Create the actions

In the **Widget Interactions and Notes** pane, click on the **Interactions** tab and double-click on the **OnClick** event. A **Case Editor** dialog box will open. Within the **Case Editor** dialog in the **Case Description** field, type `QtyZero` and perform the following steps:

To set the variable value for SubTotal, perform the following steps:

1. Under **Click to add actions**, scroll to the **Variables** drop-down menu and click on **Set Variable Value**.

2. Under **Configure actions**, in the section **Select the variables to set**, click on the checkbox next to **SubTotal**.

3. Under **Configure actions**, in the section **Set variable to**, in the first drop-down menu, select **value** and enter 0 in the text field.

To delete rows from the Repeater, perform the following steps:

1. Under **Click to add actions**, scroll to the **Repeaters** drop-down menu, click on the **Datasets** dropdown, and click on **Delete Rows**.

2. Under **Configure actions**, in the section **Select the repeaters to delete their items from**, click on the checkbox next to **MyShoppingBagRepeater**.

3. Under **Configure actions**, in the section **Select the repeaters to delete their items from**, click on the radio button next to **This**.

To move the Footer widgets, perform the following steps:

1. Under **Click to add actions**, scroll to the **Widgets** drop-down menu and click on **Move**.

2. Under **Configure actions**, in the section **Select the widgets to move**, under the **ShoppingBagFooter** dropdown, click on the checkbox next to **AboutUsLink**.

3. Under **Configure actions**, in the section **Move**, in the first drop-down menu, select **by**, and in the **y:** field, enter -220 in the text field.

4. Under **Configure actions**, in the section **Select the widgets to move**, under the **ShoppingBagFooter** dropdown, click on the checkbox next to **CopyrightLink**.

5. Under **Configure actions**, in the section **Move**, in the first drop-down menu, select **by**, and in the **y:** field, enter -220 in the text field.

6. Under **Configure actions**, in the section **Select the widgets to move**, under the **ShoppingBagFooter** dropdown, click on the checkbox next to **TermsLink**.

7. Under **Configure actions**, in the section **Move**, in the first drop-down menu, select **by**, and in the **y:** field, enter -220 in the text field.

8. Under **Configure actions**, in the section **Select the widgets to move**, under the **ShoppingBagFooter** dropdown, click on the checkbox next to **PrivacyLink**.

9. Under **Configure actions**, in the section **Move**, in the first drop-down menu, select **by**, and in the **y:** field, enter `-220` in the text field.

10. Click **OK**.

To set the text on BagNumOfItemsLabel, perform the following steps:

1. Under **Click to add actions**, scroll to the **Widgets** drop-down menu and click on **Set Text**.

2. Under **Configure actions**, in the section **Select the widgets to set text**, click on the checkbox next to **BagItemBrandRepeater**.

3. Under **Configure actions**, in the section **Set variable to**, in the first drop-down menu, select **value**. Beside the **value** text field, click on **fx** to open the **Edit Value** dialog box. In the **Edit Value** dialog box, under **Insert Variable or Function...**, type `[[LVAR1.itemcount]]`. Beneath **Local Variables** under **Add Local Variable**, in the text field, type `LVAR1`. In the first dropdown, select **value of variable**. In the second dropdown, select **MyShoppingBagRepeater**.

4. Click on **OK**.

5. Under the **OnPageLoad** event, right-click on the **NoItems** case and click on **Toggle IF/ELSE IF**.

Next, we will define the NoItems case for the OnClick event on the UpdateLineItemButton button widget.

Defining the NoItems Case

With the MyShoppingBagRepeater still open in the design area, click on the UpdateLineItemButton at the coordinates (640,20) and perform the steps given in the following section.

Create the condition

Click on the MyShoppingBagRepeater. In the **Widget Interactions and Notes** pane, click on the **Interactions** tab and double-click on the **OnItemLoad** event. A **Case Editor** dialog box will open. Within the **Case Editor** dialog in the **Case Description** field, type `NoItems` and perform the following steps:

1. Click on the **Add Condition** button.

2. In the **Condition Builder** dialog box, in the outlined condition box, perform the following steps:

   1. In the first dropdown, select **value of variable**.

   2. In the second dropdown, select **BagNumOfItemsLabel**.

   3. In the third dropdown, select **equals**.

4. In the fourth dropdown, select **value**.

5. In the text field, enter 0.

6. Click on **OK**.

To set the text on BagSubTotal, perform the following steps:

1. Under **Click to add actions**, scroll to the **Widgets** drop-down menu and click on **Set Text**.

2. Under **Configure actions**, in the section **Select the widgets to set text**, click on the checkbox next to **BagSubTotal**.

3. Under **Configure actions**, in the section **Set variable to**, in the first drop-down menu, select **value** and enter 0.00 in the text field.

4. Click on **OK**.

5. Under the **OnPageLoad** event, right-click on the **NoItems** case and click on **Toggle IF/ELSE IF**.

With the interactions completed for the **Shopping Bag Repeater Master**, we are now ready to design the Shopping Bag page.

Viewing our Shopping Bag page

The Shopping Bag page is comprised of the Header and Shopping Bag Repeater masters. The Category Repeater item on the Shopping Bag Repeater master is used to display the list of items currently in the Shopping Bag. Every item in the Shopping Bag Repeater dataset will be displayed in the order it was added to the Shopping Bag.

Once completed, our Shopping Bag page will look like this:

To build the Shopping Bag page, we will first place the Header and Shopping Bag Repeater masters. Next, we will place a **Heading 2** widget to complete the design.

Designing our Shopping Bag Page

To create the Shopping Bag page, perform the following steps:

1. In the **Sitemap** pane, double-click on the **Shopping Bag** page to open it in the design area.

2. From the **Masters** pane, drag the **Header** master and drop it at any location on the wireframe.

3. From the **Masters** pane, drag the **Shopping Bag Repeater** master and drop it at any location on the wireframe. In the **Widget Interactions and Notes** pane, in the Shopping Bag Repeater Name field, type MyShoppingBagRepeater.

4. From the **Widgets** pane, drag the **Heading 2** widget and place it at the coordinates (10,140). With the **Heading 2** widget selected, perform the following steps:

    ° Type Shopping Bag. We will see the text displayed as text on the **Heading 2** widget.

    ° In the toolbar, change the value of **w** to 191 and **h** to 32.

    ° In the **Widget Interactions and Notes** pane, click in the **Shape Name** field and type ShoppingBagHeading.

    ° In the **Widget Properties and Style** pane, with the **Style** tab selected, scroll to **Font** and change the font size to 28.

Summary

In this chapter, we created a Shopping Bag with interactions, as well as a new Shopping Bag Repeater master. The Shopping Bag page utilized a Header, Footer, and a Repeater item from the Shopping Bag Repeater master.

In the next chapter, we will complete the design and interactions for a CheckOut flow.

Self-test questions

- Why do e-commerce sites leverage shopping bags?
- What changes occur and which repeaters are updated when a user adds an item to the Shopping Bag?
- To create the MyShoppingBagRepeater, did we leverage an existing Master or create a new Repeater widget?
- How many columns does the Repeater Dataset contain for the MyShoppingBagRepeater?
- What are the names of the columns in the MyShoppingBagRepeater Dataset?
- How many cases are there and what are the names of the cases for the MyShoppingBagRepeater OnItemLoad event?
- How many and which Masters make up the Shopping Bag page?

8
Check Out Flow and Interactions

With the Shopping Cart functionality added to our prototype, we are now ready to create our checkout flow with interactions. Our check out flow will provide a progress indicator with three states and an additional confirmation page. To accomplish this, we will create a Check Out dynamic panel with four states.

In this chapter, you will learn about:

- Creating our Individual Form Field master
- Defining the Check Out dynamic panel

    ° Designing the SignIn state
    ° Designing the PaymentAndShipping state
    ° Designing the PlaceOrder state
    ° Designing the Confirmation state

Our Check Out dynamic panel will contain a streamlined header. The streamlined header will only have our logo and a process indicator. The goal for the Check Out page and dynamic panel is to remove visual clutter thereby reducing distractions. This approach allows the user to focus on completing our checkout flow.

We will create an Individual Form Field master to reduce the complexity of building our forms. We also need to identify the required states for the Check Out dynamic panel. Based on our experience and current industry trends, we determined that our checkout flow should have four steps. Our Check Out dynamic panel's four states are as follows:

- SignIn
- PaymentAndShipping

- PlaceOrder
- Confirmation

We will first create the Individual Form Field master. We will then define the Check Out dynamic panel and its states.

Creating our Individual Form Field master

Our Individual Form Field master will raise three raised events named **OnFormFieldFocus**, **OnFormFieldLostFocus**, and **OnFormFieldKeyUp**. The Individual Form Field master will also consist of the following widgets:

- Form Error Message Rectangle
- Form Error Message Label
- Form Rectangle
- Form Text Field

Design and interactions

We are now ready to create the Individual Form Field master. To create the Individual Form Field master, perform the following steps:

1. In the **Masters** pane, click on the Add Master icon. Slow-click on the master labeled **New Master 1** to select it, type `Individual Form Field`, and press *Enter*.

2. In the **Masters** pane, right-click on the icon next to **CMS Repeater**, bring your mouse over **Drop Behavior** and click on **Break Away**.

3. In the **Masters** pane, double-click on the icon next to the **Individual Form Field** master to open it in the design area.

We are now ready to place widgets and define the three raised events. To place widgets, perform the following steps:

1. From the **Widgets** pane, drag the **Rectangle** widget and place at coordinates (119,0).

2. With the **Rectangle** widget selected, perform the following steps:

   1. In the toolbar, change the value of **w** to `186` and **h** to `41`.

2. In the **Widget Interactions and Notes** pane, click in the **Shape Name** textbox and type `FormErrorMsgRectangle`.

3. In the **Widget Properties and Style** pane, scroll to **Font** with the **Style** tab selected. Perform the following steps:

    1. In the **Widget Properties and Style** pane, scroll to **Fills, Lines, + Borders** with the **Style** tab selected and click on the down arrow next to the Line Color (pencil) icon. In the **#** text field in the drop-down menu, enter `FF0000`.

    2. In the **Widget Properties and Style** pane, scroll to **Fills, Lines, + Borders** with the **Style** tab selected and click on the down arrow next to the Fill Color (paint bucket) icon. In the **#** text field in the drop-down menu, enter `FF0000`.

3. From the **Widgets** pane, drag the **Label** widget and place at coordinates (123,28).

4. With the **Label** widget selected, perform the following steps:

    1. Type `Form Error Message Label`. You will see **Form Error Message Label** displayed as text on the **Label** widget.

    2. In the toolbar, change the value of **w** to `180` and **h** to `13` and click on the checkbox next to **Hidden**.

    3. In the **Widget Interactions and Notes** pane, click in the **Shape Name** textbox and type `FormErrorMsgLabel`.

    4. In the **Widget Properties and Style** pane, scroll to **Font** with the **Style** tab selected. Perform the following steps:

        1. Change the font size to `11`.

        2. Click on the down arrow next to the Text Color icon. In the **#** text field in the drop-down menu, enter `FFFFFF`.

5. From the **Widgets** pane, drag the **Rectangle** widget and place at coordinates (122,2).

6. With the **Rectangle** widget selected, perform the following steps:

    1. In the toolbar, change the value of **w** to `180` and **h** to `25`.

    2. In the **Widget Interactions and Notes** pane, click in the **Shape Name** textbox and type `FormRectangle`.

    3. In the **Widget Properties and Style** pane, scroll to **Font** with the **Style** tab selected. Perform the following steps:

        ◦ Change the font size to `18`.

      °   Click on the down arrow next to the Text Color icon. In the **#** text field in the drop-down menu, enter `FF0000`.

    4. In the **Widget Properties and Style** pane, scroll to **Alignment + Padding** with the **Style** tab selected. Under **Alignment + Padding**, click on the third icon ▣ in the first set of icons to right-align the text on the **Rectangle** widget.

7. From the **Widgets** pane, drag the **Text Field** widget and place at coordinates (122,3).

8. With the **Text Field** widget selected, perform the following steps:

    1. Type `Form Text Field`. You will see **Form Text Field** displayed as text on the **Label** widget.

    2. In the toolbar, change the value of **w** to `157` and **h** to `23`.

    3. In the **Widget Interactions and Notes** pane, click in the **Shape Name** textbox and type `FormTextField`.

    4. In the **Widget Properties and Style** pane, scroll to **Font** with the **Style** tab selected. Click on the down arrow next to the Text Color icon. In the **#** text field in the drop-down menu, enter `666666`.

    5. In the **Widget Properties and Style** pane, click on the **Properties** tab to select. Scroll to the **Text Field** drop-down list and click on the **Hide Border** checkbox.

With the widgets placed, we are now ready to define cases and raised events as follows:

- Define the **SetFocusOnMouseEnter** case for the **OnMouseEnter** event

- Define the **RaiseEventOnFocus** case for the **OnFocus** event that creates a raised event **OnFormFieldFocus**

- Define the **RaiseEventOnLostFocus** case for the **OnLostFocus** event that creates a raised event **OnFormFieldLostFocus**

To define the interactions and the raised events, with the Individual Form Field master opened in the design area, click on the **FormTextField** at coordinates (125,3). Perform the following actions:

1. To define the **SetFocusOnMouseEnter** case for the **OnMouseEnter** event, click on the **Interactions** tab in the **Widget Interactions and Notes** pane and double-click on **OnMouseEnter**. A **Case Editor** dialog box will open. In the **Case Editor** dialog, perform the following steps to create the action; this will create the raised event:

1. In the **Case description** field, enter `SetFocusOnMouseEnter`.

2. Under **Click to add actions**, click on the **Widgets** drop-down menu and click on **Focus**.

3. Under **Configure actions**, click on the checkbox next to **This Widget** in the **Select widget to focus** section.

4. Click on **OK**.

2. To define the **RaiseEventOnFocus** case for the **OnFocus** event and the **OnFormFieldFocus** raised event, click on the **Interactions** tab in the **Widget Interactions and Notes** pane and double-click on **OnFocus**. A **Case Editor** dialog box will open. In the **Case Editor** dialog, perform the following steps to create the action; this will set focus on the **FormTextField**:

   1. In the **Case description** field, enter `RaiseEventOnFocus`.

   2. Under **Click to add actions**, click on the **Miscellaneous** drop-down menu and click on **Raise Event**.

   3. Under **Configure actions**, click on the green plus sign in the **Check the events to raise in this action** section.

   4. In the **NewEvent** field, enter `OnFormFieldFocus`. Click on the checkbox next to **OnFormFieldFocus**.

   5. Click on **OK**.

3. To define the **RaiseEventOnLostFocus** case for the **OnLostFocus** event and the **OnFormFieldLostFocus** raised event, click on the **Interactions** tab in the **Widget Interactions and Notes** pane and double-click **OnLostFocus**. A **Case Editor** dialog box will open. In the **Case Editor** dialog, perform the following steps to create the action; this will create the raised event:

   1. In the **Case description** field, enter `RaiseEventOnLostFocus`.

   2. Under **Click to add actions**, click on the **Miscellaneous** drop-down menu and click on **Raise Event**.

   3. Under **Configure actions**, in the **Check the events to raise in this action** section, click on the green plus sign.

   4. In the **NewEvent** field, enter `OnFormFieldLostFocus`. Click on the checkbox next to **OnFormFieldLostFocus**.

   5. Click on **OK**.

4. To define the **RaiseEventOnKeyUp** case for the **OnKeyUp** event and the **OnFormFieldKeyUp** raised event, click on the **Interactions** tab in the **Widget Interactions and Notes** pane, and then on **More Events** and finally on **OnKeyUp** to add to the list of events. Double-click on **OnKeyUp**. A **Case Editor** dialog box will open. In the **Case Editor** dialog, perform the following steps to create the action; this will create the raised event:

    1. In the **Case description** field, enter `RaiseEventOnKeyUp`.

    2. Under **Click to add actions**, click on the **Miscellaneous** drop-down menu and then on **Raise Event**.

    3. Under **Configure actions**, click on the green plus sign in the **Check the events to raise in this action** section.

    4. In the **NewEvent** field, enter `OnFormFieldKeyUp`. Click on the checkbox next to **OnFormFieldKeyUp**.

    5. Click on **OK**.

With the Individual Form Field master and raised events defined, you are ready to define the Check Out dynamic panel with four states.

Defining the Check Out dynamic panel

The individual states of the **Check Out** dynamic panel will be used to display associated content with the current step in our check out flow. To create the **Check Out** page and place the **CheckOutDynamicPanel** perform the following steps:

1. In the **Sitemap** pane, click on the Add Page icon and type `Check Out`. Click-and-drag the **Check Out** page to appear in the **Sitemap** after the **Shopping Bag** page.

2. In the **Sitemap** pane, double-click on the **Check Out** page to open it in the design area.

3. From the **Widgets** pane, drag the **Dynamic Panel** widget and place at coordinates (0,0). With the **Dynamic Panel** widget selected, perform the following steps:

    1. In the toolbar, change the value of **w** to `960`, **h** to `1080`, and click on the checkbox next to **Hidden**.

    2. In the **Widget Interactions and Notes** pane, click in the **Dynamic Name** textbox and type `CheckOutDynamicPanel`.

    3. In the **Widget Manager** pane, slow double-click the state named **State1** and rename to `SignIn`. Press *Enter* (that is return) to accept the change.

4. In the **Widget Manager** pane, double-click on the **SignIn** state to open it in the design area.

5. In the **Widgets** pane, click on the **Placeholder** widget. While holding down the mouse button, drag the **Placeholder** widget and place at coordinates (10,10).

6. With the **Placeholder** widget selected, type Logo. You will see **Logo** in the center of the **Placeholder** widget.

7. Next, you will name the **Placeholder** widget and add the **OnClick** interaction. With the **Placeholder** widget selected, perform the following action:

   In the **Widget Interactions and Notes** pane, click in the **Shape Name** textbox and type Logo.

8. In the **Widget Interactions and Notes** pane, click on the **Interactions** tab and click on **Create Link...**. In the **Sitemap** modal window, click on the **Home** page.

9. To create the **Check Out** progress indicator, perform the following action:

   From the **Widgets** pane, drag the **Label** widget and place at coordinates (309,92). With the **Label** widget selected, perform the following steps:

   1. Type Sign In. You will see **Sign In** displayed as text on the **Label** widget.

   2. In the **Widget Interactions and Notes** pane, click in the **Shape Name** textbox and type SignInIndicator.

   3. In the **Widget Properties and Style** pane, click on the down arrow next to the Text Color icon and scroll to **Font** with the **Style** tab selected. In the **#** text field in the drop-down menu, enter C9C9C9.

   4. Repeat step 9 four times to create additional **Label** widgets using the values given in the following table for coordinates, text displayed, shape name, and color:

Coordinates	Text displayed	Shape name	Color
(384,92)	>	**Separator1**	FF6600
(418,92)	**Payment & Shipping**	**PaymentShippingIndicator**	C9C9C9
(590,92)	>	**Separator2**	FF6600
(624,92)	**Check Out**	**PlaceOrderIndicator**	C9C9C9

10. In the **Widget Manager** pane, right-click on the **CheckOutLogIn** state and click on **Duplicate State**. In the **Widget Manager** pane, slow double-click on the state named **State1** and rename to `PaymentAndShipping`.

11. In the **Widget Manager** pane, right-click on the **CheckOutLogIn** state and click on **Duplicate State**. In the **Widget Manager** pane, slow double-click on the state named **State1** and rename to `PlaceOrder`.

12. In the **Widget Manager** pane, right-click on the **CheckOutLogIn** state and click on **Add State**. In the **Widget Manager** pane, slow double-click on the state named **State1** and rename to `Confirmation`.

With the **CheckOutDynamicPanel** placed on the **Check Out** page, you are now ready to design the **SignIn** state.

Designing the SignIn state

For the **SignIn** state on the **CheckOutDynamicPanel**, we will perform the following enhancements:

1. Change the text color of the **SignInIndicator** to indicate a selected state.

2. Add a **Heading 1** widget and use the **Inline Field Validation** and **Footer** masters.

3. Define the validation and feedback interactions.

To enhance the **SignIn** state for the **CheckOutDynamicPanel** perform the following steps:

1. In the **Widget Manager** pane under the **CheckOutDynamicPanel**, double-click on the **SignIn** state to open it in the design area.

2. In the design area, click on the **SignInIndicator** at coordinates (309,92). Perform the following action:

   In the **Widget Properties and Style** pane, scroll to **Font** with the **Style** tab selected. Click on the down arrow next to the Text Color icon. In the **#** text field in the drop-down menu, enter `515151`.

3. From the Widgets pane, drag the **Heading 1** widget and place at coordinates (308,220).

4. With the **Heading 1** widget selected, type `Sign In`.

5. In the **Widget Interactions and Notes** pane, click in the **Shape Name** textbox and type `SignInHeading1`.

6. From the **Masters** pane, drag the **Inline Field Validation** master and drop at any location on the wireframe. In the **Widget Interactions and Notes** pane, click in the **Inline Field Validation Footnote and Name** textbox and type `SignInValidationMaster`.

7. From the **Widgets** pane, drag the **Label** widget and place at coordinates (438,528).

8. With the **Label** widget selected, type `Forgot Password?`. You will see the text displayed on the **Label** widget.

9. In the **Widget Interactions and Notes** pane, click in the **Shape Name** textbox and type `ForgotPassword`.

10. In the **Widget Properties and Style** pane, scroll to **Font** with the **Style** tab selected. Perform the following steps:

    1. Change the font size to `11`.

    2. Click on the Underline icon.

    3. Click on the down arrow next to the Text Color icon. In the # text field in the drop-down menu, enter `515151`.

11. From the **Masters** pane, drag the **Footer** master and place at coordinates (10,725).

With the **SignIn** state layout for the **CheckOutDynamicPanel** completed, you are now ready to define validation and feedback interactions.

Validation and feedback on the Sign In page

To perform validation and provide user feedback on the **Sign In** page, you will leverage two of the **Inline Field Validation** master's raised events:

- **OnValidSignInEmail**
- **OnSignInSubmitClick**

You will name the instance of the **Inline Field Validation** master on the **Check Out** page **SignInValidationMaster**. For **SignInValidationMaster**, you will create new cases for both the raised events.

Defining the case for the OnValidSignInEmail event

To create the case for the **OnValidSignInEmail** event, click on the
SignInValidationMaster near coordinates (500,250) to select. In the **Widget
Interactions and Notes** pane, click on the **Interactions** tab and double-click on
OnValidSignUpEmail. A **Case Editor** dialog box will open. In the **Case Editor**
dialog, perform the following steps:

1. To set the text on the **EmailRectangle** widget, perform the following steps:

    1. Under **Click to add actions**, scroll to the **Widgets** drop-down
    menu and click on **Set Text**.

    2. Under **Configure actions**, scroll to the **SignInValidationMaster**
    drop-down, expand it, and click on the checkbox next to
    EmailRectangle.

    3. Under **Set text to**, click on the first dropdown and then on **value**.

2. To hide **SignIn/EmailMsgRectangle** and **SignIn/EmailMsgLabel**, perform
the following action:

    Under **Click to add actions**, scroll to the **Widgets** drop-down menu,
    click on the **Show/Hide** drop-down menu and then on **Hide**.

3. Under **Configure actions**, scroll to the **SignInValidationMaster** drop-down
menu, click to expand and click on the checkbox next to **EmailMsgRectangle**.

4. Click on the dropdown next to **Animate** and then on **fade**. Leave the value
of **t** set to 500 ms.

5. Under **Configure actions**, scroll to the **SignInValidationMaster** drop-
down menu, click to expand and then click on the checkbox next to
EmailMsgLabel.

6. Click on the drop-down next to **Animate** and then on **none**.

7. Click on **OK**.

Defining cases for the OnSignInSubmitClick event

For the **OnSignInSubmitClick** event, there will be three cases: Successful Default
Login, Successful New Account Login, and GlobalError. To create the cases for the
OnSignInSubmitClick event, perform the steps given in the upcoming section.

Creating the Successful Default Login case

With the **SignInValidationMaster** selected, click on the **Interactions** tab in the
Widget Interactions and Notes pane and double-click **OnSignInSubmitClick**.
A **Case Editor** dialog box will open. In the **Case Editor** dialog, perform the steps
explained in this section.

Create the conditions as follows:

1. In the **Case description** field, enter `Successful Default Login`.

2. Add the first condition by clicking on the **Add Condition** button.

   In the **Condition Builder** dialog box, perform the following steps:

   1. In the first drop-down list, select **text on widget**.

   2. In the second drop-down list, click on the **SignInValidationMaster** option to expand it and select **EmailTextField**.

   3. In the third drop-down list, select **equals**.

   4. In the fourth drop-down list, select **value of variable**.

   5. In the fifth drop-down list, select **DefaultAccountEmail**.

3. Add the second condition by clicking on the green plus sign.

   In the **Condition Builder** dialog box, perform the following steps:

   1. In the first drop-down list, select **text on widget**.

   2. In the second drop-down list, click on the **SignInValidationMaster** option to expand it and then click on **PasswordTextField**.

   3. In the third drop-down list, select **equals**.

   4. In the fourth drop-down list, select **value of variable**.

   5. In the fifth drop-down list, select **DefaultAccountPassword**.

   6. Click on **OK**.

Create the action to set the value of the **AccountVerified** variable using the following steps:

1. Under **Click to add actions**, scroll to the **Variables** drop-down menu and click on **Set Variable Value**.

2. Under **Configure actions**, click on the checkbox next to **AccountVerified**.

3. Under **Set variable to**, click on the first drop-down list and then on **text on widget**.

4. Click on the second drop-down list next to the **Set variable** field. In the drop-down menu, click on the down arrow next to **SignInValidationMaster** and then click on **EmailTextField**.

Create the actions to set the panel state of the **CheckOutDynamicPanel** using the following steps:

1. Under **Click to add actions**, click on the **Dynamic Panels** drop-down menu and then on **Set Panel State**.

2. Under **Configure actions**, click on the checkbox next to **SetCheckOutDynamicPanel** in the **Select the panels to set the state** section.

3. Under **Configure actions**, select **PaymentAndShipping** from the **Select the state** drop-down list.

4. Click on **OK**.

Creating the Successful New Account Login case

With the **SignInValidationMaster** selected, click on the **Interactions** tab in the **Widget Interactions and Notes** pane and double-click **OnSignInSubmitClick**. A **Case Editor** dialog box will open. In the **Case Editor** dialog, do the following.

We will create three conditions as follows:

1. To add the first condition, enter Successful New Account Login in the **Case description** field.

2. Click on the **Add Condition** button.

3. In the **Condition Builder** dialog box, perform the following steps:

    1. In the first drop-down list, select **text on widget**.

    2. In the second drop-down list, expand **SignInValidationMaster** and click on **EmailTextField**.

    3. In the third drop-down list, select **equals**.

    4. In the fourth drop-down list, select **value of variable**.

    5. In the fifth drop-down list, select **UserAccount1Email**.

4. Now to add the second condition, click on the green plus sign.

5. In the **Condition Builder** dialog box, perform the following steps:

    1. In the first drop-down list, select **text on widget**.

    2. In the second drop-down list, expand **SignInValidationMaster** and click on **PasswordTextField**.

    3. In the third drop-down list, select **equals**.

    4. In the fourth drop-down list, select **value of variable**.

    5. In the fifth drop-down list, select **UserAccount1Password**.

6. Click on the green plus sign to add a third condition.
7. In the **Condition Builder** dialog box, perform the following steps:
    1. In the first drop-down list, select **length of variable value**.
    2. In the second drop-down list, click on **UserAccount1Password**.
    3. In the third drop-down list, select **is greater than or equals**.
    4. In the fourth drop-down list, select **value**.
    5. In the textbox, enter 6.
8. Click on **OK**.

The following are the steps to create the action to set the panel state of the **CheckOutDynamicPanel**:

1. Under **Click to add actions**, click on the **Dynamic Panels** drop-down menu and then on **Set Panel State**.
2. Under **Configure actions**, click on the checkbox next to **SetCheckOutDynamicPanel** in the **Select the panels to set the state** section.
3. Under **Configure actions**, select **PaymentAndShipping** from the **Select the state** drop-down list.
4. Click on **OK**.

Creating the GlobalError case

With the **SignInValidationMaster** selected, click on the **Interactions** tab in the **Widget Interactions and Notes** pane and double-click on **OnSignInSubmitClick**. A **Case Editor** dialog box will open. In the **Case description** field, enter GlobalError. Perform the steps mentioned in the upcoming sections to create the actions.

To create the **Show** actions for **SignIn/GlobalErrorMsgRectangle** and **SignIn/GlobalErrorMsgLabel**, perform the following steps:

1. Under **Click to add actions**, scroll to the **Widgets** drop-down menu, expand the **Show/Hide** dropdown, and click on **Show**.
2. Under **Configure actions**, scroll to the **SignInValidationMaster** drop-down list, click to expand and then click on the checkboxes next to **GlobalErrorMsgRectangle** and **GlobalErrorMsgLabel**.

To create the horizontal shaking effect on the **SubmitButton**, you will move the **SignIn/SubmitButton** three times. Perform the steps mentioned in the upcoming sections:

The following are the steps to define the first **Move** interaction:

1. Under **Click to add actions**, scroll to the **Widgets** drop-down menu and click on **Move**.
2. Under **Configure actions**, scroll to the **SignInValidationMaster** drop-down list, click to expand, and then click on the checkbox next to **SubmitButton**.
3. In the **Move** drop-down list, select **to**. In the **x** field, enter 430. In the **y** field, enter 470.
4. In the **Animate** drop-down list, select **bounce**. In the **t** field, enter 150.

The following are the steps to define the second **Move** interaction:

1. Under **Click to add actions**, scroll to the **Widgets** drop-down menu and click on **Move**.
2. Under **Configure actions**, scroll to the **SignInValidationMaster** drop-down list, click to expand and click on the checkbox next to **SubmitButton**.
3. In the **Move** drop-down list, select **to**. In the **x** field, enter 440. In the **y** field, enter 470.
4. In the **Animate** drop-down list, select **bounce**. In the **t** field, enter 150.

The following are the steps to define the third **Move** interaction:

1. Under **Click to add actions**, scroll to the **Widgets** drop-down menu and click on **Move**.
2. Under **Configure actions**, scroll to the **SignInValidationMaster** drop-down list, click to expand and then click on the checkbox next to **SubmitButton**.
3. In the **Move** drop-down list, select **to**. In the **x** field, enter 435. In the **y** field, enter 470.
4. In the **Animate** drop-down list, select **linear**. In the **t** field, enter 100.
5. Click on **OK**.

With the **SignIn** state completed for our **CheckOutDynamicPanel**, we are now ready to design the **PaymentAndShipping** state.

Designing the PaymentAndShipping state

For the **PaymentAndShipping** state on the **CheckOutDynamicPanel**, there will be three sections:

- **Secure Checkout**
- **Billing Address**
- **Shipping Address**

Once completed, the **PaymentAndShipping** state with all error messages visible will look like the following screenshot:

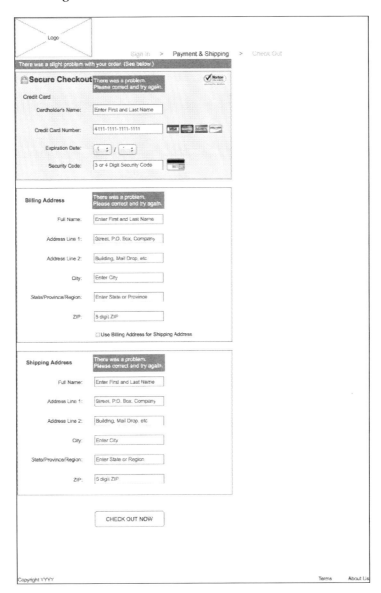

Prior to designing each section, we will update the **SignInIndicator** and place the **Footer** master. Perform the following steps:

1. In the **Widget Manager** pane under the **CheckOutDynamicPanel**, double-click on the **PaymentAndShipping** state to open it in the design area.

2. In the design area, click on the **PaymentShippingIndicator** widget at coordinates (418,92). In the **Widget Properties and Style** pane, scroll to **Font** with the **Style** tab selected. Click on the down arrow next to the Text Color icon. In the # text field in the drop-down menu, enter `515151`.

3. In the **Masters** pane, click on the **Footer** master. While holding down the mouse button, drag the **Footer** master and place at coordinates (10,985).

We will also create Global Error Variables to track the error states of three of our sections as well as place a Global Error Rectangle and Global Error Label.

To determine the state of a given field, we will use a cryptogram where each letter in the Global Error Variable corresponds to a Form Text Field. If the corresponding letter is lowercase, then the field has not been updated or the field entry was invalid. If the field was updated with a valid entry, then the corresponding letter for a Form Text Field will be uppercase. When the user updates a field, the **OnFormFieldLostFocus** event will update the appropriate Global Error Variable with the results of the form field interaction.

The following tables map the Global Error Variables sectionwise with their default values and corresponding Form Text Field states.

The following is the table for the **Secure Checkout** section; the global variable name is `SecureCheckOutError` and its default value is `abc`:

Field name	Valid entry	State Error state
CardholdersName	A	a
CreditCardNumber	B	b
SecurityCode	C	c

The following is the table for the **Billing Address** section; the global variable name is `BilllingAddressError` and its default value is `abcdef`:

Field name	Valid entry	State Error state
BillingFullName	A	a
BillingAddressLine1	B	b
BillingAddressLine2	C	c
BillingCity	D	d
BillingStateProvinceRegion	E	e
BillingZip	F	f

The following is the table for the **Shipping Address** section; the global variable name is `ShippingAddressError` and its default value is `abcdef`:

Field name	Valid entry	State Error state
ShippingFullName	A	a
ShippingAddressLine1	B	b
ShippingAddressLine2	C	c
ShippingCity	D	d
ShippingStateProvinceRegion	E	e
ShippingZip	F	f

When the user clicks on the **CheckOutNowButton**, the Global Error Rectangle and Global Error Label will be shown if any of the Global Error Variables do not match the default values.

To create Global Error Variables, navigate to **Project | Global Variables…**. In the **Global Variables** dialog, perform the following steps:

1. Click on the green plus sign and type `SecureCheckoutError`. Click in the **Default Value** textbox and type `abc`.

2. Click on the green plus sign and type `BillingAddressError`. Click in the **Default Value** textbox and type `abCdef`.

3. Click on the green plus sign and type `ShippingAddressError`. Click in the **Default Value** textbox and type `abCdef`.

To place the Global Error Rectangle and Global Error Label, perform the following steps:

1. From the **Widgets** pane, drag the **Rectangle** widget and place at coordinates (10,116). With the **Rectangle** widget selected, perform the following steps:

    1. In the toolbar, change the value of **w** to `559` and **h** to `24`. Click on the checkbox next to **Hidden**.

    2. In the **Widget Interactions and Notes** pane, click in the **Shape Name** textbox and type `GlobalErrorMsgRectangle`.

    3. In the **Widget Properties and Style** pane, scroll to **Fills, Lines, + Borders** with the **Style** tab selected and perform the following steps:

        1. Click on the down arrow next to the Line Color (pencil) icon. In the **#** text field in the drop-down menu, enter `FF0000`.

   2. Click on the down arrow next to the Fill Color (paint bucket) icon. In the **#** text field in the drop-down menu, enter `FF0000`.

2. From the **Widgets** pane, drag the **Label** widget and place at coordinates (19,119). With the **Label** widget selected, perform the following steps:

   1. Type `There was a slight problem with your order. (See below.)`. You will see the error message displayed as text on the **Label** widget.

   2. In the toolbar, change the value of **w** to `541` and **h** to `20`. Click on the checkbox next to **Hidden**.

   3. In the **Widget Interactions and Notes** pane, click in the **Shape Name** textbox and type `GlobalErrorMsgLabel`.

3. In the **Widget Properties and Style** pane, with the **Style** tab selected, scroll to **Font** and perform the following steps:

   1. Change the font size to `14`.

   2. Click on the down arrow next to the Text Color icon. In the **#** text field in the drop-down menu, enter `FFFFFF`.

4. In the **Widget Properties and Style** pane, scroll to **Fills, Lines, + Borders** with the **Style** tab selected and perform the following steps:

   1. Click on the down arrow next to the Line Color (pencil) icon. In the drop-down menu, click on the box with the red diagonal line to indicate no outline.

   2. Click on the down arrow next to the Fill Color (paint bucket) icon. In the drop-down menu, click on the box with the red diagonal line to indicate no fill.

We are now ready to fabricate the **Secure Checkout** section.

Fabricating Secure Checkout for the PaymentAndShipping state

With all widgets including error messages visible, the **Secure Checkout** section when completed will look like the following screenshot:

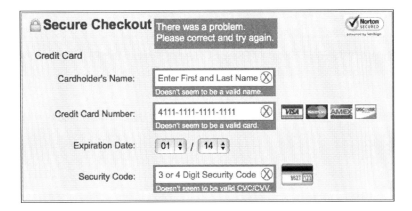

To create the **Secure Checkout** section on the **PaymentAndShipping** state of the **CheckOutDynamicPanel**, perform the following steps:

1. From the **Widgets** pane, drag the **Rectangle** widget and place at coordinates (10,146). With the **Rectangle** widget selected, perform the following steps:

   1. In the toolbar, change the value of **w** to 559 and **h** to 274.

   2. In the **Widget Interactions and Notes** pane, click in the **Shape Name** textbox and type SecureCheckoutBackground.

   3. In the **Widget Properties and Style** pane, scroll to **Font** with the **Style** tab selected. In the **Widget Properties and Style** pane, scroll to **Fills, Lines, + Borders** with the **Style** tab selected and click on the down arrow next to the Fill Color (paint bucket) icon. In the **#** text field in the drop-down menu, enter F2F2F2.

2. From the **Widgets** pane, drag the **Image** widget and place at coordinates (20,156). With the **Image** widget selected, perform the following steps:

   1. In the toolbar, change the value of **w** to 20 and **h** to 20.

   2. In the **Widget Interactions and Notes** pane, click in the **Shape Name** textbox and type ClosedLockImage.

   3. In the **Widget Properties and Style** pane, scroll to **Font** with the Style tab selected. Change the font size to **20**.

 For our closed lock icon, an image of a closed-lock emoji 🔒 sized to 20 x 20 pixels could be used. This emoji as well as other useful emojis can be found at http://emojipedia.org.

3. From the **Widgets** pane, drag the **Heading 1** widget and place at coordinates (41,156). With the **Heading 1** widget selected, perform the following steps:

   1. Right-click on the **Heading 1** widget and click on **Edit Text**. Type `Secure Checkout`.

   2. In the toolbar, change the value of **w** to `164` and **h** to `23`.

   3. In the **Widget Interactions and Notes** pane, click in the **Shape Name** textbox and type `SecureCheckoutHeading`.

   4. In the **Widget Properties and Style** pane, scroll to **Font** with the Style tab selected. Change the font size to **20**.

4. From the **Widgets** pane, drag the **Rectangle** widget and place at coordinates (210,156). With the **Rectangle** widget selected, perform the following steps:

   1. In the toolbar, change the value of **w** to `186` and **h** to `44`. Click on the checkbox next to **Hidden**.

   2. In the **Widget Interactions and Notes** pane, click in the **Shape Name** textbox and type `SecureCheckoutGlobalErrorMsgRectangle`.

   3. In the **Widget Properties and Style** pane, scroll to **Fills, Lines, + Borders** with the **Style** tab selected and perform the following steps:

      1. Click on the down arrow next to the Line Color (pencil) icon. In the **#** text field in the drop-down menu, enter `FF0000`.

      2. Click on the down arrow next to the Fill Color (paint bucket) icon. In the **#** text field in the drop-down menu, enter `FF0000`.

5. From the **Widgets** pane, drag the **Label** widget and place at coordinates (213,160). With the **Label** widget selected, perform the following steps:

   1. Type `There was a problem. Please correct and try again..` You will see the error message displayed as text on the **Label** widget.

   2. In the toolbar, change the value of **w** to `190` and **h** to `34`. Click on the checkbox next to **Hidden**.

   3. In the **Widget Interactions and Notes** pane, click in the **Shape Name** textbox and type `SecureCheckoutGlobalErrorMsgLabel`.

   4. In the **Widget Properties and Style** pane, scroll to **Font** with the **Style** tab selected and perform the following steps:

      1. Change the font size to `14`.

      2. Click on the down arrow next to the Text Color icon. In the **#** text field in the drop-down menu, enter `FFFFFF`.

3. In the **Widget Properties and Style** pane, scroll to **Fills, Lines, + Borders** with the **Style** tab selected and perform the following steps:

    1. Click on the down arrow next to the Line Color (pencil) icon. In the drop-down menu, click on the box with the red diagonal line to indicate no outline.

    2. Click on the down arrow next to the Fill Color (paint bucket) icon. In the drop-down menu, click on the box with the red diagonal line to indicate no fill.

6. From the **Widgets** pane, drag the **Heading 2** widget and place at coordinates (30,201). With the **Heading 2** widget selected, perform the following steps:

    1. Type `Credit Card`.

    2. In the toolbar, change the value of **w** to `150` and **h** to `16`.

    3. In the **Widget Interactions and Notes** pane, click in the **Shape Name** textbox and type `CreditCardH2Tag`.

    4. In the **Widget Properties and Style** pane, scroll to **Font** with the **Style** tab selected. Change the font size to `14`.

7. From the **Widgets** pane, drag the **Label** widget and place at coordinates (30,235). With the **Label** widget selected, perform the following steps:

    1. Type `Cardholder's Name:`.

    2. In the **Widget Interactions and Notes** pane, click in the **Shape Name** textbox and type `CardholdersNameLabel`.

    3. In the **Widget Properties and Style** pane, scroll to **Font** with the **Style** tab selected. Change the font size to `13`.

8. Repeat step 6 four times to create additional **Label** widgets using the following table for coordinates, text displayed, and shape name:

Coordinates	Text displayed	Shape name
(30,286)	**Credit Card Number:**	**CreditCardNumberLabel**
(30,332)	**Expiration Date:**	**ExpirationDateLabel**
(30,377)	**Security Code:**	**SecurityCodeLabel**
(264,334)	**/**	**MonthYearSeperator**

9. From the **Masters** pane, drag the **Individual Form Field** master and place at coordinates (207,228). In the **Widget Interactions and Notes** pane, click in the **Individual Form Field Name** field and type `CardholdersName`.

10. Repeat step 8 two times to create additional Individual Form Field master widgets using the following table for coordinates and Individual Form Field name:

Coordinates	Individual Form Field name
(207,277)	CreditCardNumber
(207,368)	SecurityCode

11. From the **Widgets** pane, drag the **Droplist** widget and place at coordinates (210,330). With the **Droplist** widget selected, perform the following steps:

    1. In the toolbar, change the value of **w** to 48 and **h** to 22.

    2. In the **Widget Interactions and Notes** pane, click in the **Droplist Name** textbox and type MonthDroplist.

    3. In the **Widget Properties and Style** pane, scroll to **Font** with the **Style** tab selected and change the font size to 13.

    4. Right-click on the **Droplist** and click on **Edit List Items**. Click on the **Add Many** button and enter (one per line) the integers 01 through 12.

    5. Click on **OK**.

12. From the **Widgets** pane, drag the **Droplist** widget and place at coordinates (275,330). With the **Droplist** widget selected, perform the following steps:

    1. In the toolbar, change the value of **w** to 48 and **h** to 22.

    2. In the **Widget Interactions and Notes** pane, click in the **Droplist Name** textbox and type YearDroplist.

    3. In the **Widget Properties and Style** pane, scroll to **Font** with the **Style** tab selected and change the font size to 13.

    4. Right-click on the **Droplist** and click on **Edit List Items**. Click on the **Add Many** button and enter (one per line) the integers 14 through 28.

    5. Click on **OK**.

13. From the **Widgets** pane, drag the **Image** widget and place at coordinates (496,151). With the **Label** widget selected, perform the following steps:

    1. In the toolbar, change the value of **w** to 60 and **h** to 31.

    2. In the **Widget Interactions and Notes** pane, click in the **Image Name** textbox and type VeriSignBadge.

If you want to use your own image instead of the default, double-click on the **Image** widget and follow the prompts to select the new image from your computer.

Sample images and code downloads are available at the Packt Publishing website. To download, click on the **Support** tab and then on the **Code Downloads & Errata** option.

14. Repeat step 12 two times to create additional **Image** widgets using the following table for coordinates, width, height, and image name:

Coordinates	Width (w)	Height (h)	Image name
(400,280)	145	24	CreditCardImage
(400,365)	50	35	SecurityCodeImageS

With the **Secure Checkout** section completed, we are now ready to fabricate the **Billing Address** section.

Fabricating Billing Address for the PaymentAndShipping state

With all widgets including error messages visible, the **Billing Address** section will look like the following screenshot when completed:

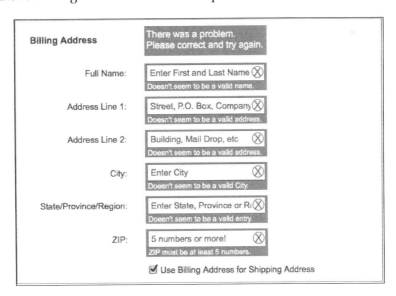

To create the **Billing Address** section on the **PaymentAndShipping** state of the **CheckOutDynamicPanel**, perform the following steps:

1. From the **Widgets** pane, drag the **Rectangle** widget and place at coordinates (10,440). With the **Rectangle** widget selected, perform the following steps:

    1. In the toolbar, change the value of **w** to 559 and **h** to 390.

    2. In the **Widget Interactions and Notes** pane, click in the **Shape Name** textbox and type BillingAddressBackground.

2. From the **Widgets** pane, drag the **Heading 1** widget and place at coordinates (30,462). With the **Heading 1** widget selected, perform the following steps:

    1. Type Billing Address.

    2. In the toolbar, change the value of **w** to 106 and the value of **h** to 16.

    3. In the **Widget Interactions and Notes** pane, click in the **Shape Name** textbox and type BillingHeading1.

    4. In the **Widget Properties and Style** pane, scroll to **Font** with the **Style** tab selected. Change the font size to 14.

3. From the **Widgets** pane, drag the **Rectangle** widget and place at coordinates (207,450). With the **Rectangle** widget selected, perform the following steps:

    1. In the toolbar, change the value of **w** to 186 and **h** to 44. Click the checkbox next to **Hidden**.

    2. In the **Widget Interactions and Notes** pane, click in the **Shape Name** textbox and type BillingGlobalErrorMsgRectangle.

    3. In the **Widget Properties and Style** pane, scroll to **Fills, Lines, + Borders** with the **Style** tab selected and perform the following steps:

        1. Click the down arrow next to the Line Color (pencil) icon. In the # text field in the drop-down menu, enter FF0000.

        2. Click the down arrow next to the Fill Color (paint bucket) icon. In the # text field in the drop-down menu, enter FF0000.

4. From the **Widgets** pane, drag the **Label** widget and place at coordinates (210,454). With the **Label** widget selected, perform the following steps:

    1. Type There was a problem. Please correct and try again.. You will see the error message displayed as text on the **Label** widget.

2. In the toolbar change the value of **w** to 190 and the value of **h** to 34. Click the checkbox next to **Hidden**.

3. In the **Widget Interactions and Notes** pane, click in the **Shape Name** textbox and type BillingGlobalErrorMsgLabel.

4. In the **Widget Properties and Style** pane, with the **Style** tab selected scroll to **Font** and perform the following steps:

   1. Change the font size to 14.

   2. Click the down arrow next to the Text Color icon. In the **#** text field in the drop-down menu, enter FFFFFF.

3. In the **Widget Properties and Style** pane, with the **Style** tab selected scroll to **Fills, Lines, + Borders** and perform the following steps:

   1. Click the down arrow next to the Line Color (pencil) icon. In the drop-down menu, click the box with the red diagonal line to indicate no outline.

   2. Click the down arrow next to the Fill Color (paint bucket) icon. In the drop-down menu, click the box with the red diagonal line to indicate no fill.

5. From the **Widgets** pane, drag the **Label** widget and place at coordinates (116,512). With the **Label** widget selected, perform the following steps:

   1. Type Full Name:.

   2. In the **Widget Interactions and Notes** pane, click in the **Shape Name** textbox and type BillingFullNameLabel.

   3. In the **Widget Properties and Style** pane, with the **Style** tab selected scroll to **Font**. Change the font size to 13.

6. Repeat step 5 five times to create additional **Label** widgets using the following table for coordinates, text displayed, and shape name:

Coordinates	Text displayed	Shape name
(88,561)	**Address Line 1:**	**BillingAddressLine1Label**
(88,610)	**Address Line 2:**	**BillingAddressLine2Label**
(152,660)	**City**	**BillingCityLabel**
(45,708)	**State/Province/Region:**	**BillingStateProvinceRegionLabel**
(154,758)	**ZIP:**	**BillingZipLabel**

7. From the **Masters** pane, drag the **Individual Form Field** master and place at coordinates (207,505). In the **Widget Interactions and Notes** pane, click in the **Individual Form Field Name** field and type `BillingFullName`.

8. Repeat step 7 five times to create additional Individual Form Field master widgets using the following table for coordinates and Individual Form Field name:

Coordinates	Individual Form Field name
(207,554)	**BillingAddressLine1**
(207,603)	**BillingAddressLine2**
(207,652)	**BillingCity**
(207,701)	**BillingStateProvinceRegion**
(207,750)	**BillingZip**

9. From the **Widgets** pane, drag the **Checkbox** widget and place at coordinates (212,803). With the **Checkbox** widget selected, type `Use Billing Address for Shipping Address`. Click the checkbox to default the checkbox to selected. In the **Widget Interactions and Notes** pane, click in the **Checkbox Footnote and Name** field and type `UseBillingForShipping`.

10. In the Widgets pane, drag the Button Shape widget and place at coordinates (210,860). With the Button Shape widget selected, perform the following steps:

    1. Type `CHECK OUT NOW`.

    2. In the toolbar, change the value of **w** to `180` and the value of **h** to `41`.

    3. In the **Widget Interactions and Notes** pane, click in the **Shape Name** field and type `CheckOutNowButton`.

    4. In the **Widget Properties and Style** pane, scroll to **Font** with the **Style** tab selected. Change the font size to **14**.

With the Billing Address design completed, we are now ready to define interactions for validation and feedback.

Validation and feedback

To provide validation and feedback for most fields on the **PaymentAndShipping** state, we will leverage two of the Individual Form Field master's raised events:

- **OnFormFieldFocus**
- **OnFormFieldLostFocus**

Defining the OnFormFieldFocus and OnFormFieldLost events

We will define interactions for these raised events on each of the Individual Form Field masters we placed on the **PaymentAndShipping** state of the **CheckOutDynamicPanel**. In the **Widget Manager** pane, double-click on the **PaymentAndShipping** state of the **CheckOutDynamicPanel** to open it in the design area. Perform the following steps:

1. Click on the Individual Form Field of **CardholdersName** at coordinates (207,228).

2. The **OnFormFieldFocus** event will have a single case named **Initialize**. We will now create the Initialize case for the **OnFormFieldFocus** event.

3. In the **Widget Interactions and Notes** pane, click on the **Interactions** tab and double-click on the **OnFormFieldFocus** event. A **Case Editor** dialog box will open. In the **Case Editor** dialog, in the **Case description** field, type Initialize.

4. Click on the **Add Condition** button to add the condition. In the **Condition Builder** dialog box, perform the following steps:

   1. In the first drop-down list, select **text on widget**.

   2. In the second drop-down list, type FormTextField in the **Search** field. Scroll to find the **CardholdersName** dropdown and click on the checkbox next to **FormTextField**.

   3. In the third drop-down list, select **equals**.

   4. In the fourth drop-down list, select **value**.

   5. In the text field, type Enter First and Last Name.

   6. Click on **OK**.

5. Create the actions. In the **Case Editor** dialog, perform the following steps:

   ° Set the text on **CardholdersName/FormTextField** with the help of the following steps:

      1. Under **Click to add actions** column, scroll to the **Widgets** drop-down menu and click on **Set Text**.

      2. Under **Configure actions** column, type FormTextField in the **Search** field under **Select the widgets to set text**. Scroll to find the **CardholdersName** dropdown and click on the checkbox next to **FormTextField** for that entry.

      3. Under **Set text to** section, click on the first drop-down list and select **value**.

4. Under **Set text to** section, clear the text in the text field. Your **Case Editor** dialog box should look like the following screenshot:

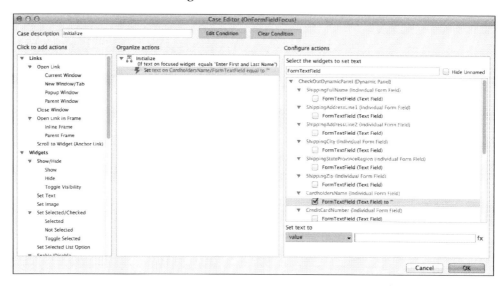

○ Set the text on **CardholdersName/FormRectangle** with the help of the following steps:

1. In the **Case Editor** dialog box in the **Configure actions** column, type `FormRectangle` in the **Search** field under **Select the widgets to set text**. Scroll to find the **CardholdersName** dropdown and click on the checkbox next to **FormRectangle** for that entry.

2. Under the **Set text to** section, click on the first drop-down list, then click on **value**, and clear the text in the text field.

3. Click on **OK**.

6. Next we will create cases for the **OnFormFieldLostFocus** event. The **OnFormFieldLostFocus** event will have three cases named as follows:
   ○ **FieldEmpty**
   ○ **FieldError**
   ○ **ValidEntry**

7. We will now create the **FieldEmpty** case for the **OnFormFieldLostFocus** event.

8. In the **Widget Interactions and Notes** pane, click on the **Interactions** tab and double-click on the **OnFormFieldLostFocus** event. A **Case Editor** dialog box will open. In the **Case Editor** dialog, type `FieldEmpty` in the **Case description** field.

9. Add the condition:

   1. Click on the **Add Condition** button.

   2. In the **Condition Builder** dialog box, perform the following steps:

      1. In the first drop-down list, select **text on widget**.

      2. In the second drop-down list, type `FormTextField` in the **Search** field. Scroll to find the **CardholdersName** drop-down list and click on the checkbox next to **FormTextField**.

      3. In the third drop-down list, select **equals**.

      4. In the fourth drop-down list, select **value**.

      5. Clear the text in the text field.

      6. Click on **OK**.

10. Create the actions. In the **Case Editor** dialog, perform the following steps:

    - To set the text on **CardholdersName/FormTextField**, perform the following steps:

      1. Under **Click to add actions**, scroll to the **Widgets** drop-down menu and click on **Set Text**.

      2. In the **Configure actions** column, type `FormTextField` in the **Search** field under **Select the widgets to set text**. Scroll to find the **CardholdersName** drop-down menu and click on the checkbox next to **FormTextField**.

      3. Under **Set text to**, click on the first drop-down menu and click on **value**.

      4. Under **Set text to**, next to the first dropdown in the text field, type `Enter First and Last Name`.

    - To set the text on **CardholdersName/FormRectangle**, perform the following steps:

      1. In the **Configure actions** column, type `FormRectangle` in the **Search** field under **Select the widgets to set text**. Scroll to find the **CardholdersName** dropdown and click on the checkbox next to **FormTextField**.

      2. Under **Set text to** click on the first dropdown and select **value**.

      3. Under **Set text to**, clear the text in the text field.

      4. Click on **OK**.

- To hide **CardholdersName/FormErrorMsgRectangle** and **CardholdersName/FormErrorMsgLabel**, perform the following steps:

   1. Under **Click to add actions**, scroll to the **Widgets** drop-down menu and click on the **Show/Hide** dropdown and then on **Hide**.

   2. In the **Configure actions** column, type `FormErrorMsgRectangle` in the **Search** field under **Select the widgets to set text**. Scroll to find the **CardholdersName** dropdown and click on the checkbox next to **FormErrorMsgRectangle**.

   3. In the **Configure actions** column, type `FormErrorMsgLabel` in the **Search** field under **Select the widgets to set text**. Scroll to find the **CardholdersName** dropdown and click on the checkbox next to **FormErrorMsgLabel**.

   4. Click on the dropdown next to **Animate** and then click on **fade**. Leave the value of **t** set to `500` ms.

   5. Click on **OK**.

11. We will now create the **FieldError** case for the **OnFormFieldLostFocus** event.

12. In the **Widget Interactions and Notes** pane, click on the **Interactions** tab and double-click on the **OnFormFieldLostFocus** event. A **Case Editor** dialog box will open. In the **Case Editor** dialog, type `FieldError` in the **Case description** field.

13. Click on the **Add Condition** button to add the condition and then in the **Condition Builder** dialog box, perform the following steps:

   1. In the first dropdown, select **text on widget**.

   2. In the second dropdown, in the **Search** field type `FormTextField`. Scroll to find the **CardholdersName** dropdown and click on the checkbox next to **FormTextField**.

   3. In the third dropdown, select **is not**.

   4. In the fourth dropdown, select **alpha**.

   5. Click on **OK**.

14. Create the actions. In the **Case Editor** dialog, perform the following steps:

   - To show the **CardholdersName/FormErrorMsgRectangle** and **CardholdersName/FormErrorMsgLabel**, perform the following steps:

      1. Under **Click to add actions**, scroll to the **Widgets** drop-down menu, click on the **Show/Hide** dropdown, and then on **Show**.

2. In the **Configure actions** column, type `FormErrorMsgRectangle` in the **Search** field under **Select the widgets to set text**. Scroll to find the **CardholdersName** dropdown and click on the checkbox next to **FormErrorMsgRectangle**.

3. In the **Configure actions** column, type `FormErrorMsgLabel` in the **Search** field under **Select the widgets to set text**. Scroll to find the **CardholdersName** dropdown and click on the checkbox next to **FormErrorMsgLabel**.

4. Click on the dropdown next to **Animate** and click on **fade**. Leave the value of **t** set to `500` ms.

○ To set the variable value for **SecureCheckOutError**, perform the following steps:

1. Under **Click to add actions**, scroll to the **Variables** drop-down menu and click on **Set Variable Value**.

2. Under **Configure actions**, click on the checkbox next to **SecureCheckOutError** in the **Select the variables to set** section.

3. Under **Configure actions**, select **value** in the **Set variable to** section in the first drop-down menu and enter the following in the text field: `[[LVAR1.replace('A','a')]]`.

○ To set the text on **CardholdersName/FormRectangle**, perform the following steps:

1. Under **Click to add actions**, scroll to the **Widgets** drop-down menu and click on **Set Text**.

2. In the **Configure actions** column, type `FormRectangle` in the **Search** field under **Select the widgets to set text**. Scroll to find the **CardholdersName** dropdown and click on the checkbox next to **FormTextField**.

3. Under **Set text to**, click on the first dropdown and select **value**. Click on the second field and enter x.

 You can enter any character into the **Set text** field by copying and pasting the character. For example: ⊗.

4. Click on **OK**.

15. We will now create the **ValidEntry** case for the **OnFormFieldLostFocus** event.

16. In the **Page Widget Interactions and Notes** pane, click on the **Interactions** tab and double-click on the **OnFormFieldLostFocus** event. A **Case Editor** dialog box will open. In the **Case Editor** dialog, type `ValidEntry` in the **Case description** field.

17. Click on the **Add Condition** button to add the condition. In the **Condition Builder** dialog box, perform the following steps:

    1. In the first dropdown, select **text**.

    2. In the second dropdown, type `FormTextField` in the **Search** field. Scroll to find the **CardholdersName** dropdown and click on the checkbox next to **FormTextField**.

    3. In the third dropdown, select **is**.

    4. In the fourth dropdown, select **alpha**.

    5. Click on **OK**.

18. Create the actions. In the **Case Editor** dialog, perform the following steps:

    ° To set the text on **CardholdersName/FormRectangle**, perform the following steps:

        1. Under **Click to add actions**, scroll to the **Widgets** drop-down menu and click on **Set Text**.

        2. In the **Configure actions** column, type `FormRectangle` in the **Search** field under **Select the widgets to set text**. Scroll to find the **CardholdersName** dropdown and click on the checkbox next to **FormTextField**.

        3. Under **Set text to**, click on the first dropdown and select **value**.

        4. Under **Set text to**, clear the text in the text field.

    ° To set the variable value for **SecureCheckOutError**, perform the following steps:

        1. Under **Click to add actions**, scroll to the **Variables** drop-down menu and click on **Set Variable Value**.

        2. Under **Configure actions**, in the **Select the variables to set** section, click on the checkbox next to **SecureCheckOutError**.

3. Under **Configure actions**, select **value** in the first drop-down menu in the **Set variable to** section and enter the following in the text field: `[[LVAR1.replace('a','A')]]`.

○ To hide the **CardholdersName/FormErrorMsgRectangle** and **CardholdersName/FormErrorMsgLabel**, perform the following steps:

1. Under **Click to add actions**, scroll to the **Widgets** drop-down menu, click on the **Show/Hide** dropdown and click on **Hide**.

2. In the **Configure actions** column, type `FormErrorMsgRectangle` in the **Search** field under **Select the widgets to set text**. Scroll to find the **CardholdersName** dropdown and click on the checkbox next to **FormErrorMsgRectangle**.

3. In the **Configure actions** column, type `FormErrorMsgLabel` in the **Search** field under **Select the widgets to set text**. Scroll to find the **CardholdersName** dropdown and click on the checkbox next to **FormErrorMsgLabel**.

4. Click on the dropdown next to **Animate** and then click on **fade**. Leave the value of **t** set at `500` ms.

5. Click on **OK**.

Next we will repeat steps 1–18 that we saw earlier to define interactions for raised events on each of the eight remaining Individual Form Field masters. For your reference, the coordinates and Individual Form Field masters names are as follows:

Coordinates	Individual Form Field name
(207,277)	**CreditCardNumber**
(207,368)	**SecurityCode**
(207,505)	**BillingFullName**
(207,554)	**BillingAddressLine1**
(207,603)	**BillingAddressLine2**
(207,652)	**BillingCity**
(207,701)	**BillingStateProvinceRegion**
(207,750)	**BillingZip**

Creating interactions for the CreditCardNumber Individual Form Field

To create interactions for the **CreditCardNumber** widget, click on the Individual Form Field of **CreditCardNumber** at coordinates (207,228). Update steps 1–18 from the *Defining the OnFormFieldFocus and OnFormFieldLost events* section while referring to the following table:

Step #	Raised event	Case	Condition	Action
4	OnFormFieldFocus	Initialize	Second dropdown: **CreditCardNumber/ FormTextField** Text field value: `4111-1111-1111-1111`	Change all previous references in this step to: • **CreditCardNumber/ FormRectangle** • **CreditCardNumber/ FormTextField**
9	OnFormFieldLostFocus	FieldEmpty	Second dropdown: **CreditCardNumber/ FormTextField**	
10	OnFormFieldLostFocus	FieldEmpty		Change all previous references in this step to: • **CreditCardNumber/ FormRectangle** • **CreditCardNumber/ FormTextField** Set text on **CardholdersName/ FormTextField** `4111-1111-1111-1111`
13	OnFormFieldLostFocus	FieldError	First dropdown: **Length of widget value** Second dropdown: **CreditCardNumber/ FormTextField** Third dropdown: **does not equal** Fourth dropdown: **value** Text field: `19`	Change all previous references in this step to: • **CreditCardNumber/ FormRectangle** • **CreditCardNumber/ FormTextField**

Step #	Raised event	Case	Condition	Action
14	OnFormFieldLostFocus	FieldError		Change all previous references in this step to: • **CreditCardNumber/ FormRectangle** • **CreditCardNumber/ FormTextField**
				Set the variable value of **SecureCheckOutError** to `[[LVAR1. replace('B','b')]]`
17	OnFormFieldLostFocus	ValidEntry	First dropdown: **Length of widget value**	Change all previous references in this step to: • **CreditCardNumber/ FormRectangle** • **CreditCardNumber/ FormTextField**
			Second dropdown: **CreditCardNumber/ FormTextField**	
			Third dropdown: **equals**	
			Fourth dropdown: **value**	
			Text field: `19`	
18	OnFormFieldLostFocus	ValidEntry		Change all previous references in this step to: • **CreditCardNumber/ FormRectangle** • **CreditCardNumber/ FormTextField**
				Set the variable value of **SecureCheckOutError** to `[[LVAR1. replace('b','B')]]`

In addition, we will leverage the **OnFormFieldKeyUp** raised event. To define **OnFormFieldKeyUp**, perform the following steps:

1. Click on the Individual Form Field of **CreditCardNumber** at coordinates (207,277).

2. The **OnFormFieldKeyUp** event will have a single case named **AddSeparator**. We will now create the **AddSeparator** case for the **OnFormFieldKeyUp** event.

3. In the **Page Widget Interactions and Notes** pane, click on the **Interactions** tab and double-click on the **OnFormFieldKeyUp** event. A **Case Editor** dialog box will open. In the **Case Editor** dialog, type `AddSeparator` in the **Case description** field.

4. Add the conditions as follows:

    1. Click on the **Add Condition** button.

    2. In the **Condition Builder** dialog box, next to **Satisfy** click on the first dropdown and then click on **any**.

    3. In the **Condition Builder** dialog box, perform the following steps:

        1. In the first dropdown, select **length of widget value**.

        2. In the second dropdown, type `FormTextField` in the **Search** field. Scroll to find the **CreditCardNumber** dropdown and click on the checkbox next to **FormTextField**.

        3. In the third dropdown, select **equals**.

        4. In the fourth dropdown, select **value**.

        5. In the text field, type 4.

        6. Click on the green plus sign to add a new condition.

    4. We will now define the second condition. Perform the following steps:

        1. In the first dropdown, select **length of widget value**.

        2. In the second dropdown, type `FormTextField` in the **Search** field. Scroll to find the **CreditCardNumber** dropdown and click on the checkbox next to **FormTextField**.

        3. In the third dropdown, select **equals**.

        4. In the fourth dropdown, select **value**.

        5. In the text field, type 9.

        6. Click on the green plus sign to add a new condition.

    5. We will now define the third condition. Perform the following steps:

        1. In the first dropdown, select **length of widget value**.

        2. In the second dropdown, type `FormTextField` in the **Search** field. Scroll to find the **CreditCardNumber** dropdown and click on the checkbox next to **FormTextField**.

        3. In the third dropdown, select **equals**.

4. In the fourth dropdown, select **value**.

5. In the text field, type 14.

6. Click on **OK**.

5. Create the action. In the **Case Editor** dialog, perform the following steps:

   To set the text on **CardholdersName/FormTextField**, perform the following steps:

   1. Under **Click to add actions**, scroll to the **Widgets** drop-down menu and click on **Set Text**.

   2. Under **Configure actions**, type FormTextField under **Select the widgets to set text** in the **Search** field. Scroll to find the **CardholdersName** dropdown and click on the checkbox next to **FormTextField**.

   3. Under **Set text to**, click on the first dropdown and then click on **value**. Click on the second field and enter [[This.text]]-.

   4. Click on **OK**.

Next we will create interactions for the **SecurityCode** Individual Form Field.

Creating interactions for the SecurityCode Individual Form Field

To create interactions for the **SecurityCode** widget, click on the Individual Form Field of **SecurityCode** at coordinates (207,368). Update steps 1-18 from the *Defining the OnFormFieldFocus and OnFormFieldLost events* section while referring to the following table:

Step #	Raised event	Case	Condition	Action
4	**OnFormFieldFocus**	Initialize	Text field value: Any 3 or 4 digit security code Second dropdown: **SecurityCode/ FormTextField**	Change all previous references in this step to: • **SecurityCode/ FormRectangle** • **SecurityCode/ FormTextField**
9	**OnFormFieldLostFocus**	FieldEmpty	Second dropdown: **SecurityCode/ FormTextField**	

Step #	Raised event	Case	Condition	Action
10	**OnFormFieldLostFocus**	**FieldEmpty**		Change all previous references in this step to: • **SecurityCode/ FormRectangle** • **SecurityCode/ FormTextField**
				Set text on **SecurityCode/ FormTextField** to 3 or 4 digit security code
13	**OnFormFieldLostFocus**	**FieldError**	First dropdown: **length of widget value**	Change all previous references in this step to: • **SecurityCode/ FormRectangle** • **SecurityCode/ FormTextField**
			Second dropdown: **SecurityCode/ FormTextField**	
			Third dropdown: **Is less than**	
			Fourth dropdown: **value**	
			Text field: 3	
14	**OnFormFieldLostFocus**	**FieldError**		Change all previous references in this step to: • **SecurityCode/ FormRectangle** • **SecurityCode/ FormTextField**
				Set the variable value of **SecureCheckOutError** to `[[LVAR1. replace('C','c')]]`
17	**OnFormFieldLostFocus**	**ValidEntry**	First dropdown: **length of widget value**	Change all previous references in this step to: • **CreditCardNumber/ FormRectangle** • **CreditCardNumber/ FormTextField**
			Second dropdown: **CreditCardNumber/ FormTextField**	
			Third dropdown: **Is greater than or equals**	
			Fourth dropdown: **value**	
			Text field: 3	

Step #	Raised event	Case	Condition	Action
18	OnFormFieldLostFocus	ValidEntry		Change all previous references in this step to: • CreditCardNumber/ FormRectangle • CreditCardNumber/ FormTextField
				Set the variable value of **SecureCheckOutError** to `[[LVAR1. replace('c','C')]]`

In addition, we need to add a condition to the **FieldError** case on the **OnFormFieldLostFocus** event. We will also leverage the **OnFormFieldKeyUp** raised event. To add the condition to the **FieldError** case and define **OnFormFieldKeyUp**, perform the following steps:

1. To add a condition to the **FieldError** case on the **OnFormFieldLostFocus** event, click on the Individual Form Field of **SecurityCode** at coordinates (207,368).

2. In the **Page Widget Interactions and Notes** pane, click on the **Interactions** tab and under the **OnFormFieldLostFocus** event, double-click on the **FieldError** case. A **Case Editor** dialog box will open. Perform the following steps:

    1. Click on the **Edit Condition** button.

    2. In the **Condition Builder** dialog box, click on the first dropdown next to **Satisfy** and then click on **any**.

    3. In the **Condition Builder** dialog box, perform the following steps:

        1. Click on the green plus sign to add a new condition.

        2. In the first dropdown, select **text on widget**.

        3. In the second dropdown, type `FormTextField` in the **Search** field. Scroll to find the **SecurityCode** dropdown and click on the checkbox next to **FormTextField**.

        4. In the third dropdown, select **is not**.

        5. In the fourth dropdown, select **numeric**.

        6. Click on **OK**.

3. The **OnFormFieldKeyUp** event will have a single case named **CheckMaxLength**. We will now create the **CheckMaxLength** case for the **OnFormFieldKeyUp** event.

4. In the **Page Widget Interactions and Notes** pane, click on the **Interactions** tab and double-click on the **OnFormFieldKeyUp** event. A **Case Editor** dialog box will open. In the **Case Editor** dialog, type CheckMaxLength in the **Case description** field.

5. Add the condition:

    1. Click on the **Add Condition** button.

    2. In the **Condition Builder** dialog box, click on the first dropdown next to **Satisfy** and click on **any**.

    3. In the **Condition Builder** dialog box, perform the following steps:

        1. In the first dropdown, select **length of widget value**.

        2. In the second dropdown, type FormTextField in the **Search** field. Scroll to find the **SecurityCode** dropdown and click on the checkbox next to **FormTextField**.

        3. In the third dropdown, select **is greater than**.

        4. In the fourth dropdown, select **value**.

        5. In the text field, type 4.

        6. Click on **OK**.

6. Create the action. In the **Case Editor** dialog, perform the following steps to show the **SecurityCode/FormErrorMsgRectangle** and **SecurityCode/FormErrorMsgLabel**:

    1. Under **Click to add actions**, scroll to the **Widgets** drop-down menu, click on the **Show/Hide** dropdown and click on **Show**.

    2. Under **Configure actions**, type FormErrorMsgRectangle in the **Search** field under **Select the widgets to set text**. Scroll to find the **SecurityCode** dropdown and click on the checkbox next to **FormErrorMsgRectangle**.

    3. Under **Configure actions**, type FormErrorMsgLabel in the **Search** field under **Select the widgets to set text**. Scroll to find the **SecurityCode** dropdown and click on the checkbox next to **FormErrorMsgLabel**.

4. Click on the dropdown next to **Animate** and then click on **fade**. Leave the value of **t** set to 500 ms.

5. Click on **OK**.

Next we will create interactions for the **Billing Address** Individual Form Fields.

Creating interactions for the Billing Address Individual Form Fields

To create interactions for all **Billing Address** form fields except the **BillingZip** form field, repeat the steps from the *Defining the OnFormFieldFocus and OnFormFieldLost events* section a total of five times for each Individual Form Field of **Billing Address**.

Click on the corresponding Individual Form Field of **BillingFullName**. The **Billing Address** Individual Form Fields we will update are listed in the reference table as follows:

Coordinates	Individual Form Field name	PlaceHolder text	Set value of BillingAddressError (FieldError case - step 14)	Set value of BillingAddressError (ValidEntry case - step 18)
(207,505)	**BillingFullName**	Enter First and Last Name	[[LVAR1. replace('A','a')]]	[[LVAR1. replace('a','A')]]
(207,554)	**BillingAddressLine1**	Street, P.O. Box, Company	[[LVAR1. replace('B','b')]]	[[LVAR1. replace('b','B')]]
(207,603)	**BillingAddressLine2**	Building, Mail Drop, etc	[[LVAR1. replace('C','c')]]	[[LVAR1. replace('c','C')]]
(207,652)	**BillingCity**	Enter City	[[LVAR1. replace('D','d')]]	[[LVAR1. replace('d','D')]]
(207,701)	**BillingStateProvinceRegion**	Enter State or Province	[[LVAR1. replace('E','e')]]	[[LVAR1. replace('e','E')]]

We will use the *PlaceHolder text* column for the following:
- **Step #4**: For text field value
- **Step #10**: To set text value to action

Update steps 1-18 from the *Defining the OnFormFieldFocus and OnFormFieldLost events* section while referring to the following table:

Step #	Raised event	Case	Condition	Action
4	OnFormFieldFocus	Initialize	Text field value: See the preceding reference table	Change all widget references to Individual Form Field widgets listed in the *Individual Form Field name* column in the preceding reference table to:
			Second dropdown: Individual Form Field name/ FormTextField	• Individual Form Field name/FormRectangle • Individual Form Field name/FormTextField
9	OnFormFieldLostFocus	FieldEmpty	Second dropdown: Individual Form Field name/ FormTextField	
10	OnFormFieldLostFocus	FieldEmpty		Change all widget references to Individual Form Field widgets listed in the *Individual Form Field name* column in the preceding reference table to: • Individual Form Field name /FormRectangle • Individual Form Field name /FormTextField
				See the preceding reference table to set text on Individual Form Field name/FormTextField
13	OnFormFieldLostFocus	FieldError	First dropdown: **length of widget value**	Change all widget references to Individual Form Field widgets listed in the *Individual Form Field name* column in the preceding reference table to:
			Second dropdown: Individual Form Field name/ FormTextField	• Individual Form Field name/FormRectangle • Individual Form Field name/FormTextField
			Third dropdown: **equals**	
			Fourth dropdown: **value**	
			Text field: 1	

Step #	Raised event	Case	Condition	Action
14	**OnFormFieldLostFocus**	**FieldError**		Change all widget references to Individual Form Field widgets listed in the *Individual Form Field name* column in the preceding reference table to: • Individual Form Field name/FormRectangle • Individual Form Field name/FormTextField See the preceding reference table to set variable value for **BillingAddressError**
17	**OnFormFieldLostFocus**	**ValidEntry**	First dropdown: **length of widget value** Second dropdown: Individual Form Field name/ FormTextField Third dropdown: **Is greater than or equals** Fourth dropdown: **value** Text field: 2	Change all widget references to Individual Form Field widgets listed in the *Individual Form Field name* column in the preceding reference table to: • Individual Form Field name/FormRectangle • Individual Form Field name/FormTextField
18	**OnFormFieldLostFocus**	**ValidEntry**		Change all widget references to Individual Form Field widgets listed in the *Individual Form Field name* column in the preceding reference table to: • Individual Form Field name/FormRectangle • Individual Form Field name/FormTextField See the preceding reference table to set variable value for **BillingAddressError**

Next we will create interactions for the **BillingZip** Individual Form Field.

Creating Interactions for the BillingZip Individual Form Field

To create interactions for the **BillingZip** widget, click on the **BillingZip** Individual Form Field at coordinates (207,750). Update steps 1-18 from the *Defining the OnFormFieldFocus and OnFormFieldLost events* section while referring to the following table:

Step #	Raised event	Case	Condition	Action
4	OnFormFieldFocus	Initialize	Text field value: five digit ZIP	Change all previous references in this step to:
			Second dropdown: **BillingZip/FormTextField**	• **BillingZip/ FormRectangle** • **BillingZip/ FormTextField**
9	OnFormFieldLostFocus	FieldEmpty	Second dropdown: **BillingZip/FormTextField**	
10	OnFormFieldLostFocus	FieldEmpty		Change all previous references in this step to:
				• **BillingZip/ FormRectangle** • **BillingZip/ FormTextField**
				Set text on **CardholdersName/ FormTextField** to five digit ZIP
13	OnFormFieldLostFocus	FieldError	First dropdown: **length of widget value**	Change all previous references in this step to:
			Second dropdown: **BillingZip/FormTextField**	• **BillingZip/ FormRectangle** • **BillingZip/ FormTextField**
			Third dropdown: **does not equal**	
			Fourth dropdown: **value**	
			Text field: 5	
14	OnFormFieldLostFocus	FieldError		Change all previous references in this step to:
				• **BillingZip/ FormRectangle** • **BillingZip/ FormTextField**
				Set variable value for **BillingAddressError** to `[[LVAR1. replace('F','f')]]`

Step #	Raised event	Case	Condition	Action
17	OnFormFieldLostFocus	ValidEntry	First dropdown: **length of widget value**	Change all previous references in this step to: • **BillingZip/ FormRectangle** • **BillingZip/ FormTextField**
			Second dropdown: **BillingZip/FormTextField**	
			Third dropdown: **equals**	
			Fourth dropdown: **value**	
			Text field: 5	
18	OnFormFieldLostFocus	ValidEntry		Change all previous references in this step to: • **BillingZip/ FormRectangle** • **BillingZip/ FormTextField**
				Set the variable value of **BillingAddressError** to `[[LVAR1. replace('f','F')]]`

In addition, we need to add a condition to the **FieldError** case on the **OnFormFieldLostFocus** event. We will also leverage the **OnFormFieldKeyUp** raised event. To add the condition to the **FieldError** case and define **OnFormFieldKeyUp**, perform the following steps:

1. To add a condition to the **FieldError** case on the **OnFormFieldLostFocus** event, click on the Individual Form Field of **BillingZip** at coordinates (207,750).

2. In the **Page Widget Interactions and Notes** pane, click on the **Interactions** tab and under the **OnFormFieldLostFocus** event, double-click on the **FieldError** case. A **Case Editor** dialog box will open. Perform the following steps:

    1. Click on the **Edit Condition** button.

    2. In the **Condition Builder** dialog box, click on the first dropdown next to **Satisfy** and then click on **any**.

    3. In the **Condition Builder** dialog box, perform the following steps:

        1. Click the green plus sign to add a new condition.

        2. In the first dropdown, select **text on widget**.

        3. In the second dropdown, type `FormTextField` in the **Search** field. Scroll to find the **SecurityCode** dropdown and click on the checkbox next to **FormTextField**.

4. In the third dropdown, select **is not**.

5. In the fourth dropdown, select **numeric**.

6. Click on **OK**.

3. The **OnFormFieldKeyUp** event will have a single case named **CheckMaxLength**. We will now create the **CheckMaxLength** case for the **OnFormFieldKeyUp** event.

4. In the **Page Widget Interactions and Notes** pane, click on the **Interactions** tab and double-click on the **OnFormFieldKeyUp** event. A **Case Editor** dialog box will open. In the **Case Editor** dialog, type `CheckMaxLength` in the **Case description** field.

5. Add the condition as follows:

   1. Click on the **Add Condition** button.

   2. In the **Condition Builder** dialog box, click on the first dropdown next to **Satisfy** and then click on **any**.

   3. In the **Condition Builder** dialog box, perform the following steps:

      1. In the first dropdown, select **length of widget value**.

      2. In the second dropdown, type `FormTextField` in the **Search** field. Scroll to find the **SecurityCode** dropdown and click on the checkbox next to **FormTextField**.

      3. In the third dropdown, select **is greater than**.

      4. In the fourth dropdown, select **value**.

      5. In the text field, type 4.

      6. Click on **OK**.

6. Create the action. In the **Case Editor** dialog, perform the following steps to show the **SecurityCode/FormErrorMsgRectangle** and **SecurityCode/FormErrorMsgLabel**:

   1. Under **Click to add actions**, scroll to the **Widgets** drop-down menu, then click on the **Show/Hide** dropdown, and finally click on **Show**.

   2. Under **Configure actions**, type `FormErrorMsgRectangle` in the **Search** field under **Select the widgets to set text**. Scroll to find the **SecurityCode** dropdown and click on the checkbox next to **FormErrorMsgRectangle**.

3. Under **Configure actions**, type `FormErrorMsgLabel` in the **Search** field under **Select the widgets to set text**. Scroll to find the **SecurityCode** dropdown and click on the checkbox next to **FormErrorMsgLabel**.

4. Click on the dropdown next to **Animate** and then click on **fade**. Leave the value of **t** set to `500` ms.

5. Click on **OK**.

Next we will create interactions for the **UseBillingForShipping** checkbox.

Creating Interactions for the UseBillingForShipping checkbox

To create interactions for the **UseBillingForShipping** checkbox, click on the **BillingZip** checkbox at coordinates (212,803). To create the **NotSelected** case for the **OnCheckedChange** event, double-click on the **OnCheckedChange** event in the **Widget Interactions and Notes** pane; a **Case Editor** dialog box will open. In the **Case Editor** dialog, perform the following steps to create the condition:

1. In the **Case description** field, enter `NotSelected`.

2. Click on the **Add Condition** button. In the **Condition Builder** dialog box perform the following steps:

   1. In the first dropdown, select **is selected of**.

   2. In the second dropdown, click on **This**.

   3. In the third dropdown, select **equals**.

   4. In the fourth dropdown, select **value**.

   5. In the fifth dropdown, select **false**.

   6. Click on **OK**.

3. Create the actions. In the **Case Editor** dialog, perform the following steps to add different actions:

   ° To set the size of the **CheckOutDynamicPanel**, perform the following steps:

      1. Under **Click to add actions**, scroll to the **Dynamic Panels** drop-down menu and click on **Set Panel Size**.

      2. Under **Configure actions**, in the **Select the dynamic panel to resize** section, click on the checkbox next to **CheckOutDynamicPanel**.

3.   Under **Configure actions**, enter 960 in the **Width** text field. In the **Height** text field, enter 1450.

○   To define the first **Move** interaction, perform the following steps:

1.   Under **Click to add actions**, scroll to the **Widgets** drop-down menu and click on **Move**.

2.   Under **Configure actions**, scroll to the **Footer** dropdown, expand it, and click on the checkbox next to **CopyrightLink**. In the **Move** dropdown, click on **to**. In the **x** field, enter 10. In the **y** field, enter 1420.

3.   Under **Configure actions**, scroll to the **Footer** dropdown, expand it and click on the checkbox next to **PrivacyLink**. In the **Move** dropdown, click on **to**. In the **x** field, enter 710. In the **y** field, enter 1420.

4.   Under **Configure actions**, scroll to the **Footer** dropdown, expand it, and click on the checkbox next to **TermsLink**. In the **Move** dropdown, click on **to**. In the **x** field, enter 790. In the **y** field, enter 1420.

5.   Under **Configure actions**, scroll to the **Footer** dropdown, expand it, and click on the checkbox next to **AboutUsLink**. In the **Move** dropdown, click on **to**. In the **x** field, enter 870. In the **y** field, enter 1420.

○   To define the second **Move** interaction, perform the following steps:

1.   Under **Click to add actions**, scroll to the **Widgets** drop-down menu, and click on **Move**.

2.   Under **Configure actions**, scroll to the **CheckOutNowButton** dropdown, expand it, and click on the checkboxe next to **CheckOutNowButton**. In the **Move** dropdown, click on **to**. In the **x** field, enter 210. In the **y** field, enter 1255.

○   To show the **SecurityCode/FormErrorMsgRectangle** and **SecurityCode/FormErrorMsgLabel**, perform the following steps:

1.   Under **Click to add actions**, scroll to the **Widgets** drop-down menu and click on the **Show/Hide** dropdown and then on **Show**.

2. In **Configure actions** column, type `ShippingHeading1` in the **Search** field under **Select the widgets to hide/show**. Click on the checkbox next to **ShippingHeading1** to select.

 For Individual Form Field/widget name pairs, type the widget name and click on the checkbox next to the widget below the Individual Form Field dropdown.

3. Repeat the previous step for widgets mentioned here:

   ○ **ShippingAddressBackground**
   ○ **ShippingFullNameLabel**
   ○ **ShippingAddressLine1Label**
   ○ **ShippingAddressLine2Label**
   ○ **ShippingCityLabel**
   ○ **ShippingStateProvinceRegionLabel**
   ○ **ShippingZipLabel**
   ○ **ShippingFullName/FormRectangle**
   ○ **ShippingFullName/FormTextField**
   ○ **ShippingAddress1/FormRectangle**
   ○ **ShippingAddress1/FormTextField**
   ○ **ShippingAddress2/FormRectangle**
   ○ **ShippingAddress2/FormTextField**
   ○ **ShippingCity/FormRectangle**
   ○ **ShippingCity/FormTextField**
   ○ **ShippingStateProvinceRegion/FormRectangle**
   ○ **ShippingStateProvinceRegion/FormTextField**
   ○ **ShippingZip/FormRectangle**
   ○ **ShippingZip/FormTextField**
   ○ **ShippingZip/FormTextField**

4. Click on **OK**.

4. To create the **Selected** case for the **OnCheckedChange** event, double-click on the **OnCheckedChange** event in the **Widget Interactions and Notes** pane. A **Case Editor** dialog box will open. Now, enter Selected in the **Case Description** field and click on the **Add Condition** button. In the **Condition Builder** dialog box, perform the following steps:

   1. In the first dropdown, select **is selected of**.
   2. In the second dropdown, click on **This**.
   3. In the third dropdown, select **equals**.
   4. In the fourth dropdown, select **value**.
   5. In the fifth dropdown, select **true**.
   6. Click on **OK**.

5. Create the actions. In the **Case Editor** dialog, perform the following steps to add different actions:

   ○ To hide the **SecurityCode/FormErrorMsgRectangle** and **SecurityCode/FormErrorMsgLabel**, perform the following steps:

      1. Under **Click to add actions**, scroll to the **Widgets** drop-down menu and click on the **Show/Hide** dropdown and then click on **Hide**.
      2. Under **Configure actions**, type ShippingHeading1 in the **Search** field under **Select the widgets to hide/show**. Click on the checkbox next to **ShippingHeading1** to select.

 For Individual Form Field/widget name pairs, type the widget name and click on the checkbox next to the widget below the Individual Form Field dropdown.

      3. Repeat this step for widgets mentioned here:
         ○ **ShippingAddressBackground**
         ○ **ShippingFullNameLabel**
         ○ **ShippingAddressLine1Label**
         ○ **ShippingAddressLine2Label**
         ○ **ShippingCityLabel**
         ○ **ShippingStateProvinceRegionLabel**
         ○ **ShippingZipLabel**

- ° **ShippingFullName/FormRectangle**
- ° **ShippingFullName/FormTextField**
- ° **ShippingAddress1/FormRectangle**
- ° **ShippingAddress1/FormTextField**
- ° **ShippingAddress2/FormRectangle**
- ° **ShippingAddress2/FormTextField**
- ° **ShippingCity/FormRectangle**
- ° **ShippingCity/FormTextField**
- ° **ShippingStateProvinceRegion/FormRectangle**
- ° **ShippingStateProvinceRegion/FormTextField**
- ° **ShippingZip/FormRectangle**
- ° **ShippingZip/FormTextField**
- ° **ShippingZip/FormTextField**

- ° To set the size of the **CheckOutDynamicPanel**, perform the following steps:

    1. Under **Click to add actions**, scroll to the **Dynamic Panels** drop-down menu and click on **Set Panel Size**.

    2. Under **Configure actions**, click on the checkbox next to **CheckOutDynamicPanel** in the section **Select the dynamic panel to resize**.

    3. Under **Configure actions**, enter 960 in the **Width** text field. In the **Height** text field, enter 1080.

- ° To define the first **Move** interaction, perform the following steps:

    1. Under **Click to add actions**, scroll to the **Widgets** drop-down menu, and click on **Move**.

    2. Under **Configure actions**, scroll to the **Footer** dropdown, expand it and click on the checkbox next to **CopyrightLink**. In the **Move** dropdown, click on **to**. In the **x** field, enter 10. In the **y** field, enter 985.

    3. Under **Configure actions**, scroll to the **Footer** dropdown, expand it and click on the checkbox next to **PrivacyLink**. In the **Move** dropdown, click on **to**. In the **x** field, enter 710. In the **y** field, enter 985.

4. Under **Configure actions**, scroll to the **Footer** dropdown, expand it and click on the checkbox next to **TermsLink**. In the **Move** dropdown, click on **to**. In the **x** field, enter 790. In the **y** field, enter 985.

5. Under **Configure actions**, scroll to the **Footer** dropdown, expand it and click on the checkbox next to **AboutUsLink**. In the **Move** dropdown, click on **to**. In the **x** field, enter 870. In the **y** field, enter 985.

° To define the second **Move** interaction, perform the following steps:

1. Under **Click to add actions**, scroll to the **Widgets** drop-down menu, and click on **Move**.

2. Under **Configure actions**, scroll to the **CheckOutNowButton** dropdown, expand it and click on the checkboxes next to **CheckOutNowButton**. In the **Move** dropdown, click on **to**. In the **x** field, enter 210. In the **y** field, enter 860.

3. Click on **OK**.

With the **UseBillingForShipping** checkbox interactions completed, we are now ready to create the **CheckOutNowButton** interactions.

Creating interactions for the CheckOutNowButton

The following are the steps to create interactions for the **CheckOutNowButton**:

1. Click on the **CheckOutNowButton** at coordinates (210,860).

2. To create the **SetFocusOnMouseEnter** case for the **OnMouseEnter** event, double-click on the **OnMouseEnter** event in the **Widget Interactions and Notes** pane.

3. A **Case Editor** dialog box will open. Perform the following steps to create the **Set Focus** action on the **CheckOutNowButton**:

1. In the **Case description** field, enter SetFocusOnMouseEnter.

2. Under **Click to add actions**, click on the **Widgets** drop-down menu and then click on **Focus**.

3. Under **Configure actions**, in the **Select widget to focus** section, type CheckOutNowButton in the **Search** textbox. Click on the checkbox next to **CheckOutNowButton**.

4. Click on **OK**.

Next we will create five cases for the **OnClick** interaction. These five cases will be as follows:

- **Check for Secure Checkout Error**
- **Check for Billing Address Error**
- **Check for Shipping Address Error**
- **Valid Entry**
- **Show Global Error Message**

To create the **Check for Secure Checkout Error** case for the **OnClick** event, click on the **Interactions** tab in the **Widget Interactions and Notes** pane and double-click on **OnClick**. A **Case Editor** dialog box will open. In the **Case Editor** dialog, perform the following steps to create the conditions:

1. In the **Case description** field, enter `Check for Secure Checkout Error`.
2. To add the condition, click on the **Add Condition** button and in the **Condition Builder** dialog box, perform the following steps:
    1. In the first dropdown, select **value of variable**.
    2. In the second dropdown, select **SecureCheckOutError**.
    3. In the third dropdown, select **does not equal**.
    4. In the fourth dropdown, select **value**.
    5. In the fifth dropdown, select **ABC**.
    6. Click on **OK**.
3. To create the **Show** action on **SecureCheckoutGlobalErrorMsgRectangle** and **SecureCheckoutGlobalErrorMsgLabel**, perform the following steps:
    1. In the **Configure actions** column, type `SecureCheckoutGlobalErrorMsgRectangle` in the **Search** field under **Select the widgets to hide/show**.
    2. Click on the checkboxes next to **SecureCheckoutGlobalErrorMsgRectangle** and **SecureCheckoutGlobalErrorMsgLabel**.

4. To create the action to set the value of the **SecureCheckoutError** variable, perform the following steps:

    1. Under **Click to add actions**, scroll to the **Variables** drop-down menu and click on **Set Variable Value**.

    2. Under **Configure actions**, click on the checkbox next to **SecureCheckoutError**.

    3. Under **Set variable to**, click on the first dropdown and click on **value**. In the text field, enter 1.

    4. Click on **OK**.

To create the **Check for Billing Address Error** case for the **OnClick** event, click on the **Interactions** tab in the **Widget Interactions and Notes** pane and double-click on **OnClick**. A **Case Editor** dialog box will open. In the **Case Editor** dialog, perform the following steps to create the conditions:

1. In the **Case description** field, enter Check for Billing Address Error.

2. Add the condition as follows:

    1. Click on the **Add Condition** button.

    2. In the **Condition Builder** dialog box, perform the following steps:

        1. In the first dropdown, select **value of variable**.

        2. In the second dropdown, select **BillingAddressError**.

        3. In the third dropdown, select **does not equal**.

        4. In the fourth dropdown, select **value**.

        5. In the fifth dropdown, select **ABCDEF**.

        6. Click on **OK**.

3. To create the **Show** action on **BillingAddressGlobalErrorMsgRectangle** and **BillingAddressGlobalErrorMsgLabel**, perform the following steps:

    1. Under **Configure actions**, type BillingAddressGlobalErrorMsgRectangle in the **Search** field under **Select the widgets to hide/show**.

    2. Click on the checkboxes next to **BillingAddressGlobalErrorMsgRectangle** and **BillingAddressGlobalErrorMsgLabel**.

4. To create the action to set the value of the **SecureCheckoutError** variable, perform the following steps:

   1. Under **Click to add actions**, scroll to the **Variables** drop-down menu and click on **Set Variable Value**.

   2. Under **Configure actions**, click on the checkbox next to **BillingAddressError**.

   3. Under **Set variable to**, click on the first dropdown and then click on **value**. In the text field, enter 1.

   4. Click on **OK**.

5. Under the **OnClick** event, right-click on the **Check for Billing Address Error** case and click on **Toggle IF/ELSE IF**.

To create the **Check for Shipping Address Error** case for the **OnClick** event, click on the **Interactions** tab in the **Widget Interactions and Notes** pane and double-click on **OnClick**. A **Case Editor** dialog box will open; in the **Case Editor** dialog, perform the following steps to create the conditions:

1. In the **Case description** field, enter Check for Shipping Address Error.

2. Add the condition using the following steps:

   1. Click on the **Add Condition** button.

   2. In the **Condition Builder** dialog box, perform the following steps:

      1. In the first dropdown, select **value of variable**.

      2. In the second dropdown, select **ShippingAddressError**.

      3. In the third dropdown, select **does not equal**.

      4. In the fourth dropdown, select **value**.

      5. In the fifth dropdown, select **ABCDEF**.

      6. Click on **OK**.

3. To create the **Show** action on **ShippingAddressGlobalErrorMsgRectangle** and **ShippingAddressGlobalErrorMsgLabel**, perform the following steps:

   1. In the **Configure actions** column, type ShippingAddressGlobalErrorMsgRectangle in the **Search** field under **Select the widgets to hide/show**.

   2. Click on the checkboxes next to **ShippingAddressGlobalErrorMsgRectangle** and **ShippingAddressGlobalErrorMsgLabel**.

4. To create the action to set the value of the **SecureCheckoutError** variable, perform the following steps:

   1. Under **Click to add actions**, scroll to the **Variables** drop-down menu and click on **Set Variable Value**.

   2. Under **Configure actions**, click on the checkbox next to **ShippingAddressError**.

   3. Under **Set variable to**, click on the first dropdown and then click on **value**. In the text field, enter 1.

   4. Click on **OK**.

5. Under the **OnClick** event, right-click on the **Check for Shipping Address Error** case and click on **Toggle IF/ELSE IF**.

To create the **Valid Entry** case for the **OnClick** event, click on the **Interactions** tab in the **Widget Interactions and Notes** pane and double-click on **OnClick**. A **Case Editor** dialog box will open. In the **Case Editor** dialog, perform the following steps to create the conditions:

1. In the **Case description** field, enter Valid Entry.

2. Add the first condition using the following steps:

   1. Click on the **Add Condition** button.

   2. In the **Condition Builder** dialog box, perform the following steps:

      1. In the first dropdown, select **value of variable**.

      2. In the second dropdown, select **SecureCheckOutError**.

      3. In the third dropdown, select **equals**.

      4. In the fourth dropdown, select **value**.

      5. In the fifth dropdown, select **0**.

3. Add the second condition using the following steps:

   1. Click on the green plus sign to add a second condition.

   2. In the **Condition Builder** dialog box, perform the following steps:

      1. In the first dropdown, select **value of variable**.

      2. In the second dropdown, select **BillingAddressError**.

      3. In the third dropdown, select **equals**.

      4. In the fourth dropdown, select **value**.

      5. In the fifth dropdown, select **0**.

4. Add the third condition using the following steps:

   1. Click on the green plus sign to add a third condition.

   2. In the **Condition Builder** dialog box, perform the following steps:

      1. In the first dropdown, select **value of variable**.

      2. In the second dropdown, select **ShippingAddressError**.

      3. In the third dropdown, select **equals**.

      4. In the fourth dropdown, select **value**.

      5. In the fifth dropdown, select **0**.

      6. Click on **OK**.

5. To create the **Set Panel State** action of the **CheckOutDynamicPanel**, perform the following steps:

   1. Under **Click to add actions**, click on the **Dynamic Panels** drop-down menu and then click on **Set Panel State**.

   2. Under **Configure actions**, in the **Select the panels to set the state** section, click on the checkbox next to **SetCheckOutDynamicPanel**.

   3. Under **Configure actions**, in the **Select the panels to set the state** section, select **PlaceOrder** next to **Select the state** in the dropdown.

   4. Click on **OK**.

6. Under the **OnClick** event, right-click on the **Valid Entry** case and click on **Toggle IF/ELSE IF**.

To create the **Show Global Error Message** case for the **OnClick** event, click on the **Interactions** tab in the **Widget Interactions and Notes** pane and double-click on **OnClick**. A **Case Editor** dialog box will open. In the **Case Editor** dialog, perform the following steps to create the conditions:

1. In the **Case description** field, enter Show Global Error Message.

2. To create the **Show** action on **GlobalErrorMsgRectangle** and **GlobalErrorMsgLabel**, perform the following steps:

   1. In the **Configure actions** column, type GlobalErrorMsgRectangle in the **Search** field under **Select the widgets to hide/show**.

   2. Scroll to find the **SignInValidationMaster** dropdown and click on the checkboxes next to **GlobalErrorMsgRectangle** and **GlobalErrorMsgLabel**.

   3. Click on **OK**.

With the **Billing Address** section completed and the interactions defined for the **CheckOutNowButton** widget, we are now ready to fabricate the **Shipping Address** section.

Fabricating the Shipping Address section

With all widgets including error messages visible, the **Shipping Address** section is almost identical to the **Billing Address** section.

To create the **Shipping Address** section, we will first copy the **Billing Address** section, place the copy on the design area, and make a few adjustments. Perform the following steps:

1. We will first select all widgets that make up the **Billing Address** section. In the design area, click near coordinates (5,425). While holding down the mouse button, drag to coordinates (600,845). This will highlight all widgets that define the **Billing Address** section. In the main menu, mouse over **Edit** and click on **Copy**. In the main menu, mouse over **Edit** and click on **Paste**. In the toolbar, change the value of **x** to 10 and the value of **h** to 850.

2. Click on the **Heading 1** widget at coordinates (30,872). Type Shipping Address. In the **Widget Interactions and Notes** pane, click in the **Shape Name** field and type ShippingHeading1.

3. In the **Widget Interactions and Notes** pane, update each widget's **Shape Name** field using the following table for coordinates and shape name:

Coordinates	Shape name
(10,850)	ShippingAddressBackground
(116,922)	ShippingFullNameLabel
(88,971)	ShippingAddressLine1Label
(88,1013)	ShippingAddressLine2Label
(152,1070)	ShippingCityLabel
(45,1118)	ShippingStateProvinceRegionLabel
(154,1168)	ShippingZipLabel
(207,860)	ShippingGlobalErrorMsgRectangle
(210,864)	ShippingGlobalErrorMsgLabel
(207,915)	ShippingFullName
(207,964)	ShippingAddress1
(207,1013)	ShippingAddress2

Coordinates	Shape name
(207,1062)	**ShippingCity**
(207,1111)	**ShippingStateProvinceRegion**
(207,1160)	**ShippingZip**

4. Click on the **Checkbox** widget at coordinates (212,803). Right-click on the **Checkbox** widget and click on **Cut**.

5. Click on the **ShippingAddressBackground** at coordinates (10,850). In the toolbar, change the value of **h** to `365`.

6. We will now hide all widgets that make up the **Shipping Address** section. In the design area, click near coordinates (5,840). While holding down the mouse button, drag to coordinates (600,1220). This will highlight all widgets that define the **Shipping Address** section. In the toolbar, click on the **Hidden** checkbox to select.

7. Right-click on the **Button Shape** widget at coordinates (210,860), mouse over **Order** and click on **Bring to Front**.

Next we need to update each Individual Form Field master's Form Text Field and Form Error Message Label. We will leverage the **OnPanelStateChange** event on the **CheckOutDynamicPanel**.

To update each Individual Form Field master in the **Sitemap** pane, double-click on the **Check Out** page to open it in the design area. Click on the **CheckOutDynamicPanel** at coordinates (0,0). In the **Widget Interactions and Notes** pane, double-click on the **OnPanelStateChange** event. A **Case Editor** dialog box will open. In the **Case Editor** dialog, perform the following steps to create the condition:

1. In the **Case description** field, enter `InitalizePaymentAndShippingFormFields`.

2. Click on the **Add Condition** button. In the **Condition Builder** dialog box, perform the following steps:

    1. In the first dropdown, select **state of panel**.

    2. In the second dropdown, click on **CheckOutDynamicPanel**.

    3. In the third dropdown, select **equals**.

    4. In the fourth dropdown, select **state**.

    5. In the fifth dropdown, select **PaymentAndShipping**.

    6. Click on **OK**.

3. We will now set the text on each Individual Form Field master's Form Text Field and Form Error Message Label. In the **Case Editor** dialog, under **Click to add actions**, scroll to the **Widgets** drop-down menu and click on **Set Text**. Under **Configure actions**, you will click on the checkbox next to the widget name and enter text in the **Set text to** field using the following table for widget and text pairings:

Widget name to set text (Individual Form Field name/widget name)	Set text to
ShippingFullName/FormTextField	Enter First and Last Name
ShippingFullName/FormErrorMsgLabel	Doesn't seem to be a valid name.
ShippingAddressLine1/FormTextField	Street, P.O. Box, Company
ShippingAddressLine1/FormErrorMsgLabel	Doesn't seem to be a valid address.
ShippingAddressLine2/FormTextField	Building, Mail Drop, etc
ShippingAddressLine2/FormErrorMsgLabel	Doesn't seem to be a valid address.
ShippingCity/FormTextField	Enter City
ShippingCity/FormErrorMsgLabel	Doesn't seem to be a valid City.
ShippingStateProvinceRegion/FormTextField	Enter State, Province or Region
ShippingStateProvinceRegion/FormErrorMsgLabel	Doesn't seem to be a valid entry.
ShippingZip/FormTextField	5 digit ZIP
ShippingZip/FormErrorMsgLabel	ZIP must be 5 digits.
BillingFullName/FormTextField	Enter First and Last Name
BillingFullName/FormErrorMsgLabel	Doesn't seem to be a valid name.
BillingAddressLine1/FormTextField	Street, P.O. Box, Company
BillingAddressLine1/FormErrorMsgLabel	Doesn't seem to be a valid address.
BillingAddressLine2/FormTextField	Building, Mail Drop, etc
BillingAddressLine2/FormErrorMsgLabel	Doesn't seem to be a valid address.
BillingCity/FormTextField	Enter City
BillingCity/FormErrorMsgLabel	Doesn't seem to be a valid City.

Widget name to set text (Individual Form Field name/widget name)	Set text to
BillingStateProvinceRegion/FormTextField	`Enter State or Province`
BillingStateProvinceRegion/ FormErrorMsgLabel	`Doesn't seem to be a valid entry.`
BillingZip/FormTextField	`5 numbers or more!`
BillingZip/FormErrorMsgLabel	`ZIP must be at least 5 numbers.`

4. In the **Case Editor** dialog, click on **OK**.

With the **Payment and Shipping** state layout for the **CheckOutDynamicPanel** completed, you are now ready to refine validation and feedback interactions for the **Shipping Address** section.

Shipping Address section validation and feedback

Since the **Shipping Address** section is almost identical to the **Billing Address** section, we created the **Shipping Address** section from a copy of the **Billing Address** section that included all interactions; thus we only need to make a few changes. We need to change the **FieldError** and **ValidEntry** cases for the **OnFormFieldLostFocus** event for each of the six Individual Form Fields in the **Shipping Address** section. The six Individual Form Fields are as follows:

- **ShippingFullName**
- **ShippingAddressLine1**
- **ShippingAddressLine2**
- **ShippingCity**
- **ShippingStateProvinceRegion**
- **ShippingZip**

Next we will update interactions for the **Shipping Address** Individual Form Fields.

Updating interactions for the Shipping Address Individual Form Fields

We will first update the **ShippingFullName** Individual Form Field by performing the following steps:

1. To update the **FieldError** case for the **OnFormFieldLostFocus** event, click on the **ShippingFullName** at coordinates (207,915).
2. In the W**idget Interactions and Notes** pane, click on the **Interactions** tab under the **OnFormFieldLostFocus** event and double-click on **FieldError**.

3. A **Case Editor** dialog box will open. In the **Case Editor** dialog, perform the following steps to change the variable for **Set** value from **BillingAddressError** to **ShippingAddressError**:

   1. Under **Organize actions**, click on the second action, **Set value**.

   2. Under **Configure action**, click on **BillingAddressError** in **Select the variables to set**. Copy the value from **BillingAddressError** to **ShippingAddressError** by clicking on the checkbox next to **ShippingAddressError**. Click on the checkbox next to **BillingAddressError** to unselect it.

   3. Click on **OK**.

4. Next we will update the **ValidEntry** case for the **OnFormFieldLostFocus** event.

5. In the **Widget Interactions and Notes** pane, click on the **Interactions** tab under the **OnFormFieldLostFocus** event and double-click on **ValidError**.

6. A **Case Editor** dialog box will open. In the **Case Editor** dialog, perform the following steps to change the variable for **Set value** from **BillingAddressError** to **ShippingAddressError**:

   1. Under **Organize actions**, click on the second action, **Set value**.

   2. Under **Configure action**, click on **BillingAddressError** in **Select the variables to set**. Copy the value from **BillingAddressError** to **ShippingAddressError** by clicking on the checkbox next to **ShippingAddressError**. Click on the checkbox next to **BillingAddressError** to unselect it.

   3. Click on **OK**.

To update the **FieldError** case on the **OnFormFieldLostFocus** event for the remaining Individual Form Fields, repeat steps 1-2 five more times using the following table for coordinates and Individual Form Field name:

Coordinates	Field name
(207,964)	ShippingAddressLine1
(207,1013)	ShippingAddressLine2
(207,1062)	ShippingCity
(207,1111)	ShippingStateProvinceRegion
(207,1160)	ShippingZip

With the **PaymentAndShipping** state completed for our **CheckOutDynamicPanel**, we are now ready to design the **PlaceOrder** state.

Designing the PlaceOrder state

The **PlaceOrder** state on the **CheckOutDynamicPanel** comprises the **Header, Footer,** and **Shopping Bag Repeater** masters. The **Category Repeater** item on the **Shopping Bag Repeater** master is used to display the list of items currently in the shopping bag. Every item in the **Shopping Bag Repeater** dataset will be displayed in the order they were added to the shopping bag.

Once completed, your **PlaceOrder** state on the **CheckOutDynamicPanel** will look like the following screenshot:

To build the **PlaceOrder** state on the **CheckOutDynamicPanel**, you will update the **PlaceOrderIndicator**, and place a **Heading 2** widget and a **Button Shape** widget. You will also place the **Shopping Bag Repeater** master and add widgets to make up our **Order Total** section to complete the design.

Building the PlaceOrder state

To design the **PlaceOrder** state, perform the following steps:

1. In the **Sitemap** pane, double-click on the **Check Out** page to open it in the design area.

2. In the **Widget Manager** pane under the **CheckOutDynamicPanel**, double-click on the **PlaceOrder** state to open it in the design area.

3. In the design area, click on the **PlaceOrderIndicator** at coordinates (624,92). In the **Widget Properties and Style** pane, scroll to **Font** with the **Style** tab selected. Click on the down arrow next to the Text Color icon. In the drop-down menu, enter 515151 in the # text field.

4. From the **Widgets** pane, drag the **Heading 2** widget and place at coordinates (10,140). With the **Heading 2** widget selected, perform the following steps:

    1. Type Review Order. You will see the text displayed on the **Heading 2** widget.

    2. In the toolbar, change the value of **w** to 182 and the value of **h** to 32.

    3. In the **Widget Interactions and Notes** pane, click in the **Shape Name** field and type CheckOutHeading.

    4. In the **Widget Properties and Style** pane, scroll to **Font** with the **Style** tab selected and change the font size to **28**.

5. From the **Widgets** pane, drag the **Button Shape** widget and place at coordinates (790,330). With the **Button Shape** widget selected, perform the following steps:

    1. Type PLACE YOUR ORDER.

    2. In the toolbar, change the value of **w** to 140 and the value of **h** to 30.

    3. In the **Widget Interactions and Notes** pane, click in the **Shape Name** field and type PlaceOrderButton.

    4. In the **Widget Properties and Style** pane, scroll to **Font** with the **Style** tab selected. Change the font size to **13**.

    5. Right-click on the **Button Shape** widget, mouse over **Order** and click on **Bring to Front**.

6. With the **Button Shape** widget selected, we will go ahead and enable our **OnClick** event that will set our dynamic panel state to the **Confirmation** state. To set the panel state of the **CheckOutDynamicPanel**, click on the **Interactions** tab in the **Widget Interactions and Notes** pane and double-click on **OnClick**. A **Case Editor** dialog box will open; in the **Case Editor** dialog, perform the following steps:

    1. Under **Click to add actions**, click on the **Dynamic Panels** drop-down menu and then click on **Set Panel State**.

    2. Under **Configure actions**, click the checkbox next to **SetCheckOutDynamicPanel** in the **Select the panels to set the state** section.

    3. Under **Configure actions**, select **Confirmation** in the dropdown next to **Select the state** in the **Select the panels to set the state** section.

    4. Click on **OK**.

7. From the **Masters** pane, drag the **Shopping Bag Repeater** master and drop at any location on the wireframe. Perform the following steps:

    1. In the **Widget Interactions and Notes** pane, type `PlaceOrderRepeater` in the **Shopping Bag Repeater Name** field.

    2. In the design area, double-click on the **PlaceOrderRepeater** at coordinates (10,260) to open the **Shopping Bag Repeater** master in the design area.

8. With the **Shopping Bag Repeater** master opened in the design area, click on the **Rectangle** widget in the **Widgets** pane. While holding down the mouse button, drag the **Rectangle** widget and place at coordinates (760,140). With the **Rectangle** widget selected, perform the following steps:

    1. In the toolbar, change the value of **w** to `200` and the value of **h** to `200` and click on the checkbox next to **Hidden**.

    2. In the **Widget Interactions and Notes** pane, click in the **Shape Name** field and type `CheckOutBackground`.

    3. Right-click on the **Rectangle** widget, mouse over **Order**, and click on **Send to Back**.

9. From the **Widgets** pane, drag the **Label** widget and place at coordinates (773,175). With the **Label** widget selected, perform the following steps:

    1. Type `Shipping`. You will see the text displayed on the **Label** widget.

    2. In the toolbar, change the value of **w** to `50` and the value of **h** to `14` and click on the checkbox next to **Hidden**.

3. In the **Widget Interactions and Notes** pane, click in the **Shape Name** field and type `ShippingSubTotalLabel`.

4. In the **Widget Properties and Style** pane, with the **Style** tab selected scroll to **Font** and change the font size to `12`.

10. From the **Widgets** pane, drag the **Label** widget and place at coordinates (891,175). With the **Label** widget selected, perform the following steps:

    1. Type `$`. You will see the text displayed on the **Label** widget.

    2. In the toolbar, change the value of **w** to `7` and the value of **h** to `12` and then click on the checkbox next to **Hidden**.

    3. In the **Widget Interactions and Notes** pane, click in the **Shape Name** field and type `ShippingCurrencySymbol`.

    4. In the **Widget Properties and Style** pane, scroll to **Font** with the **Style** tab selected and change the font size to **11**.

11. From the **Widgets** pane, drag the **Label** widget and place at coordinates (910,175). With the **Label** widget selected, perform the following steps:

    1. Type `0.00`. You will see the text displayed on the **Label** widget.

    2. In the toolbar, change the value of **w** to `22` and the value of **h** to `12` and click on the checkbox next to **Hidden**.

    3. In the **Widget Interactions and Notes** pane, click in the **Shape Name** field and type `ShippingSubTotal`.

    4. In the **Widget Properties and Style** pane, scroll to **Font** with the **Style** tab selected and change the font size to **11**.

    5. In the **Widget Properties and Style** pane, with the **Style** tab selected scroll to **Alignment + Padding**. Under A**lignment + Padding**, in the first set of icons, click on the third icon to right align the text on the **Rectangle** widget.

12. From the **Widgets** pane, drag the **Label** widget and place at coordinates (773,195). With the **Label** widget selected, perform the following steps:

    1. Type `Estimated tax`. You will see the text displayed on the **Label** widget.

    2. In the toolbar, change the value of **w** to `50` and the value of **h** to `14` and click on the checkbox next to **Hidden**.

    3. In the **Widget Interactions and Notes** pane, click in the **Shape Name** field and type `TaxSubTotalLabel`.

    4. In the **Widget Properties and Style** pane, scroll to **Font** with the **Style** tab selected and change the font size to **12**.

13. From the **Widgets** pane, drag the **Label** widget and place at coordinates (891,195). With the **Label** widget selected, perform the following steps:

    1. Type $. You will see the text displayed on the **Label** widget.

    2. In the toolbar, change the value of **w** to 7 and the value of **h** to 12 and click on the checkbox next to **Hidden**.

    3. In the **Widget Interactions and Notes** pane, click in the **Shape Name** field and type TaxCurrencySymbol.

    4. In the **Widget Properties and Style** pane, scroll to **Font** with the **Style** tab selected and change the font size to **11**.

14. From the **Widgets** pane, drag the **Label** widget and place at coordinates (922,175). With the **Label** widget selected, perform the following steps:

    1. Type 0.00. You will see the text displayed on the **Label** widget.

    2. In the toolbar, change the value of **w** to 22 and the value of **h** to 12 and click on the checkbox next to **Hidden**.

    3. In the **Widget Interactions and Notes** pane, click in the **Shape Name** field and type TaxSubTotal.

    4. In the **Widget Properties and Style** pane, scroll to **Font** with the **Style** tab selected and change the font size to **11**.

    5. In the **Widget Properties and Style** pane, scroll to **Alignment + Padding** with the **Style** tab selected. Under **Alignment + Padding**, in the first set of icons, click on the third icon to right align the text on the **Rectangle** widget.

15. From the **Widgets** pane, drag the **Horizontal Line** widget and place at coordinates (773,212). With the **Horizontal Line** widget selected, perform the following steps:

    1. In the toolbar, change the value of **w** to 177 and click on the checkbox next to **Hidden**.

    2. In the **Widget Interactions and Notes** pane, click in the **Shape Name** field and type OrderHzLine.

    3. In the **Widget Properties and Style** pane, scroll to **Font** with the **Style** tab selected and change the font size to **12**.

16. From the **Widgets** pane, drag the **Label** widget and place at coordinates (774,226). With the **Label** widget selected, perform the following steps:

    1. Type `Order Total`. You will see the text displayed on the **Label** widget.

    2. In the toolbar, change the value of **w** to `78` and the value of **h** to `16` and click on the checkbox next to **Hidden**.

    3. In the **Widget Interactions and Notes** pane, click in the **Shape Name** field and type `OrderTotalLabel`.

    4. In the **Widget Properties and Style** pane, scroll to **Font** with the **Style** tab selected and change the font size to **14**.

17. From the **Widgets** pane, drag the **Label** widget and place at coordinates (891,226). With the **Label** widget selected, perform the following steps:

    1. Type `$`. You will see the text displayed on the **Label** widget.

    2. In the toolbar, change the value of **w** to `8` and the value of **h** to `15` and click the checkbox next to **Hidden**.

    3. In the **Widget Interactions and Notes** pane, click in the **Shape Name** field and type `OrderTotatlCurrencySymbol`.

    4. In the **Widget Properties and Style** pane, scroll to **Font** with the **Style** tab selected and change the font size to **13**.

18. From the **Widgets** pane, drag the **Label** widget and place at coordinates (918,226). With the **Label** widget selected, perform the following steps:

    1. Type `###.##`. You will see the text displayed on the **Label** widget.

    2. In the toolbar, change the value of **w** to `22` and the value of **h** to `12` and click on the checkbox next to **Hidden**.

    3. In the **Widget Interactions and Notes** pane, click in the **Shape Name** field and type `OrderTotal`.

    4. In the **Widget Properties and Style** pane, scroll to **Font** with the **Style** tab selected and change the font size to **13**.

    5. In the **Widget Properties and Style** pane, scroll to **Alignment + Padding** with the **Style** tab selected. Under **Alignment + Padding**, in the first set of icons, click on the third icon to right align the text on the **Rectangle** widget.

With the design completed for the **Check Out** page, we are now ready to define interactions and feedback.

Check Out page interactions and feedback

Interactions and feedback for our **Check Out** page occur as a result of enhancements we will make to the **Shopping Cart Repeater**. We will also enable an **OnClick** event for our **CheckOutButton**.

One of the challenges we must plan for prior to enhancing the **Shopping Cart Repeater** is that Axure RP 7 currently does not maintain interim repeater state data from page to page. Normally, we design around this implementation nuance by using various states on a dynamic panel within the same page. This approach would allow us to access current interim repeater states based on various interactions with each of our repeaters (for example, faceted filtering, sort order, add or remove data rows, and so on).

Since we want to use the **Shopping Bag Repeater** master on two different pages and as a result the modification we would make to repeater data would be transient in nature, we must track the SKU, quantity, color, and size for each of the ten possible items in our shopping cart.

To accomplish this, we will create three new global variables named **ShoppingCartQty**, **ShoppingCartColor**, and **ShoppingCartSize**. We will use a single character corresponding to each SKU. The location corresponding to an SKU is indexed by the numerical location of the associated SKU integer for each variable. We will also create a **ShoppingCartIndex** variable to assist when reading and writing to the shopping cart variables.

Since we are leveraging a single character in each variable per SKU, this limits us to a maximum quantity of nine for a given SKU. We also need to transform the color and size selections to integers. The following table shows the relationship between integer values that we will store in the **ShoppingCartColor** and **ShoppingCartSize** variables and the equivalent color and size:

ColorDropList option	Integer equivalent	SizeDropList	Integer equivalent
Black	1	Small	1
White	2	Medium	2
Blue	3	Large	3
Red	4		

Next we define the new global variables and update the Shopping Cart Repeater.

Updating our Shopping Cart Repeater

To define the new global variables and update the **Shopping Cart Repeater**, perform the following steps:

1. In the main menu, click on **Project** and then click on **Global Variables...**. In the **Global Variables** dialog, perform the following steps:

    1. Click on the green plus sign and type ShoppingCartQty. Click in the **Default Value** field and type QNNNNNNNNNN.

    2. Click on the green plus sign and type ShoppingCartColor. Click in the **Default Value** field and type CNNNNNNNNNN.

    3. Click on the green plus sign and type ShoppingCartSize. Click in the **Default Value** field and type SNNNNNNNNNN.

    4. Click on the green plus sign and type ShoppingCartIndex. Click in the **Default Value** field and type 0.

2. In the **Masters** pane, double-click on the icon next to the **Shopping Bag Repeater** master to open it in the design area. Click on the **Rectangle** widget at (760,140). In the **Widget Interactions and Notes** pane, type SubtotalBackground in the **Shape Name** field.

3. Next we will define the cases to update the **ShoppingCartColor**, **ShoppingCartSize**, and **ShoppingCartQty** variables when the user clicks on the **UpdateLineItemButton**. We will define a total of seven new cases, one for each of the **ColorDropList** and **SizeDropList** options. We will also add an additional **Set Variable Value** to the **UpdateButtonClicked** case to update the **ShoppingCartQty** variable.

4. To create the **ItemColorBlack** case on the **OnClick** event for the **UpdateLineItemButton**, double-click on the **MyShoppingBagRepeater** at coordinates (10,260). Click on the **UpdateLineItemButton** at coordinates (640,20). In the **Page Widget Interactions and Notes** pane, click on the **Interactions** tab and double-click on the **OnClick** event. A **Case Editor** dialog box will open. In the **Case Editor** dialog, perform the following steps:

    1. In the **Case description** field, type ItemColorBlack.

    2. Create the condition. Click on the **Add Condition** button. In the **Condition Builder** dialog box, perform the following steps:

        1. In the first dropdown, select **selected option of**.

        2. In the second dropdown, select **ColorDropList**.

        3. In the third dropdown, select **equals**.

4. In the fourth dropdown, select **option**.

5. In the fifth dropdown, select **Black**.

6. Click on **OK**.

5. Create the action. To set the variable value for **ShoppingCartColor**, perform the following steps:

   1. Under **Click to add actions**, scroll to the **Variables** drop-down menu and click on **Set Variable Value**.

   2. Under **Configure actions**, in the **Select the variables to set** section, click on the checkbox next to **ShoppingCartColor**. In the **Set variable to** section, in the first drop-down menu, select **value** and click on **fx**. An **Edit Value** dialog box will open.

   3. In the **Edit Value** dialog box, click on the **Add Local Variable** link under **Local Variables**.

   4. To add the first local variable, type LocalVar in the first text field. In the second dropdown, select the value of the variable. In the third dropdown, select **ShoppingCartColor**.

   5. In the first textbox (under **Insert Variable or Function...**), replace the current text with `[[LocalVar.substring(0,Item.SKU) + 1 + LocalVar.substring(Item.SKU+1)]]`.

   6. Click on **OK**.

6. Repeat step 4 six more times to create the remaining cases. Refer to the following table for case description name, condition, and action:

Iteration repeating step 4	Case description name	Condition		Action	
				Variable	First text box expression
1st	**ItemColorWhite**	Second dropdown: **ColorDropList**	Fifth dropdown: **White**	**ShoppingCartColor**	`[[LocalVar.substring(0,Item.SKU) + 2 + LocalVar.substring(Item.SKU+1)]]`
2nd	**ItemColorBlue**	Second dropdown: **ColorDropList**	Fifth dropdown: **Blue**	**ShoppingCartColor**	`[[LocalVar.substring(0,Item.SKU) + 3 + LocalVar.substring(Item.SKU+1)]]`
3rd	**ItemColorRed**	Second dropdown: **ColorDropList**	Fifth dropdown: **Red**	**ShoppingCartColor**	`[[LocalVar.substring(0,Item.SKU) + 4 + LocalVar.substring(Item.SKU+1)]]`

Iteration repeating step 4	Case description name	Condition		Action	
				Variable	**First text box expression**

4th	**ItemSizeSmall**	Second dropdown: **SizeDropList**	Fifth dropdown: **Small**	**ShoppingCartSize**	`[[LocalVar.`
					`substring(0,Item.`
					`SKU) + 1 + LocalVar.`
					`substring(Item.`
					`SKU+1)]]`

5th	**ItemSizeMedium**	Second dropdown: **SizeDropList**	Fifth dropdown: **Medium**	**ShoppingCartSize**	[[LocalVar.substring(0,Item.SKU) + 2 + LocalVar.substring(Item.SKU+1)]]

6th	**ItemSizeLarge**	Second dropdown: **SizeDropList**	Fifth dropdown: **Large**	**ShoppingCartSize**	`[[LocalVar.`
					`substring(0,Item.`
					`SKU) + 3 + LocalVar.`
					`substring(Item.`
					`SKU+1)]]`

7. In the **Widget Interactions and Notes** pane, click on the **Interactions** tab, and under the **OnClick** event, double-click on the **UpdateButtonClicked** case. A **Case Editor** dialog box will open. In the **Case Editor** dialog, add the following action to set the variable value for **ShoppingCartQty** by performing the following steps:

   1. Under **Click to add actions**, scroll to the **Variables** drop-down menu and click on **Set Variable Value**.

   2. Under **Configure actions**, click the checkbox next to **ShoppingCartQty** in the **Select the variables to set** section. In the **Set variable to** section, select **value** in the first drop-down menu and click on **fx**. An **Edit Value** dialog box will open.

   3. In the **Edit Value** dialog box, click on the **Add Local Variable** link under **Local Variables**.

   4. To add the first local variable, type `LocalVar` in the first text field. In the second dropdown, select **value of variable**. In the third dropdown, select **ShoppingCartQty**.

   5. In the first text box (under **Insert Variable or Function...**), replace the current text with `[[LocalVar.substring(0,Item.SKU) + Item.ItemQty + LocalVar.substring(Item.SKU+1)]]`.

   6. Click on **OK**.

8. Next we will organize the cases for the **OnClick** event toggling IF/ELSE IF, where appropriate to change the IF condition to ELSE IF (or vice versa). Refer to the following table for case order and click on the **IF/ELSE IF** condition:

Click-and-drag each case to change the order.

To toggle IF/ELSE IF, right-click on a case name and click on **Toggle IF/ELSE IF**.

Order #	Case name	IF/ELSE IF
1	**ItemColorBlack**	IF
2	**ItemColorWhite**	ELSE IF
3	**ItemColorBlue**	ELSE IF
4	**ItemColorRed**	ELSE IF
5	**ItemSizeSmall**	IF
6	**ItemSizeMedium**	ELSE IF
7	**ItemSizeLarge**	ELSE IF
8	**UpdateButtonClicked**	IF
9	**QtyZero**	IF
10	**NoItems**	IF

With the **Shopping Cart Repeater** updated, we are now ready to add the **InitializeCheckOutState** case to the **OnPanelStateChange** event for the **CheckOutDynamicPanel**.

Adding the InitializeCheckOutState case for the OnPanelStateChange event

When our **CheckOutDynamicPanel** changes state to the **PlaceOrder** state, the **OnPanelStateChange** event's **InitalizePlaceOrder** case updates the empty **Shopping Cart Repeater** based on the data stored in our **ShoppingCartQty**, **ShoppingCartColor**, and **ShoppingCartSize** variables. Then the data stored in the **Shopping Cart Repeater** is shown on the Repeater item as defined by cases for the **OnItemLoad** event.

To update the empty **Shopping Cart Repeater** in the **Sitemap** pane, double-click on the **Check Out** page to open it in the design area. Click on the **CheckOutDynamicPanel** at coordinates (0,0). In the **Widget Interactions and Notes** pane, click on the **Interactions** tab and double-click on the **OnPanelStateChange** event. A **Case Editor** dialog box will open. In the **Case Editor** dialog, perform the following steps:

1. In the **Case description** field, enter `InitalizeCheckOutState`.

2. Create the condition. Click on the **Add Condition** button. In the **Condition Builder** dialog box, perform the following steps:

   1. In the first dropdown, select **state of panel**.

   2. In the second dropdown, select **CheckOutDynamicPanel**.

   3. In the third dropdown, select **equals**.

   4. In the fourth dropdown, select **state**.

   5. In the fifth dropdown, select **PlaceOrder**.

   6. Click on **OK**.

3. Create the first action. To hide the **PlaceOrderRepeater/SubtotalBackground** and **PlaceOrderRepeater/UpdateLineItemButton** perform the following steps:

   1. Under **Click to add actions**, scroll to the **Widgets** drop-down menu, click on the **Show/Hide** dropdown and then on **Hide**.

   2. In the **Configure actions** column, type `SubtotalBackground` in the **Search** field under **Select the widgets to hide/show**. Click on the checkbox next to **SubtotalBackground**.

   3. In the **Configure actions** column, type `UpdateLineItemButton` in the **Search** field under **Select the widgets to hide/show**. Click on the checkbox next to **UpdateLineItemButton**.

4. Create the second action. To show the widgets that make up our **Order Total** section, perform the following steps:

   1. Under **Click to add actions**, scroll to the **Widgets** drop-down menu, click on the **Show/Hide** dropdown and then on **Show**.

   2. In the **Configure actions** column, type `CheckOutBackground` in the **Search** field under **Select the widgets to hide/show**. Click on the checkbox next to **CheckOutBackground**.

3. In the **Configure actions** column, type `ShippingSubTotalLabel` in the **Search** field under **Select the widgets to hide/show**. Click on the checkbox next to **ShippingSubTotalLabel**.

4. In the **Configure actions** column, type `ShippingCurrencySymbol` in the **Search** field under **Select the widgets to hide/show**. Click on the checkbox next to **ShippingCurrencySymbol**.

5. In the **Configure actions** column, type `ShippingSubTotal` in the **Search** field under **Select the widgets to hide/show**. Click on the checkbox next to **ShippingSubTotal**.

6. In the **Configure actions** column, type `TaxSubTotalLabel` in the **Search** field under **Select the widgets to hide/show**. Click on the checkbox next to **TaxSubTotalLabel**.

7. In the **Configure actions** column, type `TaxCurrencySymbol` in the **Search** field under **Select the widgets to hide/show**. Click on the checkbox next to **TaxCurrencySymbol**.

8. In the **Configure actions** column, type `TaxSubTotal` in the **Search** field under **Select the widgets to hide/show**. Click on the checkbox next to **TaxSubTotal**.

9. In the **Configure actions** column, type `OrderHzLine` in the **Search** field under **Select the widgets to hide/show**. Click on the checkbox next to **OrderHzLine**.

10. In the **Configure actions** column, type `OrderTotalLabel` in the **Search** field under **Select the widgets to hide/show**. Click on the checkbox next to **OrderTotalLabel**.

11. In the **Configure actions** column, type `OrderTotalCurrencySymbol` in the **Search** field under **Select the widgets to hide/show**. Click on the checkbox next to **OrderTotalCurrencySymbol**.

12. In the **Configure actions** column, type `OrderTotal` in the **Search** field under **Select the widgets to hide/show**. Click on the checkbox next to **OrderTotal**.

13. Click on **OK**.

5. Create the third action. To hide the **PlaceOrderRepeater/ SubtotalBackground** and **PlaceOrderRepeater/UpdateLineItemButton** perform the following steps:

   1. Under **Click to add actions**, scroll to the **Widgets** drop-down menu, click on the **Show/Hide** dropdown and then on **Hide**.

   2. In the **Configure actions** column, type `SubtotalBackground` in the **Search** field under **Select the widgets to hide/show**. Click on the checkbox next to **SubtotalBackground**.

   3. In the **Configure actions** column, type `UpdateLineItemButton` in the **Search** field under **Select the widgets to hide/show**. Click on the checkbox next to **UpdateLineItemButton**.

With the **InitializeCheckOutState** case for the **OnPanelStateChange** event added, we are now ready to enhance the **OnItemLoad** event of **Shopping Bag Repeater** to automatically update the **OrderTotal** label.

Enhancing the OnItemLoad event of the Shopping Bag Repeater

We want to have the **OrderTotal** label updated during the **OnItemLoad** event of our **MyShoppingBagRepeater**. To do this, we will need to modify the **SetRepeater** and **NoItems** cases for the **OnItemLoad** event. In the **Masters** pane, double-click on the **Shopping Bag Repeater** master to open it in the design area. Double-click on the **MyShoppingBagRepeater** at coordinates (10,260). The **MyShoppingBagRepeater** will open in the design area. With the **MyShoppingBagRepeater** opened in the design area, perform the following steps:

1. In the **Page Widget Interactions and Notes** pane, click on the **Interactions** tab, and under the **OnItemLoad** event, double-click on the **SetRepeater** case. A **Case Editor** dialog box will open. In the **Case Editor** dialog, perform the following steps to set the text on **OrderTotal**:

   1. Under **Click to add actions**, scroll to the **Widgets** drop-down menu and click on **Set Text**.

   2. Under **Configure actions**, click on the checkbox next to **OrderTotal** in the **Select the widgets to set text** section.

   3. Under **Configure actions**, select **value** in the first drop-down menu in the **Set variable to** section, and enter `[[SubTotal.toFixed(2)]]` in the text field.

   4. Click on **OK**.

2. In the **Page Widget Interactions and Notes** pane, click on the **Interactions** tab, and under the **OnItemLoad** event, double-click on the **NoItems** case. A **Case Editor** dialog box will open. In the **Case Editor** dialog, perform the following steps to set the text on **OrderTotal**:

   1. Under **Click to add actions**, scroll to the **Widgets** drop-down menu and click on **Set Text**.
   2. Under **Configure actions**, in the **Select the widgets to set text** section, click on the checkbox next to **OrderTotal**.
   3. Under **Configure actions**, select **value** in the first drop-down menu in the **Set variable to** section, and enter `0.00` in the text field.
   4. Click on **OK**.

With the design and interactions completed for the **CheckOutDynamicPanel**, we are now ready to design the **Confirmation** state.

Designing the Confirmation state

The **Confirmation** state will consist of our **Header** master, **Heading**, **Paragraph**, and **Footer** masters.

To create the **Confirmation** state, perform the following steps:

1. In the **Widget Manager** pane under the **CheckOutDynamicPanel**, double-click on the **Confirmation** state to open it in the design area.
2. In the **Masters** pane, click on the **Header** master. While holding down the mouse button, drag the **Header** master and drop at any location on the wireframe.
3. In the **Widgets** pane, click on the **Heading 1** widget. While holding down the mouse button, drag the **Heading 1** widget and place at coordinates (312,185).
4. With the **Heading 1** widget selected, type `Thank you for your Order!`.
5. In the **Widget Interactions and Notes** pane, click in the **Shape Name** field and type `ConfirmationHeading`.
6. In the **Widgets** pane, click on the **Paragraph** widget. While holding down the mouse button, drag the **Paragraph** widget and place at coordinates (330,245).
7. In the **Widget Interactions and Notes** pane, click in the **Shape Name** field and type `ConfirmationMessage`.
8. In the **Masters** pane, click on the **Footer** master. While holding down the mouse button, drag the **Footer** master and place at coordinates (10,970).

Congratulations! With the **Confirmation** state completed for the **CheckOutDynamicPanel**, we have now completed our prototype.

Summary

In this chapter, we created a check out flow that included a dynamic progress indicator. We were able to modify our **CMS Repeater** master as well as our **Shopping Cart Repeater** to add enhanced functionality. With minimal enhancements to our design, we were able to leverage the same **Shopping Cart Repeater** for our **Review Order** state.

One goal of world-class interfaces is to provide user feedback that results in increased user confidence as well as reduced user cognitive overload. By using familiar user interface elements and common interaction paradigms (for example, inline field validation, and so on), we were able to increase user confidence. Our design allowed the user to focus on the benefits and features of the product offerings.

Once the user entered the check out flow, we provided mechanisms to enable the user to know where they were in the process as well as the ability to make last minute changes to their order. By providing the user an opportunity to make changes to the shopping cart without having to leave the check out flow, we increased the probability that the user would finalize the sale.

Self-test questions

- Why did our **Check Out** dynamic panel contain a streamlined header?
- Why did we create an Individual Form Field master?
- How many required states did we need for the **Check Out** dynamic panel?
- What were the names of the states for the **Check Out** dynamic panel?
- What is one additional experience often seen on e-commerce sites that we could add to enhance our prototype?

Answers to Self-test Questions

Together we have experienced a journey of discovery exploring both preexisting and new features of Axure RP 7. A great way to reinforce concepts is by answering questions pertaining to the concepts presented. The upcoming sections include answers to the self-test questions presented at the end of selected chapters.

Chapter 1

In this chapter, you learned about the various aspects of Axure's environment and interface. We explored the main menu, toolbar, sitemap, design area, and panes. You also became familiar with pages, widgets, and masters.

Questions and Answers

- What sections does the Axure interface comprise?

    The interface is organized into sections: a main menu, a toolbar, the design area, and the surrounding panes.

- Can you show or hide individual widgets placed on the design area?

    Yes, there are two ways. You can select or deselect the checkbox next to **Hidden** in the toolbar. You can also right-click on the widget and click on **Set Hidden** or **Set Visible**.

- When would we use a dynamic panel?

    When we need to show, hide, or swap content.

- What does it mean when you see a blue rectangle next to a dynamic panel in the **Widget Manager**?

  This indicates that the default for panel 1 is **Show in view**.

- What does it mean when you see a gray rectangle next to a dynamic panel in the **Widget Manager**?

  This indicates that the default for panel 2 is **Hide from view**.

- How many tabs are there in the **Widgets Interactions and Notes** pane and what are the names of the tabs?

  There are two tabs: **Interactions** and **Notes**.

- In the **Page** pane on the **Page Interactions** tab, how many events are shown by default and what are the names of the events?

  There are three events shown by default: **OnPageLoad**, **OnWindowResize**, and **OnWindowScroll**.

- In the **Page** pane on the **Page Interactions** tab, how would we display additional events?

  We would click on **More Events** to display the additional events available.

Chapter 2

In this chapter, we focused on creating the **Home** page for our e-commerce prototype.

Questions and Answers

- What was the first activity we performed in this chapter before we stated the Home page design?

  We completed our **Sitemap**.

- Why did we convert the widgets that make up the Header into a master?

  We convert the widgets that make up the Header into a **Header** master, so the new **Header** master could be leveraged on each page of our design.

- What **Drop Behavior** did we select for our **Header** master and why?

  We selected **Lock to Master Location** for the **Drop Behavior** of our **Header** master. As a result, the **Header** master will always appear on each page in the same location as the master.

- On the **SearchDP**, what interaction(s) on which widget(s) enable the expanding Search Bar?

  The **SearchDP** (dynamic panel) contains two states: **Collapsed** and **Expanded**. The **Collapsed** state is the default state and contains a Text Field widget. The Text Field widget responds to the **OnMouseEnter** interaction.

- How did we start the autorotation of the Carousel?

  To start the auto-rotating carousel, we leveraged the **OnPageLoad** page interaction. For each State of the **CarouselDP** dynamic panel, we used the **OnPanelStateChange** case, we waited for 2,000 ms and then verified if the user had clicked on the carousel image before we changed the state of the **CarouselDP** dynamic panel.

- Which widget stops the autorotation of the carousel on what conditions?

  The **CheckForClick** widget is used to stop the autorotation of the carousel if the carousel image, previous, or next buttons were clicked.

- Which widget did we use to embed YouTube and Vimeo videos into our prototype?

  The **Inline Frame** widget.

Chapter 3

In this chapter, we created Registration Variables, an **Inline Field Validation** master, a **Registration** page, and a **Sign In** page.

Questions and Answers

- What was the first thing we reviewed prior to creating our **Inline Field Validation** master?

  We first reviewed our Sitemap to ensure that all pages needed for the Registration and Sign-in flows had been created. We noticed that additional pages needed to be created. As a result, we created the Registration and Confirmation pages.

- What was the purpose of creating Global Registration variables?

  Global Axure variables allowed us to store the user entered e-mail and password. We also used Global variables to assist in tracking validation of the e-mail and password after the user had completed the signin process.

- What do yellow highlighted areas in the design area indicate?

  Yellow highlighted areas shown on the design area indicate that the associated widget's default visibility is hidden.

- Why did we create an **Inline Field Validation** master?

  A master is a group of widgets that is reusable. You can make a change to the master and the change is global in nature. This means that the change to the master will be seen everywhere the master has been used. The **Inline Field Validation** master was used on both the **SignIn** and **SignUp** pages.

- Why did we use raised events for the **Inline Field Validation** master?

  Raised events on the **Inline Field Validation** master allowed us to differentiate events and actions on the **SignIn** and **SignUp** pages.

- How many error message areas are defined on the **Inline Field Validation** master?

  There are three error message areas on the **Inline Field Validation** master.

- What are the names of the error message widgets for the **Inline Field Validation** master?

  GlobalErrorMsgRectangle, **GlobalErrorMsgLabel**, **EmailMsgRectangle**, **EmailMsgLabel**, **PasswordMsgRectangle**, and **PasswordMsgLabel**.

- What type and how many actions did we use to create the horizontal shaking effect for the Submit button?

  We used three **Move** actions to create the horizontal shaking effect for the Submit button.

Chapter 4

In this chapter, we leveraged a new feature of Axure RP 7 called the Repeater widget to simulate a Content Management System (CMS).

Questions and Answers

- What was the first step we took prior to designing our Catalog Repeater?

  The first step we took was to perform a Content Inventory. We then decided which content we needed for the Catalog, Category, and Product Detail designs.

- How many parts does a **Repeater** have and what are the parts typically known as?

  There are two primary parts to a Repeater: the **Repeater Dataset** and the **Repeater** item.

- Explain how a Repeater operates.

  In its simplest use, a **Repeater** iterates through the **Repeater Dataset** dynamically updating **Repeater** item widgets as specified by the **OnitemLoad** event.

- How many Repeaters did we use for the Catalog, Category, and Product Detail designs and what were the name(s) of the Repeater(s)?

  We used a single **Repeater** on the CMS Repeater master named the CategoryRepeater for the Catalog, Category, and the Product Detail designs.

- For the **Repeater** on the CMS Repeater master, how many columns did the Repeater Dataset have?

  We leveraged 17 columns.

- How did we group the columns for the Category Repeater's Dataset?
  - Column 1 was a unique integer to track individual Stock Keeping Units (SKUs) in our CMS
  - Columns 2–7 were used for the Catalog page
  - Columns 8–12 were used to update the Repeater item displayed on the Category page
  - Columns 13–17 were used for the Product Detail pages

- Name the widgets on the Repeater item for the Category Repeater.
  - **CategoryBackground**
  - **ItemImageRepeater**
  - **ItemBrandRepeater**
  - **ItemDescriptionRepeater**
  - **CurrencySymbolRepeater**
  - **ItemPriceRepeater**

- What are the minimum and maximum Cross Sell Items that our Category Repeater is designed to utilize?

  Our Category Repeater will support from one to three Cross Sell Items per individual SKU.

- For the **ItemImageRepeater**, when an item image is clicked, what Global variables are set prior to showing product details?

  ShowDetail, **SKU_CrossSell1**, **SKU_CrossSell2**, and **SKU_CrossSell3**.

- When an item **Image** is clicked, what action defined in the **ItemImageClicked** case causes the **ItemImageRepeater** to reload?

  The action Toggle Visibility for the **SetDetailCrossSellFilters** causes the **ItemImageRepeater** to reload.

Chapter 5

In this chapter, we leveraged a new feature of Axure RP 7 called the Repeater widget to simulate a Content Management System (CMS).

Questions and Answers

- What enhancements were needed to complete the **CMS Repeater** master?

  We added dynamic panels to facilitate the Category and Product Detail designs. We also added additional interactions for the **SetDetailCrossSellFilter Hot Spot**.

- What is the **SetDetailCrossSellFilter Hot Spot** widget used for?

  The **SetDetailCrossSellFilter Hot Spot** widget is used to remove and apply the Detail and Cross Sell filters on the **CategoryRepeater** widget.

- What happens when the visibility of the **SetDetailCrossSellFilter Hot Spot** is toggled?

  Toggling Visibility of the Hot Spot forces the Repeater to refresh. Once the Repeater has refreshed, content is then dynamically updated on the **Product Detail** page.

- What happens when a user clicks on a menu item in the main menu on the **Header** master?

  When a user clicks on a **Menu** item, the **ShowCatalog** global variable is set to a corresponding **Category** value and the **Catalog** page is opened in the current window.

- When we built the **Category** page, what were the first things we placed?

  We first placed the **Header**, **CMS Repeater**, and **Footer** masters.

- What actions did we define for the **Category** page **OnPageLoad** event?

  We defined the **OnPageLoad** interaction to initialize variables.

- Which social media channels did we enable interactions for on the **ItemDetailWithCrossSell** state of the **Detail** dynamic panel?

  Twitter, Pinterest, and Facebook.

Chapter 6

In this chapter, we designed a **Search Results** page and enabled Search interactions.

Questions and Answers

- What global variable did we add to support Search?

  We added the **SearchTerm** global variable.

- Which masters did we use to build the Search page?

  The **Header**, **CMS Repeater**, and **Footer** masters.

- How did we facilitate Search functionality in the **Header** master?

  We created an **OnClick** event on the **SearchRectangleExpanded** widget for the Expanded State of the **ExpandingSearchDP** dynamic panel. The **OnClick** event set the **SearchTerm** global variable and opened the Search page in the current window.

- What filter did we have to add to the **SetGlobalFilters Hot Spot**?

  We added the **SetSearchFilter** to the **SetGlobalFilters Hot Spot**.

- Which columns of the Data Set did we search for matches of our **SearchTerm** variable?

    ◦ ItemCategory
    ◦ ItemBrand
    ◦ ItemDescription

Chapter 7

In this chapter, we added **Shopping Cart** interactions to our prototype.

Questions and Answers

- Why do e-commerce sites leverage shopping bags?

  Many e-commerce sites leverage a shopping bag or shopping cart.
  This functionality allows customers to add, update, and remove items
  prior to finalizing their purchase.

- What changes occur and which Repeaters are updated when a user adds an
  item to the Shopping Bag?

  When a user adds an item to the Shopping Bag, data for that item is copied
  from the CMS Repeater master to the **Shopping Bag Repeater** master.
  The **Shopping Bag Repeater** master will also update the Quantity and
  SubTotal columns.

- To create the **MyShoppingBagRepeater**, did we leverage an existing master
  or create a new **Repeater** widget?

  We created a new **Repeater** widget.

- How many columns does the **Repeater Dataset** for the
  MyShoppingBagRepeater contain?

  There are 11 columns for the **MyShoppingBagRepeater** Dataset.

- What are the names for the columns of the **MyShoppingBagRepeater**
  Dataset?

  SKU

  ItemImage

  ItemBrand

  ItemDescription

  ItemPrice

  SKU_CrossSell1

  SKU_CrossSell2

  SKU_CrossSell3

  ItemColor

  ItemSize

  ItemQty

- How many cases are there and what are the names of the cases for the **OnItemLoad** event of **MyShoppingBagRepeater**?

  We created three cases: **SetRepeater**, **NoItems**, and **MoveMyShoppingBagFooter**.

- How many and which masters make up the Shopping Bag page?

  There are two masters used on the Shopping Bag Page: the **Header** and **Shopping Bag** Repeater.

Chapter 8

In this chapter, we created a Check Out flow that included a dynamic progress indicator.

Questions and Answers

- Why did our Check Out dynamic panel contain a streamlined header?

  To remove visual clutter while reducing distractions allowing the user to focus on completing the checkout flow.

- Why did we create an Individual Form Field master?

  We created the Individual Form Field master to reduce the complexity of building our forms.

- How many states do we require for the **Check Out** dynamic panel?

  Based on our experience and current industry trends, we determined that our Check Out flow would have four steps.

- What were the names of the states for the **Check Out** dynamic panel?
  - **SignIn**
  - **PaymentAndShipping**
  - **PlaceOrder**
  - **Confirmation**

- What is one additional experience often seen on e-commerce sites that we could add to enhance our prototype?

  We could add a preference center enabling customers to manage account information (that is login, password, billing information, and so on and e-mail preferences).

Index

Thank you for buying
Learning Axure RP Interactive Prototypes

About Packt Publishing

Packt, pronounced 'packed', published its first book, *Mastering phpMyAdmin for Effective MySQL Management*, in April 2004, and subsequently continued to specialize in publishing highly focused books on specific technologies and solutions.

Our books and publications share the experiences of your fellow IT professionals in adapting and customizing today's systems, applications, and frameworks. Our solution-based books give you the knowledge and power to customize the software and technologies you're using to get the job done. Packt books are more specific and less general than the IT books you have seen in the past. Our unique business model allows us to bring you more focused information, giving you more of what you need to know, and less of what you don't.

Packt is a modern yet unique publishing company that focuses on producing quality, cutting-edge books for communities of developers, administrators, and newbies alike. For more information, please visit our website at www.packtpub.com.

Writing for Packt

We welcome all inquiries from people who are interested in authoring. Book proposals should be sent to author@packtpub.com. If your book idea is still at an early stage and you would like to discuss it first before writing a formal book proposal, then please contact us; one of our commissioning editors will get in touch with you.

We're not just looking for published authors; if you have strong technical skills but no writing experience, our experienced editors can help you develop a writing career, or simply get some additional reward for your expertise.

Axure RP Prototyping Cookbook

ISBN: 978-1-84969-798-9   Paperback: 300 pages

Over 70 practical recipes to take your wireframing and prototyping skills to the next level using Axure

1. Create sophisticated prototypes incorporating Axure with the latest web trends and technologies, such as Responsive Web Design, Ajax, PHP, mySQL, and jQuery Mobile.

2. Customize prototypes with Social Media Badges from Facebook, Twitter, and Pinterest; logos from Apple iTunes and Google Play; Google Maps Geolocation features, and more.

3. Enhance individual and team productivity with reusable asset libraries and documentation customized for your organization and clients.

Axure RP 6 Prototyping Essentials

ISBN: 978-1-84969-164-2   Paperback: 446 pages

Creating highly compelling, interactive prototypes with Axure that will impress and excite decision makers

1. Quickly simulate complex interactions for a wide range of applications without any programming knowledge.

2. Acquire timesaving methods for constructing and annotating wireframes, interactive prototypes, and UX specifications.

3. A hands-on guide that walks you through the iterative process of UX prototyping with Axure.

Please check **www.PacktPub.com** for information on our titles

Mobile Prototyping with Axure 7

ISBN: 978-1-84969-514-5   Paperback: 118 pages

Quickly deploy innovative user experience design to mobile devices for responsive prototyping using the exciting new features of Axure 7

1. Walk through the steps needed to build mobile interactions in Axure.

2. Deploy your prototypes on devices and in users' hands.

3. Download Axure RP 7 files and get started immediately.

Instant Axure RP Starter

ISBN: 978-1-84969-516-9   Paperback: 70 pages

Start prototyping your first Axure RP project the easy way

1. Learn something new in an Instant! A short, fast, focused guide delivering immediate results.

2. Helping you learn the fundamentals of Axure RP, while making prototypes.

3. Focus on only the most important features, saving you time and helping you to start using Axure RP immediately.

4. Providing you with essential resources that will help you become an Axure master.

Please check **www.PacktPub.com** for information on our titles

Made in the USA
Lexington, KY
30 May 2019